T0306217

HESI A2*

Review

Third Edition

Kathy A. Zahler

McGraw Hill

New York Chicago San Francisco Athens London Madrid
Mexico City Milan New Delhi Singapore Sydney Toronto

1 2 3 4 5 6 7 8 9 LHS 28 27 26 25 24 23

ISBN 978-1-265-66007-9
MHID 1-265-66007-7

e-ISBN 978-1-265-66181-6
e-MHID 1-265-66181-2

For the wonderful, caring nurses at Cayuga Medical Center,
Scripps Memorial Hospital, and points in between.

Contents

CHAPTER 1

Overview

CONTENTS

This guide works well as a companion to McGraw Hill's *4 HESI A2 Practice Tests*, or it can stand alone. The goal of the book is to present a review of general skills and concepts that you may find on the test.

ABOUT HESI A2

The A2 Exam is used for admission to certain nursing schools. It is a product of Evolve Learning Systems, a division of Elsevier Publishing. Different nursing programs require different exams; for example, some schools expect applicants to take the Test of Essential Academic Skills (TEAS). Other schools give you a variety of entrance exams from which to choose. Still others require the A2 exclusively.

To know whether the school or schools of your choice require the A2, visit their websites or call their admissions offices. They may call this particular test the HESI A2 test, the Evolve Reach A2 test, or the Admission Assessment Exam. Before you begin to study, make sure that you are studying for the correct test. You may need to use McGraw Hill's *TEAS Review* or *Nursing School Entrance Exams* instead.

The exam is given at a variety of sites, often at nursing schools or community colleges. The dates of the exam may depend on the application dates for the nursing school where you take the test. Some schools offer the test every few weeks throughout the year. You may also take the exam at one of more than 350 Prometric™ testing sites around the country.

To register for an exam, set up an account at the https://evolve.elsevier.com website. To take the exam at the nursing school or community college of your choice, log on to that school's website to learn how to sign up for the next available test.

To take the exam at a Prometric site, log on to http://www.prometric.com/Elsevier. Plugging in your state, clicking "Admission Assessment," and typing your zip code lets you locate the testing site and date that best suit your needs. From there, you may use your confirmation notice to help schedule the test at a time convenient for you.

The cost of the test will vary depending on where you take it. You will pay either the business office of your school or Prometric when you set up your test date.

Check with your chosen nursing programs to find out when they need score transcripts. Then work backward from that date to determine when you should take the test.

If you take the test at the nursing school that you hope to attend, the date of the test will be designed to mesh with that school's application dates.

SCORING THE TEST

The A2 consists of eight academic modules, plus two personality profile modules. Not all nursing programs require every module. If you take the test at a nursing school or community college, the school will probably only test you on the modules that its nursing program requires. For example, some programs do not require any of the science modules. Some require Reading Comprehension and Grammar, but not Vocabulary and General Knowledge. If you wish to send transcripts to several schools, visit their websites to learn which modules they require. Then make sure that the site where you are taking the test offers all of those modules.

Your scores may be reported in three ways—as a percentage score for each module administered; as a subject-area composite score (for all science modules, for example); and as a composite score (the average score for all the modules you complete).

As soon as you complete your online test, you will receive a printed score report from the proctor. Your testing fee automatically includes the submission of scores to the school where you took the test. If you took the test at a Prometric center, or if you want your transcript sent to additional schools, order transcripts from Elsevier via their website or by calling 1-800-950-2728. Elsevier will charge a processing fee for each transcript sent.

Whether your score is acceptable depends on the program to which you are applying. Some nursing programs have specific cut-off points for each module. Others require a certain composite score.

Some nursing programs allow you to take the A2 two or three times if your first scores are unacceptable. They may require you to wait several weeks or months between exams. Again, the rules vary from program to program.

PARTS OF THE TEST

The A2 is divided into eight academic modules within three broad content areas: English language, mathematics, and science. In addition, the A2 has two ungraded modules under the heading "Learner Profile." Each test contains a few piloted items that are not scored but are used to build tests in future years.

Table 1.1 shows the number of items (which may vary from year to year) and the time suggested for each section. Because the test is given online, the times given are only suggestions that will allow you to complete the entire test within a reasonable amount of time.

Table 1.1 Parts of the Test

Content Area and Module	Number of Items	Time Suggested
ENGLISH LANGUAGE		
Reading Comprehension	50 (+ 5 pilot items)	60 minutes
Vocabulary and General Knowledge	50 (+ 5 pilot items)	50 minutes
Grammar	50 (+ 5 pilot items)	50 minutes
MATHEMATICS *Basic on-screen calculator is provided.		
Basic Math Skills	50 (+ 5 pilot items)	50 minutes
SCIENCE		
Biology	25 (+ 5 pilot items)	25 minutes
Chemistry	25 (+ 5 pilot items)	25 minutes
Anatomy and Physiology	25 (+ 5 pilot items)	25 minutes
Physics	25 (+ 5 pilot items)	50 minutes
LEARNER PROFILE		
Learning Style	14	15 minutes
Personality Profile	15	15 minutes

The Learner Profile Modules

There are two short, unscored modules in the Learner Profile: a Learning Style assessment and a Personality Profile. The Learning Style module consists of a series of questions that are designed to identify a student's preferred learning style. The module assesses three main learning styles: visual, auditory, and kinesthetic.

- Visual learners prefer to learn through visual aids such as pictures, diagrams, and videos.
- Auditory learners prefer to learn through listening, such as lectures, podcasts, and discussions.

- Kinesthetic learners prefer to learn through hands-on activities such as experiments, simulations, and interactive activities.

The Personality Profile module is designed to evaluate a student's personality traits. It consists of a series of questions that are designed to assess various personality traits such as conscientiousness, agreeableness, openness, extraversion, and neuroticism. These traits are important in the nursing profession as they can impact a nurse's ability to communicate with patients, work effectively in a team, handle stress, and make critical decisions.

HESI Critical Thinking Exam

The Critical Thinking Exam is a separate exam that complements the HESI Admission Assessment Exam. This 30-minute exam consists of a series of 30 multiple-choice questions that require students to analyze and evaluate information, make inferences and deductions, and draw conclusions based on given scenarios. The questions are designed to assess a student's ability to think logically, reason effectively, and apply critical thinking skills in very specific real-world situations. The exam also includes questions that require students to interpret graphs and charts, understand statistical data, and analyze written passages.

STRATEGIES FOR TOP SCORES

As with any test, you can use certain strategies to improve your A2 score. You already know whether you are better at math or at science, or whether your understanding of grammar is enough to score high on that part of the test. Think about your known weaknesses, and review those parts of this book that deal with those specific skills. This *HESI A2 Review* focuses on the skills that have been tested on the A2 test in the past, but it is not a textbook. You would be wise to review college textbooks, online sites, and other materials that offer comprehensive coverage of the skills and concepts that give you the most trouble.

Study Strategies

1. **Get to know the format of the exam.** The practice test in the back of this book and the four tests in McGraw Hill's *4 HESI A2 Practice Tests* are designed to be similar to what you will see on the A2.
2. **Get to know the test directions.** The A2 is similar to other multiple-choice tests you have taken over the years. There are always four choices, and most questions are stand-alone or refer to a passage or problem. Only in the math section are there occasional short-answer questions where choices are not given.
3. **Get to know what topics are covered.** The subtopics in Chapters 2–9 of this book represent the most common topics on the A2.

Test-Taking Strategies

1. **Answer all the questions!** Your time is limited across the entire test, but depending on where you take the exam, you may be able to spend more time on chemistry and less on reading comprehension if you prefer. Unfortunately, the A2 is given in a format that does not allow you to "go back" and review questions you may have had trouble on, so do your best with each question as it is presented.
2. **Use the process of elimination.** Even if you feel completely stumped, you will probably be able to eliminate one or more choices simply by using common sense. That improves your odds of selecting the right answer.
3. **When in doubt, guess.** On the A2, every question has the same value, and there are no points taken off for guessing. Use the process of elimination, but if you're baffled, go ahead and guess. On multiple-choice questions with four possible responses, you have a 25 percent chance of getting the answer right. If you leave the answer blank, your chance drops to 0.
4. **Beware of answer choices that look reasonable but are not correct.** Because most questions on the A2 are multiple choice, the test-makers have many chances to mislead you with tricky distractors (wrong answers). Focus, use scratch paper to solve problems, and use the process of elimination to help narrow your choices.

A2 TRAINING SCHEDULE

Are you ready to get started? Use this sample schedule to make a plan.

My A2 Test-Prep Schedule

Test Center: ______________________
Date: ____________ **Time:** __________

4 Weeks Before	Register for the test by setting up an account at evolve.elsevier.com/cs. Check your preferred nursing program's website to see which modules are required—or call to confirm.	
3 Weeks Before	Take a practice test or two from McGraw Hill's *4 HESI A2 Practice Tests* (required modules only). Identify your problem areas.	Number of correct answers divided by ____ questions: Problem Areas:

2 Weeks Before	Do some serious review of the problem areas you identified. Use the appropriate chapters of this book and any other resources you have available.	Reviewed: ✓ ____________ ✓ ____________ ✓ ____________
1 Week Before	Take the practice test at the end of this book (required modules only). Compare your score to the scores from two weeks ago. Identify any remaining problem areas and review those skills.	Number of correct answers divided by ____ questions: Problem Areas:

CHAPTER 2

Reading

CONTENTS

Reading comprehension is the ability to understand a reading passage. On the A2 test, you will be given a reading passage with some connection to health and medicine. It might be biographical, or it might resemble a general-interest magazine article. Rarely will you see a passage on the A2 that is overly technical or that requires specific training. All of the questions derive directly from the passage, not from any background knowledge you are expected to have in the area being discussed.

MAIN IDEA

The **main idea** of a passage is a statement that tells what the passage is mostly about. When you look at the front page of a newspaper, you get a sense of the main idea of the articles by scanning the headlines.

Main idea differs from **topic** in that it is more complex. For example, the topic of two different articles might be "vitamin supplements." However, the main ideas could differ significantly. The main idea of the first article could be "Scientists find that taking vitamin supplements is less effective than eating well-rounded meals," while the main idea of the second could be "Vitamin supplements cost more at health stores than at pharmacies."

To determine the main idea of a passage, ask yourself these questions:

- What information do I learn in the introduction and conclusion of this passage?
- What is the author trying to get me to believe or understand?
- What statement would gather together all of the details in the passage?

Stated Main Idea

Sometimes an author makes it easy for you by expressing the main idea directly in a statement. Usually that statement will appear in the opening paragraph of the passage. This passage has a statement that expresses the main idea directly.

The title of a passage is often a clue about its topic and can help you focus on the main idea. →	Dangers of CO Poisoning Carbon monoxide is a dangerous gas that can build up in areas of poor air circulation. Because the symptoms of CO poisoning are so similar to those of other illnesses, people sometimes do not recognize the dangers until
This sentence connects to every other part of the passage. It is a direct statement of the main idea. →	they are deathly ill. It is critical to be aware of the sources and symptoms of CO poisoning so that you can avoid serious illness or death.
The next paragraphs add details that connect to the main idea. This paragraph is on <u>sources</u> of CO. →	First, look for areas where fumes might build up in the home. Does your stove have a good vent, and do you use it correctly? Do you start your car in the garage and leave it running without opening the garage door? Do you have any old appliances such as boilers or water heaters that have not been serviced recently? Even old cans of paint remover can be dangerous if they are leaking fumes.
This paragraph is on <u>symptoms</u> of CO poisoning.	Second, be sure that you recognize the symptoms of CO poisoning. Does everyone in the family complain of headaches or dizziness? Are family members waking up feeling weak and nauseated? Get out of the house until you find the source of the carbon monoxide. See a doctor if your symptoms are serious; CO poisoning can cause brain damage. It is no joke.

Implied Main Idea

Often, there is no direct statement that tells you the main idea of the passage. You need to **infer** the main idea from the details in the text. Consider the focus of each paragraph and decide how the details fit together to form a common viewpoint, argument, or theory. Imagine you read a passage whose topic is yoga for the elderly. (See Figure 2.1.)

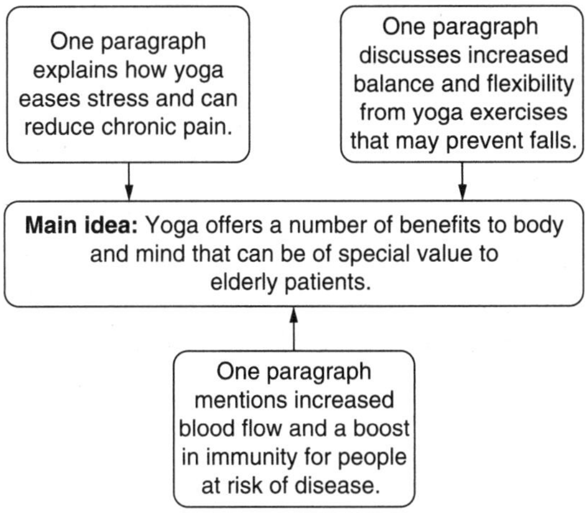

Figure 2.1 Inferring Main Idea

Test Yourself

Read the passage. Then answer the questions.

Virtual Reality Comes to the Gym

You've probably spent time riding on a stationary bike or running on a treadmill. Maybe you wear headphones and listen to music, or maybe you watch the TV in the gym. That's old school, and you know how dull it can be! Today, you can turn your exercise machine into a giant virtual reality (VR) game and bike through the south of France before jogging on a Hawaiian beach. What other incentive do you need to up your routine and improve your health?

A headset and computer plunge you into a virtual environment. As you run or pedal harder, you move faster through the environment you choose. A few early studies indicate that VR exercise promotes a decreased level of perceived exertion and an increased level of enjoyment, meaning that people exercise longer and get all the benefits of a longer routine without feeling bored or exhausted by the end.

There are a variety of VR exercises that involve sword fighting or that allow you to feel that instead of riding a stationary bike, you are piloting a helicopter. The possibilities seem endless and exciting. Instead of playing a video game and exercising only your thumbs, you can now get a full-body workout indoors while enjoying the flights of fancy that virtual reality provides for you. It's a win-win, and we hope to see many more of these opportunities in gyms across the nation.

1. This passage is mostly about ___________ and its effect on ___________.

2. List some of the plusses of virtual reality in the gym.

   Paragraph 1: ___________
   Paragraph 2: ___________
   Paragraph 3: ___________

3. Give the passage a different title that tells about its main idea.

   ____

4. The main idea of the final paragraph seems to be that virtual reality makes exercise ___________.

5. What is the main idea of the passage?

   A. Virtual reality lets runners jog on a beach and bikers ride through France.
   B. Virtual reality can be a welcome and incentivizing addition to an exercise routine.
   C. Adding a headset and computer to an exercise room can make people work harder.
   D. Adding the fantasy of virtual reality can make indoor exercise as beneficial as working out in the open air.

Answers

1. virtual reality; exercise
2. Paragraph 1: It lets you pretend to be in great settings.
   Paragraph 2: It decreases perceived exertion and increases enjoyment.
   Paragraph 3: It offers the fun of video games plus a full-body workout.
3. Possible answer: Virtual Reality Makes Exercise Fun
4. Possible answers: entertaining, exciting, fun
5. B. Choices A and C are too limited, and choice D goes beyond the scope of the passage.

SUPPORTING DETAILS

Supporting details in a reading passage are all of the facts, descriptions, and examples that make up the body of a passage and support the main idea.

5 W's

It is sometimes helpful to think like a journalist as you approach a complex passage. Think about the answers to what journalists call the 5 W's:

- **Who** (or what) is this about?
- **What** happened?
- **When** did it happen?
- **Where** did it happen?
- **Why** did it happen?

WHY DO I NEED THIS?

As you read medical reports as a professional nurse, you must identify at a glance any key details.

The answers are all supporting details.

Evidence

In a piece of writing that states an opinion or presents an argument, supporting details constitute **evidence** in support of the opinion or argument.

Suppose that an author claims the following:

> Homemade baby food is preferable to store-bought.

In support of that claim, the author might offer a variety of facts, descriptions, and examples.

- **Evidence 1:** Baby food fruit in jars contains five grams more sugar than kitchen-mashed fruit.
- **Evidence 2:** Store-bought food may look shiny and appetizing, but that may be due to added food coloring.
- **Evidence 3:** The fillers in one brand included starches that babies could not easily digest.

All of these details add up to a condemnation of store-bought baby food and strong support of the author's claim.

Test Yourself

Read the passage. Then answer the questions.

The Master of Vaccines

His is not a household name, but Maurice Hilleman saved more lives than any doctor, firefighter, or soldier. Born in 1919 in rural Montana, he very nearly ended up as a farmer before obtaining help to attend college. From there, his career took off, and his PhD dissertation proved that chlamydia, thought to be viral, was in fact caused by bacteria. His fascination with microbiology would never wane.

Instead of continuing with a university, Hilleman went into industry, where he developed a vaccine against a virulent type of encephalitis. He used his own daughter's cells from the back of the infected girl's throat to invent a mumps vaccine, which he later expanded to include vaccination against measles and rubella in the MMR multiple virus vaccine that children still receive today.

Over the years, Hilleman would be the primary researcher and developer of dozens of vaccines, including those that prevent chickenpox, some strains of influenza, and hepatitis A and B. He was known as a driven man who put up with little nonsense in the lab and fought his corporate overseers to achieve what he thought was needed. He died in 2005, little remembered except by his peers, but deserving of much respect.

1. What did Hilleman use to create the mumps vaccine?

   ____

2. How old was Hilleman when he died?

   ____

3. The MMR vaccine protects against ___________, ___________, and ___________.

4. What did Hilleman do instead of going on in academia?

   ____

5. Which of the following diseases is not mentioned as one that Hilleman's vaccines help to prevent?

   A. Influenza
   B. Rubella
   C. Smallpox
   D. Encephalitis

Answers

1. He used cells from his daughter's throat.
2. 85 or 86. He was born in 1919 and died in 2005, making him 85 or 86.
3. measles, mumps, rubella
4. He went into industry.
5. C. Choice A appears in paragraph 3, and choices B and D appear in paragraph 2.

WORDS IN CONTEXT

Technical writing and complex texts often include vocabulary that may be unfamiliar. You must infer the meaning of such words by using **context clues**—semantic and syntactic clues that appear in the text surrounding the unknown word.

If you saw a nonsense word out of context, it would simply be nonsense:

brufle

But if you read it in context, you could draw some conclusions about its meaning:

When confronted, Jack tends to brufle and look away.

Its use in this sentence (its **syntax**) suggests that *brufle* is a verb. It apparently describes an action that a person might do when confronted by someone else.

See? Even if the word is completely foreign to you, you can determine a lot about it from its context in a sentence and by the meaning of the words around it (**semantics**).

There are various semantic and syntactic clues that make determining the meanings of words in context easier. Here are just a few.

Definition/explanation

Sometimes the word in question is defined directly by a phrase that clarifies its meaning.

- The tonic was salubrious, offering a variety of healthful benefits.
- Five of the nurses gathered in amity, an aura of goodwill and friendship.

Restatement/synonym

A word that means the same thing may make the meaning of an unfamiliar word clear.

- Her experiment was an unalloyed, total disaster.
- His office was a maelstrom, with a whirlwind of papers flying around.

Contrast/antonym

A word that means the opposite of the unknown word may help to illuminate its meaning. Words such as *unlike* and *whereas* may signal this contrast.

- Whereas the doctor was magnanimous, his wife was stingy.
- I prefer honesty and truthfulness to deceit and artifice.

Inference

As with the nonsense word *brufle* above, sometimes you must simply use syntactic and semantic clues as well as your own prior knowledge about the English language and the topic being discussed to decipher an unknown word.

- His statement seemed specious, so we chose to ignore it.
- It takes a certain mettle to survive such a difficult childhood.

Test Yourself

1. Underline the synonym that suggests the meaning of the underlined word.

   I would rather you steal my goods than purloin my ideas.

2. Underline the phrase that explains the underlined word.

   She reviewed my work dispassionately, with no sign of emotion.

3. Underline the antonym that helps define the underlined word.

   Although Dave found the film soporific, Meg thought it was invigorating.

4. Choose the best meaning of the underlined word.

   Norm prefers a pedestrian career to one with wild variations.

   A. Routine
   B. Rambling
   C. Disorderly
   D. Sophisticated

5. What is the meaning of *mercenary* as used in this paragraph?

   Most people become doctors out of a desire to help others. A few, however, have mercenary motivations. They are attracted more by the perks of medicine than by its virtues.

   A. Humble
   B. Combative
   C. Greedy
   D. Worthwhile

Answers

1. steal
2. with no sign of emotion
3. invigorating
4. A. A career that is routine would have few wild variations.
5. C. Instead of being attracted by a desire to help others, people with mercenary motivations are attracted by the chance to make money.

AUTHOR'S PURPOSE

Writing is two-way communication between an author and a reader. Authors write with a purpose in mind. Understanding that purpose can help you to interpret their writing more easily.

Persuasion

Authors who write to persuade want something from their readers. They may want the readers to change their minds about a contentious topic. They may want the readers to take action.

Persuasive writing expresses an opinion, states a claim, and/or presents an argument. Typically, persuasive writers use one or more of these modes of rhetoric, shown in Table 2.1.

Table 2.1 Rhetorical Techniques from the Ancient Greeks

Technique	Appeals to . . .	Example
ethos	Ethics	As a scientist, I assure you that early treatment works.
pathos	Emotion	If you fail to get early treatment, the results may be dire.
logos	Logic	Patients who got early treatment had good results 90 percent of the time.
kairos	Setting	Since all of you patients share a diagnosis, I encourage you to try early treatment.
telos	Purpose	Since we all wish to regain our strength, let us all try early treatment.

If a passage expresses the author's concerns, beliefs, or opinions, its purpose is probably persuasive. Look for persuasive words and phrases like those below.

- Without a doubt
- I am convinced
- I believe
- You should know
- You can see
- Clearly
- Obviously
- Unmistakably

Information

Most of what you read and write in college and in nursing school is likely to be informational, or **expository**, writing. Informational writing relies on facts. Its purpose is to explain a process or an event, to describe something in detail, or to inform the reader.

Informational writing is impersonal and largely unbiased. It may compare and contrast two things but will not choose sides. It may tell the reader how to do something but will not tell the reader that he or she should do that thing.

Examples of Informational Writing

biography	newspaper article	textbook	directions
handbook	field guide	encyclopedia	report
abstract	almanac	feature article	legal document

If a passage is filled with names, dates, statistics, and quotes, it is probably informational.

Entertainment

Authors of fiction, drama, or poetry write primarily to entertain. Entertaining writing may engage the reader using suspense, humor, tragedy, or fascinating characters and settings. When we talk about "creative writing," we are usually talking about writing whose purpose is to entertain.

Examples of Entertaining Writing

short story	novel	one-act play	television script
movie script	song	narrative	ballad
monologue	anecdote	limerick	character sketch

Reflection

Sometimes, authors write to reflect upon personal experiences or to share personal responses. This sort of personal writing differs from persuasion in that the author is not trying to convince the reader of anything. The author may be writing to explore his or her own thoughts or to gain self-knowledge while involving the reader in that personal journey. Reflective writing turns up in certain memoirs, essays, poetry, and solo performances.

Test Yourself

1. Match each written work with its primary purpose.

King Lear	persuasion
The Diary of Anne Frank	information
A Brief History of Time	entertainment
"I Have a Dream"	reflection

2. Which part of a newspaper has a primary purpose of persuasion?

   ____

3. Typically, a memoir would have a primary purpose of ____________.

Read the passage. Then answer questions 4 and 5.

Infants and Sleep

Ninety percent of sudden infant death syndrome cases occur during the first six months of infancy, with the other 10 percent occurring during the second six months. Research indicates that the sleep positions of babies affect their risk.

It has become clear that room sharing is critically important for infants in their first year of life. Having infants within arms' reach allows parents to monitor them easily. This does not imply that parents should share a bed with their infants; this is a dangerous practice that should be discouraged.

4. What is the author's primary purpose in writing paragraph 1?

   A. To persuade
   B. To inform
   C. To entertain
   D. To reflect

5. What is the author's primary purpose in writing paragraph 2?

   A. To persuade
   B. To inform
   C. To entertain
   D. To reflect

Answers

1. *King Lear*—entertainment; *The Diary of Anne Frank*—reflection; *A Brief History of Time*—information; "I Have a Dream"—persuasion
2. op-ed or letters to the editor
3. reflection
4. B. This paragraph includes facts and statistics.
5. A. This paragraph is filled with appeals to emotion and logic.

FACT AND OPINION

Determining whether a statement is fact or opinion is not the same as determining whether it is accurate or untrue. Most of what you read as a medical professional will involve multiple facts. Recognizing when the author's bias pushes into the writing with ideas that may not be verifiable is a useful skill to have.

Facts

A statement of fact is **objective** and can be checked or proved. It may be true or false, but it is always provable one way or the other.

- The patient is currently in room 305A.
- The patient's name is Lucia Alvarez.
- The patient's fever reached 102 degrees.

Opinions

A statement of opinion is **subjective** and cannot be checked or proved. It may represent one person's judgment or the beliefs of thousands, but it is not verifiable through any scientific means.

- The patient's diet was appalling.
- The patient should not be moved yet.
- The patient deserves our attention.

A Few Words That Signal Opinions

always	believe	best	might
most	ought	perhaps	probably
should	think	usually	worst

Sentences that contain vivid adjectives and adverbs usually indicate judgment and are probably opinions rather than facts.

- The patient has an unpleasant odor.
- The patient's skin feels leathery.
- The patient treats the nurses rudely.

WHY DO I NEED THIS?

Nursing reports should be dispassionate and objective—filled with facts and information, not personal opinions.

Test Yourself

1. Underline the word or words that signal an opinion.

After lunch, Corinne washed the glassware carelessly.
People in the commissary should clean up their waste.
I think that the café serves the best coffee around.

2. Underline the sentence that states a fact.

Most of our patients spend fewer than two nights in the hospital.
Most of our patients need more time in the hospital than they receive.

3. Complete the sentence to make it state an opinion.

In my opinion, hospitals ______________________________.

Read the passage. Then answer questions 4 and 5.

ATTN: New Employees

Corbyn Health Center has added 12 new staff members since September. That brings our total workforce to 89, including several part-time staff. Since Corbyn opened in 2010, this is our largest staff ever. The quality of our employees is unparalleled, and we welcome our newcomers.

Initiation for new employees is scheduled for Friday at 4 P.M. You should arrive early if possible to have time to ask questions. Initiation is always interesting, and this year is no exception. A respected speaker will give you an inspirational overview.

4. Which sentence in the first paragraph states an opinion?

A. Corbyn Health Center has added 12 new staff members since September.
B. That brings our total workforce to 89, including several part-time staff.
C. Since Corbyn opened in 2010, this is our largest staff ever.
D. The quality of our employees is unparalleled, and we welcome our newcomers.

5. Which sentence in the second paragraph states a fact?

A. Initiation for new employees is scheduled for Friday at 4 P.M.
B. You should arrive early if possible to have time to ask questions.
C. Initiation is always interesting, and this year is no exception.
D. A respected speaker will give you an inspirational overview.

Answers

1. carelessly; should; think; best
2. Most of our patients spend fewer than two nights in the hospital.
3. Possible answers: are hotbeds for diseases, serve patients well, get an undeserved bad reputation.
4. D. *Unparalleled* is a judgment. The other statements can be checked.
5. A. Either initiation is scheduled for that time or it isn't; either way, the schedule may be confirmed.

DRAWING CONCLUSIONS AND MAKING INFERENCES

As you read, whether you are aware of it or not, you apply what you know and clues from the text to draw conclusions or make inferences about what you are reading. For example, if you receive political mail around election time, you can probably easily tell which party sent it without even looking for a party insignia. Your knowledge of local political parties and their interests and focuses added to the information in the text allows you to infer the identity of the sender.

Drawing conclusions and making inferences are part of being an active reader. Instead of expecting an author to deliver everything you need to know in a text and to explain how you should think or react, you must determine for yourself how facts and details fit together; what information is not provided but can be guessed at or surmised; and how the information given supports additional conjectures, predictions, or judgments.

Using What You Know

When you draw conclusions or make inferences, you apply your own background knowledge to a text to make assumptions. An author, therefore, must be fairly aware of his or her audience in order to get readers to draw the desired conclusions.

Imagine this sentence in a text:

> The old man's chest rose almost imperceptibly, and his bony fingers grasped at nothing.

A child reading this might not be able to conclude what an adult would—that the man's health is failing, and he may be near death. Only life experience and a lifetime of reading would let a reader draw that conclusion.

Here is another example:

> The yacht's wake was the only blemish on the turquoise Aegean, and the caw of whirling gulls the only sound to disturb our languor.

The author does not bother to remind you that yachts are not an ordinary form of transportation or to tell you where the Aegean might be. If you know about yachts, the Aegean, and languor, you can conclude that the people being described are wealthy.

The more you live and the more you read, the better you will be at making inferences and drawing conclusions from a text.

Using Textual Clues

An author does not tell a reader everything, but he or she does tell the reader some things. Using the clues that are given in the text can help you to draw conclusions and make inferences.

Consider this example:

> The antipersonnel mines indiscriminately kill civilians or soldiers, young children or old women.

The word *mines* has a variety of meanings, but you can determine from the surrounding text which meaning is implied. Coal mines might be harmful to some workers, but they would not kill soldiers, children, or old women. This sentence refers to land mines, explosive devices designed to kill.

Here is another example:

> Following the opening of the high-end organic grocery down the block, the bodega appeared to lose first its bustling exterior, then its scrubbed storefront, and finally most of the contents of its shelves.

The author does not directly tell you what happened to the bodega, but the loss of *bustling, scrubbed*, and, finally, *contents* implies a slow decline in its success. The fact that this is linked to the "opening of the high-end organic grocery" tells you that the author wants you to infer that the cause of the decline is the appearance of the new grocery.

Test Yourself

1. For each description, write an inference about that person's emotions.

He shook his fist and gritted his teeth.	He feels ___________.
She dropped her eyes and blushed.	She feels ___________.
His sweaty hands trembled.	He feels ___________.

Read the passage. Then answer the questions.

Tablets and Patient Care

Patients at certain hospitals around the nation are connecting to their own medical records and learning about their treatment through the use of tablets that allow them to see their own charts. They can input questions and reminders to help connect to their doctors and nurses and remain active in their own care.

Midnight texts to the nursing station may soon take the place of buttons and alarms on the floors where such tablets are being tested, and both patients and nurses seem to appreciate the option. Not all patients are taking full advantage of the tablets, but those who are seem impressed.

"When my doctor is presenting options to me, I sometimes can't quite follow everything she is saying," says patient Janelle Vincent. "But if she can send me the options on the tablet, I can study all about them at my own pace. I feel I'm making choices with a clear mind."

Vincent's doctor, Ann Weeks, says that this is exactly the point. "I want Janelle and all my patients to be involved in their own treatment, both here and in my general practice," she says. "I firmly believe that being an active patient rather than a passive recipient aids in recovery."

2. What clues let you know which meaning of *tablet* the author is using?

____

____

3. Which statement would *not* be inferred by the reader?

   A. Patients can communicate with staff using their tablets.
   B. Nurses may get calls from patients in the middle of the night.
   C. Dr. Weeks has other patients besides Janelle in the hospital.
   D. Tablets will soon be available to patients in most hospitals.

4. A reader might infer from the third paragraph that Janelle ____________.

   A. does not speak English as a native language
   B. feels comfortable doing some research on her own
   C. is currently studying to become a health professional
   D. has never used electronic devices before

5. A reader might infer from the last paragraph that Dr. Weeks ____________.

   A. no longer has to monitor Janelle closely
   B. thinks that Janelle is not involved in her own treatment
   C. strongly supports the use of tablets in the hospital
   D. fears the use of tablets as a replacement for medical care

Answers

1. angry or upset; shy or embarrassed; anxious or fearful
2. Clues include the fact that patients can read things on tablets and send texts on them.
3. D. This choice goes beyond what the passage suggests. Tablets may be working for some doctors and patients, but you cannot conclude that they will "soon" be available to patients in many hospitals, much less "most."
4. B. Janelle doesn't always understand everything her doctor says, but that could just mean that her doctor is technical, not that Janelle doesn't understand English (choice A). Although she studies her options, Janelle is not studying to become a health professional (choice C). There is no evidence to support choice D, but there is evidence to suggest that Janelle appreciates the chance to research her options with her doctor's guidance, making choice B correct.
5. C. Dr. Weeks wants her patients to be involved in their own treatment because she thinks it aids in recovery. For that reason, she would support tablets in the hospital, since they allow patients to be involved in their own treatment. None of the other choices finds support in the passage.

SUMMARIZING

When you summarize a paragraph or longer passage, you restate the main idea and key details expressed in the writing. A summary answers the question, "What is this mostly about?"

Good summaries follow the Goldilocks precept that applies to the three bears' chairs. A good summary is not too big—it does not cover material or ideas that do not appear in the original writing. A good summary is not too small—it does not focus narrowly on a single point in the original writing. A good summary is "just right"—it is a brief restatement of the key points in the original writing.

Summaries

TOO BIG: Nursing school is hard, so you need to prepare yourself in a variety of critical ways.

TOO SMALL: Carefully choose the nursing program you want based on the requirements you have fulfilled.

JUST RIGHT: To get into nursing school, check the requirements, follow the guidelines for applying, and take the required test.

Passage

Before you get into the nursing school of your dreams, you must follow some critical steps. Make sure that you have completed the requirements for the nursing career path of your choice. You may even adapt your plan based on the requirements you have completed. Find the guidelines for applying to the program of your choice and follow them religiously. Meet all deadlines and complete all application materials. Finally, take whichever entrance exam your chosen program requires. Locate the testing site, apply for a specific testing date, and review and practice until you are ready.

WHY DO I NEED THIS?

You will often need to write an abstract or summary as part of a report on a study or piece of research.

Test Yourself

Read the passage. Then answer the questions.

A Weird, Metallic Taste

Dysgeusia is the name for a condition in which a particular taste sensation persists in the mouth without an obvious cause. Often, the taste is described as metallic. Usually a metallic taste has a benign underlying cause. Occasionally, though, the cause is more serious.

Sometimes, a lingering metallic taste is linked to actual metals entering the body. For example, a vitamin supplement may contain significant amounts of copper or zinc. Other times, the metal source is not obvious, but the taste sensation connects to drugs the patient is taking, such as steroids, some antibiotics, and some antihistamines.

A sinus infection or allergies that block sinus passages may lead to a metallic taste. Once the sinuses are clear, the taste sensation clears as well.

Waste buildup in the kidneys can cause a metallic taste in the mouth. This origin of dysgeusia is dangerous; the buildup may indicate kidney failure. In general, a metallic taste that does not go away and seems not to be connected to sinusitis, vitamin or medicine ingestion, or a benign cause such as pregnancy should be checked out by a physician.

1. What is the topic of the passage?

____

2. Choose the best summary of paragraph 2.

A. A metallic taste may derive from metals in vitamins or from medication.
B. A lingering metallic taste may indicate that metals are being ingested.
C. Copper and zinc are two examples of metals that can cause a metallic taste.
D. The taste sensation from vitamins may be metallic, or it may be more medicinal.

3. Write a quick summary of paragraph 3.

____

4. Choose the best summary of paragraph 4.

A. Dysgeusia is not always dangerous, but sometimes it is.
B. Some dysgeusia is not clearly connected to benign causes.
C. Dysgeusia may signal a dangerous condition such as kidney failure.
D. Most dysgeusia merits being checked out by a medical professional.

5. Choose the best summary of the passage.

A. Copper, zinc, drugs, or allergens are just some of the many outside influences that can lead to the odd taste sensation called *dysgeusia.*

B. A lingering metallic taste in the mouth may have a benign cause, such as vitamin use or sinusitis, or a dangerous cause, such as kidney failure.

C. When pregnant women experience a metallic taste, they need not see a doctor, but when kidney patients experience such a taste, they should.

D. Vitamin supplements that contain a lot of metal and some antibiotics and antihistamines may result in the side effect known as *dysgeusia.*

Answers

1. dysgeusia, a strange taste sensation

2. A. Paragraph 2 is about dysgeusia as a side effect both of certain vitamin supplements and of certain other medications. Choices B and C are too small—too specific—and choice D is too large and goes beyond the scope of the paragraph.

3. Possible answer: Sinus problems may cause a metallic taste that vanishes when the problems clear up.

4. C. Paragraph 4 switches to discuss dangerous causes of dysgeusia, specifically kidney failure. Choices A and B are vague, and choice D contradicts information in the passage.

5. B. This choice covers the main points in the passage—both the benign and the dangerous reasons for dysgeusia. Choices A and D are too small and specific. Choice C focuses on pregnant women, who are only mentioned as an aside in the last sentence.

AUTHOR'S TONE

An author's tone indicates the author's attitude toward the subject matter. That attitude determines the words the author chooses, and those words in turn indicate the author's point of view.

Figure 2.2 shows just a few examples of words that may be used to describe an author's tone.

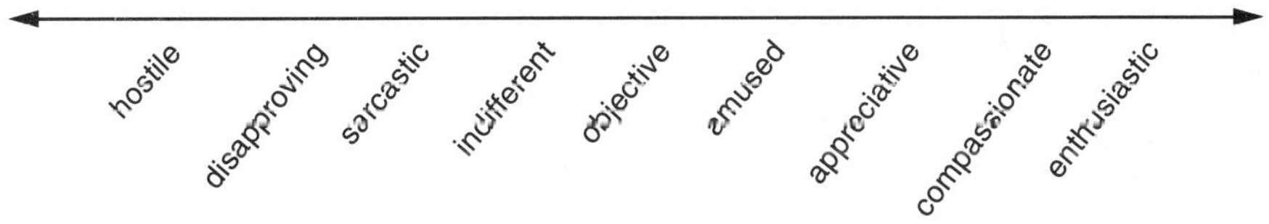

Figure 2.2 Tone Scale from Negative to Positive

Test Yourself

Use a word from the box to describe the tone of each example below. Use each word only once.

ambivalent	approving	critical	sympathetic

1. It defies understanding that doctors would continue to prescribe this drug without further testing.

____

2. Patients who took the drug are struggling to recover from devastating side effects.

____

3. The *Jutland Standard* won a well-deserved Pulitzer Prize for their reporting on this product.

____

4. Although early results of the drug therapy were positive, it appears that troubling consequences may occur.

____

Read the passage. Then answer question 5.

Knee Replacement in Obese Patients

There is positive news coming out today for morbidly obese patients who have chronic knee pain. If a patient is healthy enough to tolerate surgery, it turns out that even the most obese patient can benefit from knee replacement, with outcomes similar to those in patients of normal weight. Obese patients tend to develop osteoarthritis at a faster rate than normal-weight patients—thanks to the damaging pressure on their joints from too much body weight—but now it appears that their pain can be alleviated through the surgery, and their joints can return to normal function in a reasonable and predictable length of time.

5. Identify the overall tone of the passage.

A. Formal
B. Impartial
C. Optimistic
D. Scornful

Answers

1. critical. The author is shocked and thinks the doctors' actions "defy understanding."
2. sympathetic. The words *struggling* and *devastating* indicate the author's sympathy.
3. approving. The author believes that the newspaper deserves the award.
4. ambivalent. The author is weighing two sides of an issue—the drug had positive results but now seems to have troubling consequences.
5. C. Phrases such as "it turns out" and "thanks to" keep this from being formal (choice A), and phrases such as "positive news" keep it from being impartial (choice B). On the whole, the author thinks this is good news for obese people with knee pain, making the tone optimistic.

CHAPTER 3

Vocabulary and General Knowledge

CONTENTS

A mature vocabulary helps you to read with comprehension, write professionally, and speak astutely on a variety of issues. The A2 test not only expects you to have a relatively broad general vocabulary but also to recognize certain terms that are related to health care.

HEALTH CARE CONTEXTS

You may have seen some of the words in Table 3.1 in different contexts, unrelated to health care. Other words on the chart are specific to the medical profession.

Table 3.1 Health-Related Words

Word	Meaning	Sentence
aberration *n.*	deviation, irregularity	Those low T cell counts seem to be an *aberration.*
abrasion *n.*	scrape, scratch	A minor *abrasion* rarely requires a bandage.
acrid *adj.*	bitter, caustic, pungent	The *acrid* smoke made our eyes water.
acute *adj.*	experienced to a severe degree	He suffered from *acute* pain after eating.
adverse *adj.*	unfavorable, harmful	The *adverse* effects of overeating are well known.
ambulate *v.*	to walk, saunter, stroll	Patients *ambulate* or wheel themselves down the hall.

Table 3.1 Health-Related Words (*Continued*)

Word	Meaning	Sentence
anomalous *adj.*	abnormal, atypical, deviant	His *anomalous* opinions irritated his colleagues.
aspirate *v.*	to inhale, to withdraw fluid	Turn the patient so that he does not *aspirate* fluid.
assuage *v.*	to alleviate, allay, ease	A bit of aloe will *assuage* the itch of a mosquito bite.
atrophy *v.*	waste away, wither, weaken	The unused limb began to *atrophy*.
benign *adj.*	not harmful, noncancerous	The tumor was *benign* and was easily removed.
bifurcate *v.*	to divide, branch, fork	The arteries *bifurcate* into external and internal arteries.
cadaver *n.*	corpse, dead body	The trainees worked together to dissect the *cadaver*.
cathartic *adj.*	invigorating, therapeutic, liberating	A plunge into the cold lake can be *cathartic*.
caustic *adj.*	corrosive, biting, acerbic	Wear gloves when working with *caustic* chemicals.
cauterize *v.*	to burn for curative purposes	They will *cauterize* the wound to prevent infection.
chronic *adj.*	persistent, long-lasting	Her nose drips as though she has a *chronic* cold.
coagulate *v.*	clot, congeal, solidify	Healthy blood will *coagulate* in 30 seconds or less.
contagion *n.*	infection, contamination	The *contagion* spread rapidly through the hospital.
contusion *n.*	bruise, discoloration	Bumping the table left a *contusion* on his knee.
corporeal *adj.*	bodily, physical	He prefers the life of the mind to *corporeal* reality.
corpulent *adj.*	fleshy, overweight, fat	My *corpulent* dachshund needs to exercise more.
deliquesce *v.*	to melt, liquefy	The powder will *deliquesce* and coat the tubing.
delirium *n.*	confusion, disorientation	In her *delirium*, she thought she saw bugs on the wall.
dilation *n.*	expansion, stretching, enlargement	Bright light causes *dilation* of the pupils.
dilute *v.*	to water down, weaken	Add cold water to *dilute* the sample.
distend *v.*	stretch, swell, expand	Overeating will *distend* your stomach temporarily.

Table 3.1 Health-Related Words (*Continued*)

Word	Meaning	Sentence
efficacy *n.*	effectiveness, value	The drug's *efficacy* has not yet been proved.
endemic *adj.*	prevalent, widespread	Are tick bites *endemic* in this area?
enervate *v.*	to weaken, debilitate, enfeeble	Surgery can *enervate* an elderly patient.
excise *v.*	to remove, eliminate	The dermatologist will *excise* that oddly shaped mole.
febrile *adj.*	feverish, flushed	She placed a damp cloth on the child's *febrile* forehead.
fissure *n.*	cleft, crack, crevice	Dripping water caused a *fissure* in the foundation.
flaccid *adj.*	sagging, limp, lifeless	My muscles were *flaccid* after weeks in a cast.
flex *v.*	to bend, contract	Can you *flex* your wrist with that bandage on it?
gait *n.*	walking, movement	His *gait* appears unsteady following the operation.
geriatric *adj.*	elderly, senior	An aging population makes *geriatric* medicine popular.
gestation *n.*	pregnancy, development in the womb	Track the mother through *gestation* and after the birth.
gravid *adj.*	pregnant	All *gravid* patients belong on the third floor.
impervious *adj.*	impermeable, resilient, impenetrable	Those *impervious* gloves will protect your hands.
infestation *n.*	invasion, as by a parasite	An *infestation* of lice can be hard to get rid of.
inflammation *n.*	irritation, swelling, redness	Expect mild *inflammation* around the injection site.
innocuous *adj.*	harmless, unobjectionable, inoffensive	Eat something mild and *innocuous*, such as toast.
insidious *adj.*	stealthy, sinister	An *insidious* disease often shows no visible symptoms.
juxtapose *v.*	to place side by side, compare	If you *juxtapose* his fingers, you can see that one is bent.
latent *adj.*	dormant, underlying, potential	The virus is *latent* and has produced no symptoms yet.
lesion *n.*	cut, wound, damaged region	The frightened cat left a *lesion* on my arm.

Table 3.1 Health-Related Words (*Continued*)

Word	Meaning	Sentence
lethargic *adj.*	weary, sluggish, inactive	The hot weather made all of us feel *lethargic* and dull.
malaise *n.*	dissatisfaction, discomfort, unease	Following the layoffs, a sort of *malaise* set in at the company.
malignant *adj.*	cancerous, menacing	Radiation will slow the growth of the *malignant* tumor.
masticate *v.*	to chew, munch, chomp	Cows *masticate* their cuds all day long.
nostrum *n.*	remedy, potion, panacea	Herbs are considered a *nostrum* for many ailments.
noxious *adj.*	harmful, lethal, toxic	Propane leaks can be *noxious*, so watch your grill.
obesity *n.*	fatness, heaviness	Her diabetes may stem from youthful *obesity*.
ossify *v.*	to harden, solidify, set	As the baby grows, the tissue will begin to *ossify*.
palliative *adj.*	soothing, relieving, easing	Finding no cure, the doctors ordered *palliative* measures.
palpable *adj.*	tangible, obvious, physical	There is a *palpable* lump under the skin.
papule *n.*	pimple, swelling	The *papule* turned red and itched for a week.
paroxysm *n.*	outburst, convulsion, spasm	She burst into a *paroxysm* of uncontrollable coughing.
penumbra *n.*	shadow, obscurity, shade	The tumor showed up as a *penumbra* on the x-ray.
permeable *adj.*	porous, leaky, penetrable	*Permeable* bandages allow air to circulate.
pernicious *adj.*	deadly, destructive, harmful	Food advertising can have a *pernicious* effect on my diet.
postmortem *n.*	autopsy, inquest, examination	Every suspicious death warrants a *postmortem*.
prognosis *n.*	projection, prediction	What is the *prognosis* for that woman's recovery?
prone *adj.*	lying facedown	If you lie in a *prone* position, he will massage your back.
putrefy *v.*	to decay, rot, molder	Meat will soon *putrefy* if it is left out on a counter.
quarantine *n.*	seclusion, confinement	We placed them in *quarantine* to prevent further infection.
quiescent *adj.*	latent, inert, dormant	The virus may be *quiescent* for months before causing illness.

Table 3.1 Health-Related Words (*Continued*)

Word	Meaning	Sentence
reflex *n.*	reaction, impulse, spontaneous effect	Test the biceps, *reflex* by tapping the tendon.
resilient *adj.*	flexible, hardy, durable	A *resilient* child easily overcomes obstacles.
respiration *n.*	breathing	His *respiration* seems forced; each breath is labored.
respite *n.*	reprieve, break, rest	We took a short *respite* to stretch our legs.
senescent *adj.*	aging, maturing	My *senescent* brain has trouble recalling names.
soporific *adj.*	monotonous, hypnotic, sleep-inducing	The *soporific* drug had him drowsy within minutes.
spasm *n.*	tremor, contraction	Tickling her feet caused a small *spasm* in her legs.
stanch *v.*	stop, restrict	Use a clean cloth to *stanch* the bleeding.
succor *n.*	assistance, help, aid	Paramedics offered *succor* to the accident victims.
supine *adj.*	lying on the back	While the patient is *supine*, raise the legs one at a time.
suppurating *adj.*	festering, discharging pus	Civil War soldiers often died of *suppurating* injuries.
suture *n.*	stitching, seam, junction	A *suture* held the edges of the wound together.
syndrome *n.*	pattern of symptoms and signs	The *syndrome* starts with numbness and tingling.
tepid *adj.*	lukewarm, unenthusiastic, apathetic	Pour *tepid* water into the vaporizer.
torpor *n.*	lethargy, languor, inactivity	After ten at night, a *torpor* came over our study group.
toxic *adj.*	poisonous, lethal	Wild mushrooms may be *toxic*.
transverse *adj.*	crosswise, oblique, slanted	We observed the *transverse* image of the bone.
trauma *n.*	injury, damage, suffering	After physical *trauma*, some people go into shock.
tremulous *adj.*	quivering, shaky, wavering	Her legs seemed *tremulous* as she rose from the bed.
valve *n.*	controller, as of material through a passage	With the *valve* closed, no liquid can flow.

Table 3.1 Health-Related Words (*Continued*)

Word	Meaning	Sentence
vertiginous *adj.*	dizzy, giddy, reeling	Four rides on the carousel gave me a *vertiginous* feeling.
virulent *adj.*	infectious, contagious	That *virulent* strain of flu infected the whole school.

Test Yourself

Use a word from the box to complete each sentence below. Use each word only once.

quiescent	senescent	lethargic

1. A young person with low energy might be described as ____________.

2. Before emerging as butterflies, caterpillars go through a ____________ phase.

3. Loss of skin resilience is typical of someone who is ____________.

4. Which word meaning "to weaken" best fits in the sentence?

The terrible humidity can exhaust and ____________ most people.

A. infest
B. ossify
C. enervate
D. assuage

5. A palliative measure offers ____________.

A. relief
B. healing
C. potency
D. options

6. Which of these would be permeable?

A. Rubber gloves
B. Concrete steps
C. Mesh fabric
D. Zip-lock bag

7. Which of these might lead to an infestation?

A. E. coli
B. Viruses
C. Termites
D. Bacilli

8. A tremulous voice is one that is ____________.

A. shaky
B. vibrant
C. harsh
D. high-pitched

9. Which of these might be called a contusion?

A. Black eye
B. Broken arm
C. Split lip
D. Hair loss

10. A doctor may have you walk around the room to check your ____________.

A. reflexes
B. torpor
C. lesion
D. gait

Answers

1. lethargic. *Senescence* applies only to older people.
2. quiescent. In the chrysalis, caterpillars are inert, or quiescent.
3. senescent. Skin's loss of elasticity is typical of old age.
4. C. If you are enervated, you are drained and devitalized.
5. A. Something that is palliative does not offer a cure (choice B), but it does offer comfort, or relief.
6. C. Something permeable lets air or water flow through it.
7. C. Choices A, B, and D may lead to an infection.
8. A. To be tremulous is to be quivering or shaky.
9. A. A contusion is a bruise.
10. D. Your gait is your manner of walking.

GENERAL KNOWLEDGE

Most of your vocabulary knowledge derives from reading and conversation. However, there are certain words that you may have heard or read but have never bothered to define. Table 3.2 of difficult vocabulary words offers some useful words with their definitions.

Table 3.2 Difficult Vocabulary Words

Word	Meaning	Sentence
abdicate *v.*	to relinquish power, renounce, abandon, resign	The queen will *abdicate* her throne on behalf of her son.
abrogate *v.*	to do away with, abolish, annul	The board may *abrogate* the public's right to speak.
abscond *v.*	to leave quickly, flee	Did the puppy *abscond* with the steak bones?
abstemious *adj.*	self-disciplined, temperate, moderate	Be *abstemious* when your boss is paying for your meal.
accede *v.*	to give in, agree, consent	Will the workers *accede* to the proposed contract?
acme *n.*	pinnacle, summit, culmination	That award marks the *acme* of her acting career.
acumen *n.*	insight, wisdom, quickness	She is known for having outstanding business *acumen*.
adamant *adj.*	unyielding, obstinate, inflexible	The professor was *adamant* that all work be in by Friday.
adjudicate *v.*	to pass judgment, arbitrate, referee	A panel of musicians will *adjudicate* the performances.
advent *n.*	arrival, beginning, initiation	Daffodils often indicate the *advent* of warmer weather.
aegis *n.*	protection, guidance, tutelage	The students were under the *aegis* of a group of experts.
affinity *n.*	attraction, sympathy, resemblance	Judging by her wardrobe, she has an *affinity* for ruffles.
aggrandize *v.*	to exaggerate, enhance, overdo	He tends to *aggrandize* his rather minor achievements.
agnate *adj.*	related on the father's side	In some tribes, the family connection is strictly *agnate*.
alacrity *n.*	enthusiasm, readiness, eagerness	We responded to his suggestion with *alacrity*.
albeit *conj.*	notwithstanding, although	After his fall, his recovery was steady, *albeit* slow.
allege *v.*	to contend, claim, assert	They continue to *allege* that the accountant lost their files.

Table 3.2 Difficult Vocabulary Words (*Continued*)

Word	Meaning	Sentence
amalgamate *v.*	to combine, merge, integrate	Our village may *amalgamate* with the town next door.
ambient *adj.*	surrounding, encircling	All of the *ambient* noises made it hard to converse.
ameliorate *v.*	to improve, upgrade, enhance	Those upgrades will *ameliorate* Internet access.
amicable *adj.*	friendly, cordial, harmonious	Their divorce was *amicable* and went forward quickly.
amphora *n.*	jar, jug	Feathers in a clay *amphora* decorated the entrance.
anchorite *n.*	recluse, hermit	He lived as an *anchorite* with just a cot and his Bible.
anima *n.*	soul, spirit	She believes that her *anima* controls her actions.
animus *n.*	ill will, hostility, enmity	My *animus* toward that writer stems from years of abuse.
anneal *v.*	to strengthen, harden	To *anneal* glass, you must let it cool slowly.
antebellum *adj.*	prewar	The house's columns date from the *antebellum* era.
antediluvian *adj.*	ancient, prehistoric, primitive	Caves held the bones of *antediluvian* creatures.
apiculture *n.*	beekeeping	He wore a helmet and gloves when engaging in *apiculture*.
aplomb *n.*	self-confidence, composure, assurance	Despite her youth, she performed with *aplomb*.
apoplectic *adj.*	irate, angry, furious	The coach was *apoplectic* when his team appeared to give up.
apostate *n.*	renegade, disbeliever, runaway	Having left the mosque, he was considered an *apostate*.
approbation *n.*	approval, praise, commendation	Their splendid duet was greeted by great *approbation*.
arboreal *adj.*	tree-dwelling	*Arboreal* species often have long, grasping tails.
archetype *n.*	standard, model, prototype	Beelzebub is considered an *archetype* of evil.
arduous *adj.*	laborious, difficult, demanding	Few jobs are more *arduous* than coal mining.
arras *n.*	wall hanging, tapestry	A woven *arras* covered one wall of the castle.

Table 3.2 Difficult Vocabulary Words (*Continued*)

Word	Meaning	Sentence
artisan *n.*	craftsperson	I bought the wooden toys from an *artisan* at the market.
ascertain *v.*	to discover, determine, ensure	Were you able to *ascertain* the cost of that property?
aspersion *n.*	insinuation, defamation, slur	His nasty *aspersion* made his opponent look better to me.
assiduous *adj.*	industrious, diligent, persistent	They are *assiduous* workers who never seem to tire.
atelier *n.*	studio, workshop	Degas painted daily in his Parisian *atelier*.
audacious *adj.*	bold, overconfident, reckless	Her *audacious* plan reflected her fearless attitude.
august *adj.*	grand, impressive, majestic	The judge made an *august* entrance in his flowing robes.
aureole *n.*	halo, aura	In the painting, a white *aureole* surrounds Mary.
auspicious *adj.*	lucky, favorable, fortunate	Sailors believed that a red sunset was an *auspicious* sign.
austere *adj.*	sober, plain, severe	The Mennonite workers dressed in *austere* garments.
avaricious *adj.*	greedy, acquisitive, grasping	An *avaricious* fox is bothering the chickens.
avuncular *adj.*	like an uncle	He welcomed his students with an *avuncular* greeting.
axiom *n.*	maxim, truth, principle	One common *axiom* states that two points define a line.
babel *n.*	din, confusion, noise	The *babel* of the marketplace meant that we had to shout.
badinage *n.*	banter, repartee, chitchat	She liked to engage in flirtatious *badinage* with her classmates.
bagatelle *n.*	trifle, triviality	Their request was a mere *bagatelle* for the skilled chef.
bailiwick *n.*	specialty, field of expertise	Her *bailiwick* is the study of freshwater sustainability.
baleful *adj.*	sinister, menacing, malevolent	The vulture gave us a *baleful* glance before flapping off.
banal *adj.*	clichéd, trite, hackneyed	Please omit *banal* phrases from your academic writing.
bane *n.*	blight, curse, injury	Their ancient plumbing is the *bane* of those homeowners.

Table 3.2 Difficult Vocabulary Words (*Continued*)

Word	Meaning	Sentence
bastion *n.*	mainstay, stronghold	That particular institute is a *bastion* of conservativism.
bazaar *n.*	open-air market, flea market	We furnished the room with rare finds from the *bazaar*.
beatific *adj.*	saintly, blessed, venerable	The monks wrote about their *beatific* vision of St. Jerome.
beguile *v.*	to entice, charm, captivate	We tried to *beguile* the famous author to join us at the table.
behest *n.*	command, request, order	At the queen's *behest*, the knights patrolled the town.
belay *v.*	to secure, make fast	As the boats reach the dock, deckhands *belay* each rope.
beleaguer *v.*	to harass, bother, pester	Swarms of flies *beleaguer* the cows in the pasture.
belie *v.*	to contradict, misrepresent, disprove	The new data *belie* what we had believed earlier.
bellicose *adj.*	warlike, aggressive, contentious	His *bellicose* attitude makes him seem out of control.
belligerent *adj.*	hostile, quarrelsome, argumentative	Drunks may become *belligerent* or clumsy.
beneficent *adj.*	kind, charitable, of assistance	She is known for her *beneficent* support of local schools.
berate *v.*	to scold, reproach, criticize	Do not *berate* me for doing what I think is right.
berserk *adj.*	frenzied, crazy, uncontrollable	Catnip makes my cat run in *berserk* circles.
beseech *v.*	to beg, plead, implore	The people *beseech* their king to keep their nation out of war.
bibliophile *n.*	book collector	My aunt is a *bibliophile* who specializes in first editions.
bilk *v.*	to cheat, swindle, defraud	Their plot could *bilk* retirees out of their pensions.
blandish *v.*	to cajole, wheedle, sweet-talk	Don't try to *blandish* me just to gain my forgiveness.
blight *v.*	to damage, ruin, disfigure	An infestation may *blight* the entire crop of corn.
bludgeon *v.*	to club, beat, bash	Did he use a bat to *bludgeon* the escaping thief?
boisterous *adj.*	rowdy, noisy, unruly	A *boisterous* crowd ran through the streets after the game.

Table 3.2 Difficult Vocabulary Words (*Continued*)

Word	Meaning	Sentence
bolster *v.*	to prop up, support, encourage	You can *bolster* the campaign by contributing money.
bombast *n.*	bluster, pomposity, bravado	The boy's *bombast* and swagger covered up his insecurity.
boycott *v.*	to reject, abstain from	We will *boycott* that store until they pay a living wage.
brackish *adj.*	salty, briny	*Brackish* water filled the small inlet.
brusque *adj.*	curt, abrupt, brisk	She acts *brusque* when she is under stress or in a hurry.
bulwark *n.*	fortification, rampart, embankment	Before the battle, soldiers lined up along the *bulwark*.
burgeon *v.*	to sprout, proliferate, multiply	Mini-marts and fast-food sites *burgeon* along the highway.
cabal *n.*	faction, conspiracy, plot	The rebels formed a *cabal* that met twice a week.
cache *n.*	hiding place, hoard, store	They found a *cache* of old films in the basement of the library.
cacophonous *adj.*	inharmonious, dissonant, jarring	That *cacophonous* din is his attempt to play the trombone.
cadence *n.*	rhythm, pace, lilt	The train's gentle *cadence* soon lulled us to sleep.
cajole *v.*	to coax, persuade, entice	Can we *cajole* you into spending the day with us?
calumny *n.*	slander, defamation, slur	His vile *calumny* against her may lead to a lawsuit.
canon *n.*	rule, law, tenet	The *canon* of the council of Nicaea advises fasting for Lent.
capacious *adj.*	roomy, voluminous, sizeable	She fits her laptop and books into that *capacious* carpetbag.
capitulate *v.*	to yield, surrender, submit	Their army will soon *capitulate* to our demands.
capricious *adj.*	impulsive, whimsical, variable	Her *capricious* nature keeps us guessing what she'll do next.
caveat *n.*	caution, warning, stipulation	The doctor's only *caveat* was to avoid fried foods.
celerity *n.*	swiftness, speed, haste	With incredible *celerity*, the pit crew replaced all four tires.

Table 3.2 Difficult Vocabulary Words (*Continued*)

Word	Meaning	Sentence
chagrin *n.*	embarrassment, mortification, disappointment	Her *chagrin* at losing the game was visible on her face.
charisma *n.*	charm, magnetism, appeal	A politician's *charisma* can help her to attract supporters.
chary *adj.*	wary, cautious, suspicious	After losing money, she is *chary* of using that stockbroker again.
chicanery *n.*	trickery, deception, fraud	The con men used *chicanery* to learn about their victims.
chide *v.*	to scold, rebuke, reprimand	Both nannies *chide* their charges after the sandbox battle.
chivalrous *adj.*	gallant, well-mannered, courteous	His *chivalrous* manners seem to come from an earlier age.
choleric *adj.*	bad-tempered, irritable, belligerent	A *choleric* disposition rarely leads to successful friendships.
churlish *adj.*	rude, coarse, boorish	It would be *churlish* to refuse his kind hospitality.
circumscribe *v.*	to restrict, limit, encircle	Barbed-wire fences *circumscribe* the ranchland.
clamor *v.*	to demand, exclaim, shout	Excited children *clamor* for the pitcher's autograph.
cleave *v.*	to split, slice, chop	Use the sharpened axe to *cleave* the firewood easily.
clemency *n.*	mercy, leniency, compassion	The judge may grant *clemency* if she finds his remorse sincere.
cloying *adj.*	syrupy, sugary, nauseating	The overly sweet sauce tasted unpleasantly *cloying*.
cogent *adj.*	logical, convincing, coherent	Your argument is both *cogent* and well-reasoned.
collier *n.*	coal miner	The *collier* descended into the shaft on a rickety elevator.
collusion *n.*	conspiracy, scheme, complicity	Their whispered conversations seemed to imply a *collusion*.
comestible *adj.*	edible, safe to eat	Do you know which of the wild mushrooms are *comestible*?

Table 3.2 Difficult Vocabulary Words (*Continued*)

Word	Meaning	Sentence
commensurate *adj.*	proportionate, corresponding, matching	We expect a salary *commensurate* with our skills.
commiserate *v.*	to empathize, sympathize, show compassion	I *commiserate* with the workers who lost their jobs this week.
commodious *adj.*	ample, spacious, roomy	One *commodious* handbag can hold everything you need.
compendium *n.*	summary, abstract, list	The appendix includes a *compendium* of early works.
complacent *adj.*	contented, self-satisfied, unconcerned	Knowing that she has tenure gives her a *complacent* air.
compunction *n.*	regret, qualm, uneasiness	He had no *compunction* about firing the sloppy painters.
conciliate *v.*	to pacify, appease, mollify	The boss made some changes to *conciliate* upset workers.
condone *v.*	to pardon, overlook, forgive	I could never *condone* their crude behavior.
conflagration *n.*	fire, inferno, blaze	By the time firetrucks arrived, a *conflagration* had erupted.
conjecture *n.*	guess, speculation, theory	My *conjecture* about his motives proved to be incorrect.
construe *v.*	to interpret, analyze, decipher	Were you able to *construe* the meaning of this old text?
contentious *adj.*	controversial, argumentative, debatable	Her *contentious* remarks led to a forceful and heated discussion.
contiguous *adj.*	adjacent, abutting, bordering	The farmer's fields are *contiguous* with state land.
contrition *n.*	repentance, penitence, remorse	The burglar's obvious *contrition* may earn him a short sentence.
conundrum *n.*	riddle, puzzle, mystery	That geometric proof is a complete *conundrum* to me.
convivial *adj.*	hospitable, cordial, sociable	Our hosts were *convivial* and made our trip delightful.
coquette *n.*	flirt, tease	She is shy in real life but plays a *coquette* on television.
cosmopolitan *adj.*	sophisticated, international, multi-ethnic	Toronto is a *cosmopolitan* city with foods from every land.

Table 3.2 Difficult Vocabulary Words (*Continued*)

Word	Meaning	Sentence
cotillion *n.*	ball, dance, prom	Our club holds a formal *cotillion* once a year.
countenance *n.*	appearance, face, expression	The child's *countenance* mixed excitement with fear.
covenant *n.*	agreement, pledge, contract	The classmates made a *covenant* to meet again in 20 years.
credible *adj.*	believable, plausible, probable	Is that theory *credible*, or does it lack substance?
cryptic *adj.*	puzzling, mysterious, secret	Did you receive a *cryptic* message from your father?
cudgel *n.*	club, stick, truncheon	He used a *cudgel* to beat away the thorn bushes.
culvert *n.*	drain, sewer, channel	Ducks were swimming in the *culvert* after the rainstorm.
curate *n.*	clergyman, cleric	A *curate* greeted us at the door of the church.
cursory *adj.*	superficial, hasty, perfunctory	I only had time to give your essay a *cursory* look.
dander *n.*	ire, temper, anger	Don't get your *dander* up just because he behaves rudely.
daub *v.*	to smear, spread, paint	The clowns *daub* their cheeks with red face paint.
debonair *adj.*	refined, suave, elegant	James Bond is a character known for *debonair* good looks.
deferential *adj.*	obsequious, respectful, reverent	The young priests are *deferential* toward the bishop.
deleterious *adj.*	harmful, injurious, damaging	Caffeine may have a *deleterious* effect on blood pressure.
demeanor *n.*	bearing, behavior, conduct	A subdued *demeanor* is appropriate at a funeral.
demur *v.*	to object, protest, balk	I must *demur* at your description of her presentation.
denigrate *v.*	to belittle, vilify, disparage	Try not to *denigrate* people whom you do not understand.

Table 3.2 Difficult Vocabulary Words (*Continued*)

Word	Meaning	Sentence
denizen *n.*	resident, citizen, native	She is a *denizen* of Chicago, having lived there for decades.
deprecate *v.*	to condemn, denounce, criticize	Some students *deprecate* the value of writing seminars.
dereliction *n.*	abandonment, neglect, desertion	Parts of the city were marked by *dereliction* and ruin.
despoil *v.*	to ruin, plunder, damage	Did the Vikings *despoil* these coastal towns?
desultory *adj.*	haphazard, aimless, random	Our conversation became *desultory* and finally died out.
detritus *n.*	debris, remains, fragments	A storm left shells and other *detritus* along the sand.
devolve *v.*	to delegate, entrust, transfer	Slowly, the king will *devolve* power to his ministers.
diaphanous *adj.*	sheer, filmy, translucent	*Diaphanous* curtains let in the morning light.
diatribe *n.*	invective, tirade, rant	Your *diatribe* at the meeting just made you seem hysterical.
didactic *adj.*	informative, educational, instructive	The poem is *didactic* and has a clear moral.
diffident *adj.*	shy, reticent, timid	His *diffident* actions can seem unfriendly.
dilatory *adj.*	lagging, slow, sluggish	They used *dilatory* tactics to delay the proceedings.
discomfit *v.*	to embarrass, mortify, disconcert	Dad's hilarity is designed to *discomfit* his daughter.
disparage *v.*	to belittle, mock, criticize	He chose to *disparage* his staff rather than supporting them.
dissemble *v.*	to evade, feign, disguise	If you are sincere, you rarely *dissemble* or hide your feelings.
dissonance *n.*	discord, conflict, noise	Eastern music can sound like *dissonance* to untrained ears.
doctrinaire *adj.*	inflexible, dogmatic, strict	I find his ideas too *doctrinaire* to be practical.
dogmatic *adj.*	rigid, unbending, stubborn	Your *dogmatic* statements are not necessarily true.
dolor *n.*	sorrow, grief, misery	Lost in her *dolor*, the widow neglected her job and home.

Table 3.2 Difficult Vocabulary Words (*Continued*)

Word	Meaning	Sentence
dour *adj.*	grim, gloomy, forbidding	That *dour* expression makes you look perpetually angry.
dragoon *v.*	force, coerce, intimidate	It was once popular to *dragoon* boys into military service.
drivel *n.*	idiocy, foolishness, nonsense	Do not spout *drivel* and expect us to believe you.
duplicity *n.*	deception, betrayal, treachery	Their *duplicity* led everyone to turn against them.
ebullient *adj.*	enthusiastic, merry, jovial	She was *ebullient* when her boss offered her a promotion.
echelon *n.*	rank, level, division	Only family members occupy the top *echelon* of the company.
eclectic *adj.*	mixed, varied, diverse	Her appetite is *eclectic*; she likes Thai food and barbecue.
edification *n.*	enlightenment, learning, instruction	For your *edification*, here are some informative brochures.
efficacious *adj.*	effective, successful, efficient	That therapy is *efficacious* in patients with muscle loss.
effrontery *n.*	boldness, impudence, impertinence	Her grandfather scolded her for her *effrontery*.
empirical *adj.*	experiential, verifiable, observed	The *empirical* evidence seems to prove our theory.
emulate *v.*	to imitate, copy, replicate	Children tend to *emulate* the adults in their lives.
encomium *n.*	praise, tribute, accolade	We offered an *encomium* for his work in the community.
enigma *n.*	puzzle, mystery, riddle	The coin's disappearance was an *enigma* we could not solve.
ennui *n.*	boredom, world-weariness, tedium	She suffers from *ennui*; nothing seems to interest her.
entreaty *n.*	plea, appeal, supplication	An *entreaty* to the teacher led to a new, more feasible deadline.
ephemeral *adj.*	transient, fleeting, short-lived	Summer was *ephemeral*; before long, it was chilly again.
epigram *n.*	saying, witticism, axiom	Above the counter is an *epigram* that amuses everyone.

Table 3.2 Difficult Vocabulary Words (*Continued*)

Word	Meaning	Sentence
epistle *n.*	letter, communiqué, dispatch	Our town owns an *epistle* from Lincoln to a childhood friend.
equivocal *adj.*	ambiguous, unclear, indefinite	Test results were *equivocal*, so more tests were scheduled.
eremite *n.*	hermit, recluse, ascetic	An *eremite* lives alone in the woods behind the village.
ersatz *adj.*	phony, fake, artificial	*Ersatz* coffee was all that was available during wartime.
escarp *n.*	cliff, slope, precipice	Climbing the *escarp* requires skill and good equipment.
ethos *n.*	culture, character, philosophy	New York's *ethos* in the 1980s centered on making money.
eulogize *v.*	to praise, extol, honor	Several colleagues stood to *eulogize* their fallen friend.
euphoric *adj.*	ecstatic, joyous, elated	We were *euphoric* when our band was chosen to play.
evanesce *v.*	to dissipate, vaporize, disappear	Bubbles *evanesce* as she pours the champagne.
evocative *adj.*	reminiscent, suggestive, extracting	That *evocative* poem appeals to anyone who loves nature.
exacerbate *v.*	to worsen, aggravate, inflame	Don't *exacerbate* your injury by exercising too soon.
excoriate *v.*	to rebuke, attack, censure	Other journalists *excoriate* him for stealing from their work.
exculpate *v.*	to clear, absolve, exonerate	New evidence will serve to *exculpate* the congressman.
execrable *adj.*	deplorable, disgusting, hateful	This cherry-flavored toothpaste is *execrable* and nasty.
exegesis *n.*	interpretation, analysis, construal	Did you read his *exegesis* of the ancient scrolls?
exhort *v.*	to encourage, urge, insist	We tried to *exhort* our coach into taking us out tonight.
exonerate *v.*	to acquit, pardon, vindicate	Did the judge *exonerate* him of all wrongdoing?
extirpate *v.*	to pull up, uproot, abolish	Let us *extirpate* all inequity from our public schools.
extricate *v.*	to disentangle, free, rescue	The kitten fought to *extricate* itself from the tangle of yarn.

Table 3.2 Difficult Vocabulary Words (*Continued*)

Word	Meaning	Sentence
exuberant *adj.*	enthusiastic, fervent, high-spirited	Several *exuberant* fans waited backstage for the performers.
fabricate *v.*	to manufacture, construct, concoct	Let's *fabricate* a shed to hold all of our gardening tools.
fabulist *n.*	liar, impostor, fraud	He's a noted *fabulist*; his words often deceive strangers.
facetious *adj.*	flippant, humorous, playful	That *facetious* remark does not help to fix the problem.
facile *adj.*	superficial, effortless, simplistic	His response to this complex problem is too *facile* for me.
factotum *n.*	aide, assistant, subordinate	A young *factotum* carried the boss's overcoat and briefcase.
fastidious *adj.*	painstaking, finicky, fussy	No one can compete with that tailor's fine and *fastidious* work.
fatuous *adj.*	inane, foolish, idiotic	I immediately regretted my *fatuous* response to his question.
fealty *n.*	allegiance, loyalty, faithfulness	The players' *fealty* to their coach was inspiring to see.
fecund *adj.*	fruitful, productive, fertile	The land was *fecund* and well-irrigated.
felicitous *adj.*	lucky, fortuitous, apt	A rainbow can appear to be a *felicitous* sign.
fervid *adj.*	zealous, passionate, ardent	She is a *fervid* supporter of that congressional candidate.
filial *adj.*	relating to a son or daughter	He considered assisting his father to be his *filial* duty.
flagrant *adj.*	blatant, brazen, overt	That hit was a *flagrant* violation of the rules.
flippant *adj.*	facetious, glib, offhand	The senator's *flippant* remark annoyed the reporter.
flout *v.*	to disobey, defy, contravene	It is unwise to *flout* the university's regulations.
foment *v.*	to provoke, incite, agitate	Did the union *foment* protest or just support it?
founder *v.*	to sink, fail, collapse	The business began to *founder* under the weight of its debt.
fracas *n.*	disturbance, brawl, quarrel	A *fracas* broke out between supporters of the two teams.

Table 3.2 Difficult Vocabulary Words (*Continued*)

Word	Meaning	Sentence
fractious *adj.*	peevish, irritable, ill-tempered	He is most *fractious* when he first awakens from a nap.
fraternal *adj.*	relating to a brother	The boys seem to lack any *fraternal* affection.
fraught *adj.*	burdened, laden, full	Her memoir was *fraught* with emotion and pain.
fulsome *adj.*	flattering, overgenerous, unctuous	*Fulsome* praise can sometimes seem insincere.
furtive *adj.*	sly, secretive, stealthy	The dog gave its owner a *furtive* glance as it licked the plate.
gaffe *n.*	error, blunder, faux pas	The reporter's unfortunate *gaffe* harmed her reputation.
gallantry *n.*	courtliness, chivalry, heroism	The knight's *gallantry* impressed even his enemies.
galvanize *v.*	to rouse, stimulate, incite	Injustice may *galvanize* even the laziest people to protest.
gamut *n.*	range, extent, scope	His class covers the *gamut* of East Indian literature.
garrulous *adj.*	talkative, voluble, chatty	She became *garrulous* when she was nervous or tense.
gelid *adj.*	frozen, cold, icy	The *gelid* drink was perfect for such a hot day.
gesticulate *v.*	to gesture, signal	Don't just *gesticulate* wildly; use your words.
gird *v.*	to encircle, surround, enclose	Silver belts *gird* the waists of those models.
glib *adj.*	smooth, persuasive, offhand	His *glib* answer sounded good despite its lack of meaning.
gradient *n.*	slope, incline, hill	The road has a shallow *gradient* in front of their house.
grandiose *adj.*	pompous, ostentatious, flamboyant	Don't make *grandiose* statements about your skills.
grandiloquent *adj.*	pretentious, pompous, overbearing	The actor's *grandiloquent* entrance showed her vanity.
gratuitous *adj.*	free, unnecessary, superfluous	We found his advice *gratuitous* and inappropriate.
guile *n.*	deception, trickery, cunning	It will take all of her *guile* to escape this messy situation.
gullible *adj.*	naïve, trusting, credulous	She was *gullible* and believed his flattering words.

Table 3.2 Difficult Vocabulary Words (*Continued*)

Word	Meaning	Sentence
hackneyed *adj.*	overused, trite, clichéd	Replace that *hackneyed* slogan with something fresher.
halcyon *adj.*	peaceful, tranquil, quiet	The *halcyon* days of childhood linger in our minds.
hapless *adj.*	unlucky, unfortunate, wretched	That *hapless* fellow seems to live under his own cloud.
harangue *n.*	tirade, rant, lecture	Some parents *harangue* their children for poor grades.
harbinger *n.*	omen, forerunner, portent	Is a raven considered to be a *harbinger* of trouble?
hauteur *n.*	arrogance, self-importance, haughtiness	Her *hauteur* makes her look snobbish, not distinguished.
heinous *adj.*	odious, shocking, monstrous	It was a *heinous* crime that people still discuss years later.
heresy *n.*	unorthodoxy, sacrilege, deviation	His refusal to wear a suit is considered *heresy* at the firm.
hiatus *n.*	break, pause, interval	The class took a short *hiatus* before resuming the discussion.
homage *n.*	deference, worship, respect	That statue pays *homage* to the soldiers who fought in Iraq.
hovel *n.*	hut, slum, shack	Their home was little more than a *hovel* made of scrap wood.
hubris *n.*	pride, arrogance, audacity	Excessive *hubris* does not endear you to others.
humbug *n.*	hypocrisy, duplicity, insincerity	Her analysis reeked of *humbug* and double standards.
iconoclast *n.*	dissident, rebel, radical	He is an *iconoclast* who rejects the usual party line.
idyllic *adj.*	tranquil, relaxing, carefree	They spent an *idyllic* weekend enjoying the quiet cabin.
ignoble *adj.*	reprehensible, dastardly, shameful	She was ashamed of her *ignoble* feelings of envy.
ignominy *n.*	disgrace, humiliation, shame	The discredited CEO ended his career in *ignominy*.
illicit *adj.*	illegal, illegitimate, criminal	Their *illicit* activities are bound to land them in jail.
imbroglio *n.*	entanglement, embarrassment, fix	Caught up in the *imbroglio*, she hired a PR firm to guide her.

Table 3.2 Difficult Vocabulary Words (*Continued*)

Word	Meaning	Sentence
immaterial *adj.*	irrelevant, unimportant, insignificant	Whether he started the fight is *immaterial* to this case.
impecunious *adj.*	destitute, poor, penniless	Despite a few land holdings, the family is *impecunious*.
implacable *adj.*	ruthless, relentless, merciless	Gunfire marked the *implacable* advance of the Union army.
importune *v.*	to beg, beset, pester	The children *importune* their grandparents for sweets.
imprecate *v.*	to curse, hex	The criminals *imprecate* the snitch for turning them in.
impugn *v.*	to accuse, challenge, attack	Why did she *impugn* your motives at the board meeting?
inchoate *adj.*	unformed, undeveloped, incomplete	The structures of the new nation were still *inchoate*.
incontrovertible *adj.*	unquestionable, indisputable, irrefutable	It is *incontrovertible* that last winter was unusually warm.
inculcate *v.*	to instill, indoctrinate, instruct	Parents hope to *inculcate* their children with their values.
indigent *adj.*	poor, impoverished, needy	*Indigent* families are welcome at the food bank.
indomitable *adj.*	unconquerable, invincible, strong	Her *indomitable* optimism inspired her team members.
ineffable *adj.*	inexpressible, indescribable, indefinable	The *ineffable* grandeur of the canyon took our breath away.
infamy *n.*	disgrace, notoriety, disrepute	The mayor's *infamy* ruined the name of his home town.
ingenuous *adj.*	unsophisticated, naive, candid	Her *ingenuous* character led her to trust the wrong people.
inimical *adj.*	detrimental, injurious, unfavorable	Salty foods may be *inimical* to one's health.
iniquity *n.*	wickedness, evil, injustice	In *The Scarlet Letter*, the heroine is charged with *iniquity*.
inscrutable *adj.*	impenetrable, enigmatic, mysterious	His face was *inscrutable*, so no one knew what to expect.
insipid *adj.*	trite, dull, colorless	Because the songs were *insipid*, the crowd lost interest.
intrepid *adj.*	bold, resolute, valiant	Lewis and Clark were *intrepid* explorers of the West.

Table 3.2 Difficult Vocabulary Words (*Continued*)

Word	Meaning	Sentence
invidious *adj.*	offensive, unpleasant, undesirable	That *invidious* comparison will just annoy both writers.
irascible *adj.*	short-tempered, irritable, cranky	She was *irascible* when attacked but kind to her defenders.
jaded *adj.*	world-weary, cynical, blasé	A youth with too much freedom and money soon grows *jaded*.
jejune *adj.*	immature, unsophisticated, sophomoric	Your *jejune* behavior proves that you are not ready.
jettison *v.*	to throw away, discard, dump	Let's *jettison* all of the unused junk in the garage.
juggernaut *n.*	force, deity	Her company was a *juggernaut* in the city's economy.
keen *v.*	to lament, bemoan, wail	Aunts and cousins *keen* behind the casket in the procession.
ken *n.*	knowledge, understanding, comprehension	Advanced calculus is far beyond my *ken*.
knave *n.*	villain, criminal, scoundrel	That *knave* conned his clients out of their hard-earned cash.
kowtow *v.*	to conform, fawn, grovel	You need not *kowtow* to your boss's every command.
lachrymose *adj.*	tearful, weepy, sentimental	She grew *lachrymose* when we mentioned her late husband.
lackey *n.*	minion, assistant, servant	A *lackey* took our coats at the door of the mansion.
laggard *n.*	straggler, idler, slacker	We do not have time to wait for any *laggard*.
lambaste *v.*	to beat, berate, scold	I had to *lambaste* him for his poorly written report.
languid *adj.*	leisurely, lethargic, unhurried	She raised one *languid* arm to signal the waiter.
laud *v.*	to praise, glorify, acclaim	My speech will *laud* the senator for her support of state colleges.
levity *n.*	frivolity, wit, flippancy	A little *levity* can brighten a stressful day.
lithe *adj.*	supple, lissome, graceful	Nimbly, the dancer stretched her *lithe* limbs along the barre.
loquacious *adj.*	talkative, garrulous, wordy	Is he usually this *loquacious*, or does he ever pause to think?

Table 3.2 Difficult Vocabulary Words (*Continued*)

Word	Meaning	Sentence
lugubrious *adj.*	mournful, doleful, melancholy	A heavy, *lugubrious* melody emerged from the pipe organ.
lurid *adj.*	shocking, explicit, vivid	All of the *lurid* details of the crime were in the newspaper.
lyrical *adj.*	expressive, poetic, emotional	She uses a *lyrical* style to describe even ordinary scenes.
macabre *adj.*	gruesome, ghoulish, horrid	That *macabre* mask will scare away trick-or-treaters.
macerate *v.*	to soak, steep, pulp	Let the fruit *macerate* in a sweet sugar syrup.
machinate *v.*	to plot, conspire, scheme	The group will *machinate* to rid the town of its supervisor.
maelstrom *n.*	whirlpool, vortex, turbulence	Trash whirled in the *maelstrom* after the flood.
maladroit *adj.*	gawky, awkward, inept	Teenagers may be *maladroit* as they grow into their bodies.
malefactor *n.*	scoundrel, criminal, evildoer	We hope that the *malefactor* receives ample punishment.
malice *n.*	spite, hatred, wickedness	She criticized them out of *malice*, not out of concern.
malign *v.*	to smear, slander, disparage	Don't *malign* the police chief for doing his job.
malleable *adj.*	yielding, dutiful, adaptable	She was *malleable* to our suggestions and eager to help.
manumit *v.*	to free, emancipate, liberate	When did Great Britain *manumit* African slaves?
martinet *n.*	despot, disciplinarian, tyrant	The colonel, a *martinet*, is feared by his troops.
melee *n.*	fracas, brawl, skirmish	Adults broke up a brief *melee* on the playground.
mellifluous *adj.*	smooth, sweet, honeyed	His saxophone has a pleasant, *mellifluous* tone.
mendacity *n.*	deceit, dishonesty, untruthfulness	Her constant *mendacity* has lost her a group of loyal friends.
mendicant *n.*	beggar, almsman, pauper	A *mendicant* walked through the subway, hat in hand.
mentor *n.*	counselor, tutor, adviser	I serve as a *mentor* for several entering freshmen.
mercenary *adj.*	money-oriented, acquisitive, grasping	A day trader may benefit from a *mercenary* attitude.

Table 3.2 Difficult Vocabulary Words (*Continued*)

Word	Meaning	Sentence
mere *n.*	pond, lake, marsh	Herons hunted small frogs in the area around the *mere*.
meretricious *adj.*	vulgar, gaudy, specious	Those *meretricious* trinkets are not worth a dollar.
meticulous *adj.*	painstaking, careful, thorough	She does *meticulous* work as she repairs the old books.
mettle *n.*	courage, fortitude, pluck	The soldiers showed *mettle* as they patrolled the village.
mien *n.*	bearing, appearance, demeanor	Even under stress, her *mien* is always regal and calm.
misanthropic *adj.*	mistrustful, skeptical, scornful	A *misanthropic* attitude will never win you friends.
mitigate *v.*	to moderate, alleviate, ease	Early education may *mitigate* poverty in some cases.
modulate *v.*	to adjust, modify, vary	Please *modulate* your voice as you enter the hospital.
mollify *v.*	to pacify, calm, soothe	After the team's loss, no words could *mollify* the players.
moribund *adj.*	dying, declining, failing	It is a *moribund* town with few remaining businesses.
mundane *adj.*	commonplace, ordinary, dull	A vacation can break you out of your *mundane* existence.
munificent *adj.*	generous, charitable, benevolent	Her *munificent* deeds helped many in our community.
mutable *adj.*	alterable, changeable, variable	The hummingbird's colors are *mutable* as it flies.
nabob *n.*	ruler, noble, aristocrat	He is considered something of a *nabob* in his city of residence.
nadir *n.*	low point, depths, bottom	The loss of her job was the *nadir* of her misfortune.
naiveté *n.*	innocence, ingenuousness, artlessness	A child's *naiveté* makes every experience seem wondrous.
narcissism *n.*	self-love, conceit, vanity	*Narcissism* led her to challenge any critique of her work.
nascent *adj.*	blossoming, budding, emerging	The *nascent* windmill industry has transformed the town.
nebulous *adj.*	cloudy, hazy, imprecise	His *nebulous* explanation just confused matters.

Table 3.2 Difficult Vocabulary Words (*Continued*)

Word	Meaning	Sentence
nemesis *n.*	arch-enemy, rival, retribution	Othello's *nemesis* is clearly his adviser, Iago.
nettle *v.*	to irritate, vex, annoy	Her constant nitpicking will just *nettle* her coworkers.
nicety *n.*	detail, subtlety, fastidiousness	Using the proper fork is a *nicety* of table manners.
niggardly *adj.*	grasping, parsimonious, stingy	He was especially *niggardly* at handing out compliments.
noisome *adj.*	offensive, foul, rank	What is that *noisome* odor coming from the kitchen?
nonchalant *adj.*	unconcerned, indifferent, cool	Act *nonchalant*, and they will never suspect a thing.
nugatory *adj.*	trifling, invalid, unimportant	Leave those *nugatory* details out of the report.
numismatist *n.*	coin collector	The *numismatist* has coins found on a sunken ship.
obdurate *adj.*	stubborn, obstinate, unyielding	An *obdurate* refusal to learn will not help you to succeed.
obese *adj.*	fat, stout, corpulent	If he becomes more *obese*, it will affect his heart and liver.
obfuscate *v.*	to complicate, confuse, obscure	Don't *obfuscate* the truth with unimportant details.
obsequious *adj.*	sycophantic, flattering, fawning	Her *obsequious* behavior made her seem oily and passive.
obsolete *adj.*	outdated, passé, archaic	That computer is *obsolete*; you can no longer buy parts for it.
obstreperous *adj.*	defiant, confrontational, aggressive	The *obstreperous* girl spent time in the principal's office.
obtrusive *adj.*	blatant, prominent, brash	The solar panels blend in and are not too *obtrusive*.
obviate *v.*	preclude, avert, hinder	A good carpet can *obviate* the need to refinish the floors.
odious *adj.*	abhorrent, hateful, vile	That *odious* person deserves no one's pity.
oeuvre *n.*	composition, masterwork, lifework	Her *oeuvre* contains poetry as well as prose.
officious *adj.*	self-important, bureaucratic, overbearing	With an *officious* manner, the woman directed us to sit down.

Table 3.2 Difficult Vocabulary Words (*Continued*)

Word	Meaning	Sentence
oligarchy *n.*	government by the few	My town is a democracy, but yours is more of an *oligarchy*.
omnipotent *adj.*	all-powerful, invincible, almighty	Zeus was *omnipotent*, but he still got into trouble.
onerous *adj.*	burdensome, oppressive, troublesome	Filling out tax forms can be an *onerous* task.
opaque *adj.*	dense, obscure, unclear	The tiles are *opaque* to hide the shower stall.
opprobrium *n.*	disgrace, ignominy, dishonor	He left town to escape any *opprobrium* for his misdeeds.
oracle *n.*	seer, soothsayer, visionary	An *oracle* warned him that he would face many enemies.
oratory *n.*	speechifying, rhetoric, eloquence	Plainspoken Harry Truman was not known for his *oratory*.
oscillate *v.*	to swing, vacillate, sway	The breeze caused the swings to *oscillate* gently.
osculate *v.*	to kiss, buss, contact	The two pool balls *osculate* as they come to rest.
ostentatious *adj.*	showy, flamboyant, pretentious	That *ostentatious* display does not inspire me to buy his hats.
palaver *n.*	chatter, gossip, chitchat	After an hour of *palaver*, club members got down to business.
palisade *n.*	picket, fence, fortification	We set up a *palisade* around the orchard to keep out the deer.
paltry *adj.*	trivial, trifling, unimportant	Leave that *paltry* task and join our more important discussion.
panache *n.*	flair, élan, style	He wears his unusual outfits with *panache*.
panegyric *n.*	tribute, encomium, compliment	She delivered a *panegyric* in memory of her father.
paradigm *n.*	model, example, archetype	Is Romeo the *paradigm* of the star-crossed lover?
paramount *adj.*	dominant, supreme, principal	Raising wages is *paramount* in our plan for reform.
pariah *n.*	outcast, exile, untouchable	His odd appearance made him a *pariah* in the village.

Table 3.2 Difficult Vocabulary Words (*Continued*)

Word	Meaning	Sentence
parsimony *n.*	stinginess, frugality, economy	*Parsimony* led her to live in rags when she could afford better.
pathos *n.*	pity, sympathy, sorrow	The *pathos* in the music made the audience somber and still.
patois *n.*	dialect, regionalism, vernacular	He speaks an unusual *patois* that mixes French and English.
paucity *n.*	scarceness, lack, rarity	There is a *paucity* of fresh seafood in my inland city.
peccadillo *n.*	offense, transgression, sin	A minor *peccadillo* will not result in much punishment.
pecuniary *adj.*	monetary, financial, economic	His *pecuniary* difficulties led him to seek new employment.
pedagogy *n.*	teaching, education, instruction	My education professor teaches theories of *pedagogy*.
pedantic *adj.*	dull, doctrinaire, obscure	The speaker's *pedantic* tone nearly put me to sleep.
penitence *n.*	atonement, repentance, regret	As *penitence* for being late, she promised to pay for dinner.
pensive *adj.*	thoughtful, brooding, meditative	In a *pensive* mood, he meditated on his life.
penurious *adj.*	indigent, destitute, stingy	The *penurious* family scratched out a living on five acres.
peon *n.*	laborer, farm worker, drudge	Rather than valuing my input, my boss treats me like a *peon*.
perambulate *v.*	to roam, stroll, amble	My parents like to *perambulate* along the paths in the park.
perfidy *n.*	betrayal, treachery, disloyalty	His earlier *perfidy* means that no one trusts him now.
perfunctory *adj.*	mechanical, unthinking, indifferent	I only gave the instructions a quick, *perfunctory* look.
peripatetic *adj.*	wandering, roving, itinerant	Her career has been *peripatetic*, taking her to six different cities.
persiflage *n.*	banter, chat, repartee	Their silly *persiflage* was meant to amuse the listener.
perspicacious *adj.*	astute, insightful, shrewd	One *perspicacious* remark led me to reconsider my plans.

Table 3.2 Difficult Vocabulary Words (*Continued*)

Word	Meaning	Sentence
petulant *adj.*	irritable, peevish, bad-tempered	That *petulant* child deserves a short time-out.
phalanx *n.*	formation, configuration, arrangement	A *phalanx* of armed horsemen appeared on the hillside.
phantasm *n.*	apparition, specter, ghost	Wispy fog can make you think that you have seen a *phantasm*.
Pharisee *n.*	hypocrite, goody-goody	His know-it-all superiority made us call him a *Pharisee*.
philanthropic *adj.*	benevolent, altruistic, charitable	*Philanthropic* works are expected of the very rich.
philatelist *n.*	stamp collector	Does that *philatelist* have any stamps that are valuable?
philistine *n.*	boor, barbarian, lout	Does my dislike of opera make me some kind of *philistine*?
phlegmatic *adj.*	placid, undemonstrative, apathetic	As others become passionate, he becomes more *phlegmatic*.
picayune *adj.*	trivial, paltry, worthless	That was a *picayune* waste of everyone's time.
piebald *adj.*	spotted, mottled, multicolored	The child rode a russet and white *piebald* pony.
piety *n.*	devotion, faithfulness, reverence	We expect nuns to display more *piety* than the average person.
pilfer *v.*	to steal, embezzle, filch	If you *pilfer* writing supplies from work, is that a crime?
pinion *v.*	to shackle, immobilize, bind	Both wrestlers *pinion* their opponents easily.
placate *v.*	to calm, pacify, appease	His quiet explanation seemed to *placate* the children.
platitude *n.*	cliché, banality, truism	Responding with a *platitude* will not make her feel better.
plaudit *n.*	acclaim, recognition, approval	She earned every *plaudit* that she received for her work.
plethora *n.*	excess, overabundance, surplus	The shop houses a *plethora* of worthless castoffs.
polemic *n.*	argument, controversy, refutation	His *polemic* against the two-party system made us mad.
politic *adj.*	artful, shrewd, diplomatic	Your outburst was not *politic* and merely upset people.

Table 3.2 Difficult Vocabulary Words (*Continued*)

Word	Meaning	Sentence
portentous *adj.*	ominous, significant, pompous	A *portentous* dark cloud seemed to hover over the hero.
portico *n.*	entry, walkway, porch	They stood under the *portico* to greet their guests.
postulate *v.*	hypothesize, assert, assume	What did early scientists *postulate* about lunar eclipses?
pragmatic *adj.*	practical, sensible, down-to-earth	She gave her son *pragmatic* advice as he set off for college.
prate *v.*	to chatter, jabber, babble	Don't *prate* about your day when I am trying to work.
precipitant *adj.*	headlong, rash, impulsive	Thoughtful preparation is better than *precipitant* action.
precocious *adj.*	advanced, gifted, premature	Her *precocious* daughter could read by the age of three.
predilection *n.*	partiality, tendency, preference	In bakeries, my *predilection* is for anything chocolate.
preponderant *adj.*	prevalent, predominant, influential	Wineries are *preponderant* in the land between the lakes.
prerogative *n.*	right, privilege, sanction	It is their *prerogative* to ask for a legal opinion.
prescient *adj.*	clairvoyant, psychic, perceptive	She seemed *prescient* when she correctly predicted the winner.
prevaricate *v.*	to lie, evade, hedge	Do not *prevaricate*; tell the panel what really happened.
probity *n.*	integrity, honesty, morality	They believe that his *probity* is beyond reproach.
proclivity *n.*	penchant, tendency, liking	A *proclivity* for sweets may lead to tooth decay.
prodigal *adj.*	profligate, wasteful, dissolute	Her *prodigal* habits made her father put her on an allowance.
prodigious *adj.*	extraordinary, phenomenal, immense	The table held a *prodigious* number of desserts.
profligate *adj.*	dissolute, decadent, extravagant	*Profligate* spending will bankrupt them in no time.
prognosticate *v.*	to predict, forecast, portend	What do you *prognosticate* about next week's weather?
proliferate *v.*	to multiply, breed, reproduce	Wildflowers *proliferate* the moment it gets warm.

Table 3.2 Difficult Vocabulary Words (*Continued*)

Word	Meaning	Sentence
prolix *adj.*	verbose, wordy, long-winded	His *prolix* speech confused and exhausted his audience.
promulgate *v.*	to broadcast, publicize, disseminate	Candidates *promulgate* their messages through social media.
propinquity *n.*	closeness, proximity, relationship	The *propinquity* of the shop to the highway made it desirable.
propitious *adj.*	favorable, auspicious, promising	It is a *propitious* time to buy that particular stock.
prosaic *adj.*	straightforward, matter-of-fact, pedestrian	*Prosaic* worries prevent us from seeing the beauty around us.
proscribe *v.*	to forbid, ban, prohibit	Do the rules *proscribe* bringing more than one guest?
provisional *adj.*	temporary, interim, short-term	It is a *provisional* appointment until we see how you perform.
prowess *n.*	skill, competence, expertise	The gymnast's *prowess* on the uneven bars amazed us.
prurient *adj.*	lascivious, salacious, lecherous	Keep that *prurient* literature out of the hands of children.
puerile *adj.*	juvenile, childish, immature	His *puerile* conduct would have seemed silly in a child of five.
pugnacious *adj.*	combative, belligerent, argumentative	Being agreeable may beat being *pugnacious* in this situation.
pulverize *v.*	to crush, macerate, mash	That machine is used in winemaking to *pulverize* grapes.
purloin *v.*	to steal, pilfer, rob	She would *purloin* a quarter or two from his change jar.
pusillanimous *adj.*	cowardly, timid, spineless	The *pusillanimous* officer ran away at the first sign of battle.
putative *adj.*	supposed, alleged, presumed	Who was the *putative* winner of last night's election?
quaff *v.*	to drink, imbibe, guzzle	*Quaff* that beer, and let's be on our way.
quagmire *n.*	predicament, quandary, dilemma	Deciding on a graduate school felt like a *quagmire* to him.

Table 3.2 Difficult Vocabulary Words (*Continued*)

Word	Meaning	Sentence
quash *v.*	to defeat, suppress, nullify	Don't *quash* their ideas; they have a right to express them.
quay *n.*	wharf, dock, jetty	Several people were fishing from the end of the *quay*.
querulous *adj.*	petulant, complaining, whiny	Her *querulous* objections followed me down the hallway.
quintessential *adj.*	exemplary, prototypical, classic	He is the *quintessential* leading man—articulate and attractive.
quixotic *adj.*	idealistic, romantic, impulsive	My *quixotic* vision is of a world at peace.
quotidian *adj.*	everyday, commonplace, usual	They continued to follow their *quotidian* routine.
rabid *adj.*	zealous, fanatical, fervent	They are both *rabid* believers in the need for alternative energy.
raffish *adj.*	carefree, breezy, jaunty	She tossed on her colorful scarf with a *raffish* air.
raillery *n.*	teasing, banter, ridicule	His *raillery* was meant in fun but felt hurtful.
rambunctious *adj.*	boisterous, unruly, disorderly	The *rambunctious* girls pushed rudely through the crowd.
rampant *adj.*	unrestrained, widespread, extensive	Rodents were *rampant* in the basement of the old museum.
rapport *n.*	affinity, bond, relationship	We built up a *rapport* after working together for weeks.
rarefied *adj.*	esoteric, obscure, highbrow	College life can seem *rarefied* to young blue-collar workers.
ratiocinate *v.*	to reason, calculate, deduce	I can't *ratiocinate* if you keep adding more information.
ravenous *adj.*	starving, famished, voracious	We were *ravenous* and stopped at the next diner we saw.
recalcitrant *adj.*	unmanageable, unruly, defiant	*Recalcitrant* middle-schoolers can be difficult to teach.
recant *v.*	disavow, retract, renounce	Galileo would not *recant* his statements about the sun.
reciprocate *v.*	interchange, return, counter	We would like to *reciprocate* your hospitality sometime.

Table 3.2 Difficult Vocabulary Words (*Continued*)

Word	Meaning	Sentence
recondite *adj.*	abstruse, ambiguous, complex	The article contains *recondite* facts about an unknown event.
recreant *adj.*	faithless, disloyal, craven	His *recreant* behavior led his supervisor to demote him.
rectitude *n.*	decency, morality, virtue	I want *rectitude* and honesty in my representatives.
redolent *adj.*	aromatic, fragrant, reminiscent	The shop was *redolent* with the smell of honey.
redress *v.*	to rectify, equalize, remedy	How can I *redress* my unintended harm to you?
redundant *adj.*	unnecessary, superfluous, excessive	We made the *redundant* bedroom into a library.
refractory *adj.*	disobedient, willful, resistant	We hired a trainer for our *refractory* dogs.
refute *v.*	to contest, disprove, rebut	It's hard to *refute* his insistence that the game was rigged.
reiterate *v.*	to repeat, restate, reaffirm	I will *reiterate* my statement in case you were not listening.
reliquary *n.*	receptacle, shrine, coffer	In the churchyard, a *reliquary* holds the bones of a saint.
remiss *adj.*	negligent, careless, slipshod	It was *remiss* of me not to call you when the twins were born.
remonstrate *v.*	to argue, dispute, protest	*Remonstrate* with me all you like; I will not change my mind.
reparation *n.*	amends, compensation, reimbursement	How do they intend to make *reparation* to their victims?
replete *adj.*	full, sated, stuffed	Following their five-course dinner, they felt *replete*.
reprobate *n.*	degenerate, rascal, troublemaker	That *reprobate* should pay for his wickedness.
resolute *adj.*	determined, steadfast, unyielding	I am *resolute* in my desire to attain a doctoral degree.
respite *n.*	reprieve, break, rest	We took a short *respite* to stretch our legs.
revile *v.*	to censure, berate, abuse	We *revile* television hosts who humiliate their guests.

Table 3.2 Difficult Vocabulary Words (*Continued*)

Word	Meaning	Sentence
rhapsodize *v.*	to enthuse, rave, gush	She continued to *rhapsodize* over the great Broadway show.
rhetoric *n.*	discourse, oratory, expression	Ability to use *rhetoric* well can help a politician.
ribald *adj.*	bawdy, lewd, vulgar	The *ribald* revue shocked some members of the audience.
rift *n.*	fissure, crevice, schism	There was a growing *rift* in the Republican Party.
rigorous *adj.*	demanding, laborious, meticulous	*Rigorous* exercise is only for those who are already healthy.
risible *adj.*	laughable, humorous, ludicrous	Your *risible* argument will convince no one at all.
rostrum *n.*	pulpit, dais, podium	On the *rostrum* were his notes and a bottle of water.
rout *n.*	defeat, disorder, retreat	The battle was a *rout*, and the army pulled back to the forest.
rubicund *adj.*	rosy, ruddy, red	Hals painted a drunk with *rubicund* nose and cheeks.
rue *v.*	to regret, lament, repent	I don't want to *rue* missing my child's important event.
ruminate *v.*	to ponder, mull over, reflect	I must *ruminate* on the choices that led me to this point.
saccharine *adj.*	sugary, cloying, syrupy	That song is too *saccharine* for such a powerful singer.
sacrilege *n.*	irreverence, blasphemy, profanation	Her use of psalms in artworks looked like *sacrilege* to some.
sacrosanct *adj.*	sacred, inviolable, hallowed	Our traditions are *sacrosanct* and may not be altered.
salacious *adj.*	immoral, indecent, lascivious	The *salacious* comic is not a hit with older audiences.
salubrious *adj.*	healthful, wholesome, beneficial	Taking a day off made a *salubrious* change in my mood.
salutary *adj.*	constructive, remedial, wholesome	One *salutary* effect of the storm was that I finished my book.

Table 3.2 Difficult Vocabulary Words (*Continued*)

Word	Meaning	Sentence
sanction *v.*	to permit, authorize, endorse	Will you *sanction* a short break for the workers?
sanguine *adj.*	upbeat, confident, optimistic	She is more *sanguine* about the upcoming election than I am.
sapient *adj.*	wise, astute, discerning	The professor bestowed some *sapient* advice on his students.
sardonic *adj.*	sarcastic, derisive, mocking	A *sardonic* wit may disguise the speaker's anxiety.
satrap *n.*	ruler, sovereign, emperor	The *satrap* had complete control over his people.
schism *n.*	division, rift, rupture	A *schism* in the Church took place in the 1300s.
scintilla *n.*	iota, bit, speck	I see no *scintilla* of evidence that his theory is correct.
screed *n.*	sermon, harangue, lecture	The magazine published his *screed* on global warming.
scrupulous *adj.*	painstaking, conscientious, thorough	He is *scrupulous* about washing his car every week in summer.
scurrilous *adj.*	defamatory, scandalous, abusive	That *scurrilous* gossip will ruin her reputation.
sectarian *adj.*	partisan, parochial	The *sectarian* struggle could turn into civil war.
secular *adj.*	worldly, lay, humanistic	The cathedral is surrounded by more *secular* shops and homes.
sedition *n.*	treason, subversion, rebellion	The traitor will probably be tried for *sedition*.
segue *n.*	transition, conversion	The conversation made a *segue* from personal to political issues.
seminal *adj.*	influential, decisive, creative	His most *seminal* work is about the influence of religion.
sententious *adj.*	moralizing, pompous, didactic	Your *sententious* speech was more patronizing than inspiring.
sepulcher *n.*	tomb, crypt, mausoleum	The raised *sepulcher* dominated the graveyard.
serendipity *n.*	chance, destiny, accident	They met by *serendipity* at a concert in the park.

Table 3.2 Difficult Vocabulary Words (*Continued*)

Word	Meaning	Sentence
servile *adj.*	submissive, docile, subservient	The dog wagged and crept low in a *servile* manner.
simulate *v.*	to imitate, replicate, model	Clay balls are meant to *simulate* autos in this replica of the town.
slue *v.*	to pivot, rotate, veer	Your tires may *slue* on the slushy driveway.
sluice *n.*	channel, valve, floodgate	The *sluice* opens once a day to drain the runoff.
soigné *adj.*	elegant, sophisticated, fashionable	Her *soigné* party attracted several movie stars.
solace *n.*	consolation, comfort, succor	Find *solace* in the fact that he is no longer suffering.
solicitous *adj.*	concerned, anxious, caring	The nurse was *solicitous* and anticipated our every need.
somnolent *adj.*	sleepy, drowsy, lethargic	The swinging hammock sent me into a *somnolent* stupor.
sonorous *adj.*	resonant, echoing, loud	From the steeple, a *sonorous* bell chimed the hour.
sordid *adj.*	foul, repugnant, squalid	It was a *sordid* tale of petty crime and obnoxious people.
sororal *adj.*	relating to a sister	The twins' *sororal* connection was very apparent.
spectral *adj.*	ghostly, ethereal, vaporous	A *spectral* light rose over the darkened city.
splenetic *adj.*	irritable, ill-humored, surly	He has a *splenetic* tantrum whenever he is frustrated.
spurious *adj.*	bogus, unauthentic, illegitimate	His excuses were *spurious* and failed to convince us.
spurn *v.*	to reject, scorn, disdain	She will *spurn* any suitor who does not amuse her.
stalwart *adj.*	valiant, sturdy, steadfast	The *stalwart* guard stood watch all night long.
static *adj.*	fixed, unmoving, stationary	We replaced the *static* sign with a vibrant, digital banner.
staunch *adj.*	faithful, loyal, dependable	Her bulldog is a *staunch* defender of the home.
stentorian *adj.*	loud, booming, thunderous	In *stentorian* tones, he expressed his displeasure.
stigma *n.*	disgrace, shame, ignominy	A failing grade can be a *stigma* for those students.

Table 3.2 Difficult Vocabulary Words (*Continued*)

Word	Meaning	Sentence
stipulate *v.*	to specify, require, demand	Signs *stipulate* that no smoking may take place here.
stodgy *adj.*	dull, stuffy, unimaginative	Her books are brilliant, but her lectures are *stodgy*.
stoic *adj.*	indifferent, unresponsive, apathetic	As they stitched up his wound, he remained *stoic* and brave.
strident *adj.*	shrill, discordant, clamorous	My alarm clock's *strident* ring scared the cat.
stultify *v.*	to cripple, deaden, hamper	Hot weather may *stultify* our preparations for the 10K race.
stupefy *v.*	to daze, bewilder, stun	A blow to the head can *stupefy* the strongest athlete.
suave *adj.*	smooth, debonair, urbane	In movies he is *suave*, but in real life he's a bit of a slob.
subjugate *v.*	to overpower, conquer, defeat	Tyrants tend to *subjugate* and oppress their citizens.
sublime *adj.*	impressive, majestic, supreme	The waterfall was a *sublime* example of nature at its best.
subtle *adj.*	elusive, abstruse, indefinable	There is a *subtle* difference between the two plans.
succulent *adj.*	juicy, luscious, delectable	Pears are most *succulent* when picked ripe from the tree.
supercilious *adj.*	disdainful, patronizing, haughty	With a *supercilious* smile, she banished them from the room.
supersede *v.*	to replace, supplant, succeed	Members of the board may *supersede* the CEO for now.
surmise *v.*	to infer, deduce, conclude	One might *surmise* from your actions that you are furious.
surreptitious *adj.*	sneaky, stealthy, clandestine	With a *surreptitious* movement, he passed her the note.
sybaritic *adj.*	sensuous, luxurious, pleasurable	They enjoyed the *sybaritic* features of the spa.
sycophant *n.*	flatterer, toady, yes-man	A *sycophant* rarely gains the respect of his or her supervisor.
symposium *n.*	meeting, conference, convention	At the *symposium* we learned more about international law.
synchronous *adj.*	simultaneous, contemporary, concurrent	Earthquakes were *synchronous* in all three counties.

Table 3.2 Difficult Vocabulary Words (*Continued*)

Word	Meaning	Sentence
synthesize *v.*	to integrate, amalgamate, manufacture	The new CD will *synthesize* country and alt rock.
tacit *adj.*	unspoken, implied, inferred	They had a *tacit* agreement about household chores.
taciturn *adj.*	reserved, reticent, silent	He remained *taciturn* when accused of wrongdoing.
tangible *adj.*	palpable, corporeal, substantial	We found no *tangible* evidence of marine life in the bay.
tawdry *adj.*	crude, gaudy, cheap	Her *tawdry* makeup gave her a clown-like appearance.
temerity *n.*	recklessness, gall, audacity	She had the *temerity* to accuse me of misconduct.
temperance *n.*	self-restraint, moderation, abstinence	He lived to be 96 by practicing *temperance* in all things.
tenable *adj.*	plausible, defensible, justifiable	If the plan is not *tenable*, go back to the drawing board.
tenacity *n.*	persistence, obstinacy, doggedness	I admire your *tenacity* in sticking to an exercise plan.
tendentious *adj.*	partisan, biased, opinionated	The flyer gave a *tendentious* account of city politics.
tenebrous *adj.*	shady, gloomy, murky	We could not see far into the *tenebrous* alley.
tenet *n.*	belief, precept, doctrine	He lives by the *tenet* most call "The Golden Rule."
tenuous *adj.*	unconvincing, fragile, weak	His oddball theories have a *tenuous* link to reality.
thespian *adj.*	dramatic, theatrical, staged	She tries out for every *thespian* activity on campus.
timorous *adj.*	timid, fearful, anxious	His *timorous* voice was nearly impossible to hear.
torrid *adj.*	sweltering, hot, sizzling	In the *torrid* zones, ships might founder for lack of wind power.
tortuous *adj.*	winding, circuitous, meandering	The trail up the cliff was *tortuous* and unmarked.
tractable *adj.*	obedient, dutiful, governable	Only the most *tractable* animals make good service dogs.
transitory *adj.*	short-lived, impermanent, fleeting	Butterflies make a *transitory* appearance here in July.

Table 3.2 Difficult Vocabulary Words (*Continued*)

Word	Meaning	Sentence
trenchant *adj.*	forceful, effective, incisive	He made a *trenchant* argument in support of the proposal.
trepidation *n.*	apprehension, foreboding, dread	I approach the first day of any new job with *trepidation*.
trite *adj.*	stale, hackneyed, pedestrian	Do not use *trite* phrases to present an imaginative idea.
truculent *adj.*	quarrelsome, argumentative, defiant	The man grew *truculent* as they pulled him from the police car.
truism *n.*	cliché, platitude, maxim	It is a *truism* that good always triumphs over evil.
tumult *n.*	clamor, commotion, hubbub	In the *tumult*, we called out for our missing friends.
ubiquitous *adj.*	omnipresent, everywhere	Cell phones are now *ubiquitous* among middle schoolers.
ululate *v.*	to lament, wail, howl	As the mourners passed, we heard people *ululate*.
umbrage *n.*	offense, resentment, indignation	Do not take *umbrage* at his clumsy remarks.
unctuous *adj.*	oily, ingratiating, obsequious	The *unctuous* butler seemed to slither around his employer.
undulate *v.*	to ripple, surge, heave	Waves *undulate* gently all along the seashore.
upbraid *v.*	to scold, berate, chastise	I had to *upbraid* the children for staying up past their bedtimes.
urbane *adj.*	suave, refined, elegant	Living in Paris for two years gave him an *urbane* manner.
usurp *v.*	to appropriate, commandeer, seize	The prince plans to *usurp* power from his uncle.
uxorial *adj.*	relating to a wife	*Uxorial* duties changed as more women entered the workplace.
vacillate *v.*	to fluctuate, hesitate, waver	I continue to *vacillate* between law school and teaching.
vacuous *adj.*	empty, inane, vacant	Not a single emotion flickered across his *vacuous* face.
validate *v.*	to sanction, confirm, corroborate	The results seem to *validate* our original theory.

Table 3.2 Difficult Vocabulary Words (*Continued*)

Word	Meaning	Sentence
vapid *adj.*	bland, lifeless, insipid	The movie was cheerful and bubbly but had a *vapid* plot.
vaunt *v.*	to boast, brag, crow	The students *vaunt* about their lab's breakthrough discovery.
vehement *adj.*	forceful, fervid, passionate	He was *vehement* in his denial of wrongdoing.
venal *adj.*	mercenary, corruptible	That *venal* pair took part in three bank robberies.
venerable *adj.*	esteemed, respected, honored	Everyone admires the *venerable* old bishop.
verbose *adj.*	wordy, garrulous, loquacious	It is better to be concise and clear than to be *verbose*.
verdant *adj.*	green, grassy, fertile	*Verdant* fields lay under the bluest of skies.
verisimilitude *n.*	truth, reality, authenticity	Randomly placed objects add *verisimilitude* to his portraits.
vernacular *n.*	dialect, idiom, argot	Her command of the native *vernacular* is impressive.
vicarious *adj.*	secondhand, delegated	She gets *vicarious* joy from her child's accomplishments.
vicissitude *n.*	variation, mutation, complication	My company's closing is just one more *vicissitude* of life.
vilify *v.*	to malign, disparage, defame	Her column seems to *vilify* the members of the board.
virtuosity *n.*	genius, talent, skill	The violinist showed great *virtuosity* at a young age.
vitriol *n.*	wrath, ire, spleen	Parents showered *vitriol* on the coach of the opposite team.
vociferous *adj.*	voluble, noisy, raucous	Silence the *vociferous* students before starting your speech.
voracious *adj.*	ravenous, greedy, insatiable	Wolves may be *voracious* after a long, cold winter.
vouchsafe *v.*	to grant, deign, bestow	The queen will *vouchsafe* the ambassador's safe return.
wanton *adj.*	immodest, unchaste, lewd	The actors were dressed as *wanton* women of the streets.
wastrel *n.*	spendthrift, squanderer, profligate	She has the habits of a *wastrel* and fritters away money.

Table 3.2 Difficult Vocabulary Words (*Continued*)

Word	Meaning	Sentence
wheedle *v.*	to cajole, inveigle, coax	Could you *wheedle* the kitten to come out from under the sofa?
whet *v.*	to sharpen, hone, stimulate	Use this tool to *whet* the carving knife.
wily *adj.*	sly, cunning, devious	An owl is considered wise, and a fox is believed to be *wily*.
winnow *v.*	to sift, separate, extract	Toss the grain in the air to *winnow* away the chaff.
wizened *adj.*	shriveled, wrinkled, withered	The fallen apples were *wizened* and dried.
wrangle *v.*	to quarrel, bicker, argue	My brothers often *wrangle* over who has the better job.
xeric *adj.*	dry, sere, desert	The Mojave Desert is one example of a *xeric* environment.
yaw *v.*	to swerve, veer, weave	The sailboat may *yaw* to avoid other boats in the harbor.
zenith *n.*	summit, apex, pinnacle	When the sun is at its *zenith*, stay inside or risk sunburn.

Test Yourself

Use a word from the box to complete each sentence below. Use each word only once.

parsimony	perfidy	persiflage

1. You might accuse gossipy teens of ____________.

2. You might accuse someone who never picks up the check of ____________.

3. You might accuse a coworker who tattles to the boss of ____________.

4. Select the meaning of the underlined word in the sentence.

The child's fractious behavior in preschool made us reconsider sending her.

A. guileful
B. introverted
C. ill-tempered
D. outspoken

5. A wizened face is ___________.

A. angry
B. wrinkled
C. intelligent
D. puzzled

6. If you take umbrage, you are ___________.

A. responsible
B. protected
C. surprised
D. offended

7. Levity is the same as ___________.

A. floating
B. humor
C. knowledge
D. solemnity

8. A curate might work in a ___________.

A. stable
B. kitchen
C. church
D. theater

9. To prognosticate is to ___________.

A. predict
B. consider
C. obstruct
D. dawdle

10. If you vilify someone in print, you ___________ him or her.

A. compliment
B. validate
C. analyze
D. denounce

Answers

1. persiflage. Persiflage is silly, harmless banter.
2. parsimony. Someone who is parsimonious is cheap.
3. perfidy. Perfidy is treachery or betrayal.
4. C. A child who is fractious is irritable and quarrelsome.
5. B. A face that is wizened is wrinkled with age.
6. D. To take umbrage is to take offense.
7. B. Levity is humor or wit.
8. C. A curate is a member of the clergy.
9. A. To prognisticate is to foretell future events.
10. D. To vilify someone is to speak or write about him or her in a critical, denunciatory way.

STRATEGIES: CONTEXT

Figuring out the meaning of a word through context is an important reading skill that involves using the surrounding words and phrases to infer the meaning of an unfamiliar word. Here are some steps to follow:

1. Read the entire sentence: It is important to read the entire sentence to understand the context in which the unfamiliar word is being used.
2. Look for context clues: Look for clues within the sentence or passage that can help you understand the meaning of the unfamiliar word. Context clues can include other words in the sentence, the tone or mood of the passage, and any additional information that may help you make sense of the word.
3. Identify the type of context clue: There are different types of context clues that can help you figure out the meaning of a word. These include:
   - Definition clues: The meaning of the unfamiliar word is given in the sentence or passage.
   - Example clues: An example is given to help illustrate the meaning of the unfamiliar word.
   - Synonym clues: A synonym or word with a similar meaning is used in the sentence or passage.
   - Antonym clues: An antonym or word with an opposite meaning is used in the sentence or passage.
4. Make an educated guess: Use the context clues you have identified to make an educated guess about the meaning of the unfamiliar word. Consider the tone and mood of the passage, the topic being discussed, and the purpose of the sentence or passage.

Test Yourself

Try to figure out the meaning of the underlined word from the context of the sentence.

1. Mayor Landon was very effusive in his praise for the new law.

A. Angry
B. Eager
C. Enthusiastic
D. Careful

2. The family's abject poverty prevented them from buying basic necessities.

A. Severe
B. Minimal
C. Pleasant
D. Painful

3. Dr. Ryan prescribed a potent painkiller that completely alleviated the patient's discomfort.

A. Weak
B. Strong
C. Mild
D. Unnecessary

4. Evelyn's prodigious talent in gymnastics earned her a place on the Olympic team.

A. Average
B. Small
C. Strange
D. Amazing

5. The teacher's admonition to study harder motivated Vivian to improve.

A. Warning
B. Praise
C. Agreement
D. Disinterest

Answers

1. C. *Effusive* means to express feelings of gratitude or pleasure in an unrestrained or enthusiastic way. *Praise* gives you the context clue here.
2. A. *Abject* means extremely severe and unpleasant. The level of poverty must be severe if the family cannot buy necessities.
3. B. *Potent* means having a strong effect. If the pain was completely gone, the medicine must have been powerful.
4. D. *Prodigious* means remarkably or impressively great in extent, size, or degree. To make the Olympic team, one must have extreme talent.
5. A. An *admonition* is a warning or reprimand about conduct. The fact that Vivian began to study tells you that her teacher warned her.

STRATEGIES: WORD PARTS

Understanding word parts helps you to define unfamiliar words. This is especially true in the field of medicine, where knowledge of some key Greek and Latin roots and affixes can help you to decipher the most complicated manual.

Roots

There are hundreds of important root words that help you to decode medical terminology. Table 3.3 gives you just a handful of useful roots.

Table 3.3 Useful Roots

Root	Meaning	Examples
andr/o	man	android, polyandrous
cardi/o	heart	cardiology, cardiogram
cephal/o	head	encephalitis, hydrocephaly
chrom/o	color	chromatograph, chromosome
crani/o	skull	cranial, cranium
cyan/o	blue	cyanide, cyanotic
dactyl/o	finger	polydactyl, pterodactyl
derm/o	skin	dermatitis, epidermis
enter/o	intestine	enterocolitis, enteritis
erythr/o	red	erythroblast, erythromycin
gastr/o	stomach	gastric, gastritis
gyn/o	woman	androgynous, gynecology
hem/o	blood	hemoglobin, hemorrhage

Table 3.3 Useful Roots (*Continued*)

Root	Meaning	Examples
hyp/o	below	hypodermic, hypotonic
leuc(k)/o	white	leucoplast, leukemia
my/o	muscle	myocardial, myofilament
myel/o	spinal cord	myelopathy, poliomyelitis
nephr/o	kidney	nephritic, nephrology
oste/o	bone	osteoarthritis, osteopath
necr/o	dead	necrotic, necrophilia
path/o	disease	homeopath, pathology
phag/o	eating	esophagus, microphage
phleb/o	vein	phlebitis, phlebotomy
pulm/o	lungs	cardiopulmonary, pulmonic
scler/o	hard	arteriosclerosis, scleroderma
thromb/o	clot	antithrombin, thrombosis
vas/o	vessel	vascular, vasoconstrictor

WHY DO I NEED THIS?

The same roots are repeated in a variety of medical terms. If you know the root, you can interpret the word.

Prefixes

You know many of the prefixes in Table 3.4 from everyday life. Many will appear in medical terms you read.

Table 3.4 Useful Prefixes

Prefix	Meaning	Examples
a-, ac-, ad-, af-, ag-, al-, an-, ap-, as-, at-	to, toward, in addition to, according to	ahead, accompany, adhere, affix, aggravate, alarm, appall, assent, attempt
a-, an-	without	amoral, analgesic
ab-, abs-	away from	abdicate, absence
ante-	before	antebellum, anterior
anti-	against	antiwar, antipathy
auto-	self	automobile, autobiography

Table 3.4 Useful Prefixes (*Continued*)

Prefix	Meaning	Examples
bi-	two	biannual, bicycle
circum-	around	circumnavigate, circumvent
co-, cog-, col-, com-, con-, cor-	with, together, mutually	coherent, cognizant, collapse, companion, concur, correspond
contra-	against, opposite	contradict, contravene
de-	to do the opposite of	decriminalize, degenerate
dis-	not, opposite of	disagree, disfavor
e-, ex-	out of, away from	egress, extension
em-, en-	to put into, to cause to be	endear, embody
epi-	upon, over	epidermis, epitaph
extra-	outside, beyond	extracurricular, extraordinary
il-, im-, in-, ir-	not	illicit, impossible, incorrect, irresponsible
inter-	between, among	intercom, international
intro-	into	introduce, introvert
mal-	bad	maladjusted, malformed
mis-	wrong	misnomer, misunderstood
mono-	one	monotone, monogamy
multi-	many	multifaceted, multimillions
non-	no, not	nonentity, nonsensical
ob-, oc-, of-, op-	toward, against	object, occlude, offend, opposite
over-	above, more than	overachieve, overcharge
para-	beside	paradigm, paragraph
per-	through, throughout	perambulate, perambulate
peri-	around, about	peripatetic, periodic
poly-	many	polychromatic, polygamist
post-	after	postdate, posthumous
pre-	before	prediction, preexist
pro-	for, supporting	procreate, promotion
re-	back, again	recall, recapture
retro-	backward, behind	retrofit, retrospective
semi-	half	semicircle, semiconscious

Table 3.4 Useful Prefixes (*Continued*)

Prefix	Meaning	Examples
sub-, suc-, suf-, sup-, sus-	below, under	subarctic, succumb, suffer, suppress, suspend
super-	over, above	superfluous, superscript
sur-	over, above	surpass, surrealism
sym-, syn-	together	sympathetic, synthesize
trans-	across	transatlantic, transmission
tri-	three	tricycle, trilogy
un-	not, opposite of	unlikely, unravel
uni-	one	uniform, unisex

Suffixes

When placed at the end of a word, suffixes, such as those in Table 3.5, change the part of speech.

Table 3.5 Useful Suffixes

Suffix	Function and Meaning	Examples
-able, -ible	adjective-forming; capable of, worthy of	laudable, flexible
-acy, -cy	noun-forming; state, quality	literacy, bankruptcy
-age	noun-forming; action	breakage, blockage
-al	adjective-forming; state, quality	communal, supplemental
-an, -ian	noun-forming; one who	artisan, librarian
-ance, -ence	noun-forming; action, state, quality	performance, adherence
-ancy, -ency	noun-forming; state, quality	buoyancy, fluency
-ant, -ent	noun-forming; one who	deodorant, antecedent
-ant, -ent, -ient	adjective forming; indicating	compliant, dependent, lenient
-ar, -ary	adjective-forming; related to	solar, imaginary
-ate	verb-forming; cause to be	percolate, graduate
-ation	noun-forming; action	hibernation, strangulation
-dom	noun-forming; place, condition	kingdom, freedom
-en	adjective-forming; made of	flaxen, wooden
-en	verb-forming; cause to be	cheapen, dampen
-er, -or	noun-forming; one who	painter, sailor

Table 3.5 Useful Suffixes (*Continued*)

Suffix	Function and Meaning	Examples
-fold	adverb-forming; divided or multiplied by	threefold, hundredfold
-ful	adjective-forming; full of	joyful, playful
-ful	noun-forming; amount	cupful, bucketful
-fy, -ify	verb-forming; cause to be	liquefy, justify
-ia	noun-forming; disease	inertia, anemia
-iatry	noun-forming; medical treatment	psychiatry, podiatry
-ic	adjective-forming; having the qualities of	futuristic, academic
-ician	noun-forming; one who	physician, mortician
-ics	noun-forming; science of	athletics, physics
-ion	noun-forming; action	completion, dilution
-ish	adjective-forming; having the quality of	foolish, boyish
-ism	noun-forming; doctrine	pacifism, jingoism
-ist	noun-forming; person who	jurist, polemicist
-ity, -ty	noun-forming; state, quality	reality, cruelty
-ive, -ative, -itive	adjective-forming; having the quality of	supportive, talkative, definitive
-ize	verb-forming; cause to be	demonize, dramatize
-less	adjective-forming; without	careless, hopeless
-ly	adverb-forming; in the manner of	loudly, suddenly
-ment	noun-forming; action	argument, statement
-ness	noun-forming; state, quality	kindness, abruptness
-ous, -eous, -ose, -ious	adjective-forming; having the quality of	porous, gaseous, jocose, bilious
-ship	noun-forming; condition	scholarship, friendship
-ure	noun-forming; action, condition	erasure, portraiture
-ward	adverb-forming; in the direction of	forward, windward
-wise	adverb-forming; in the manner of	otherwise, clockwise
-y	adjective-forming; having the quality of	chilly, crazy
-y	noun-forming; state, condition	jealousy, custody

Test Yourself

For questions 1–3, use the charts to put together the word parts. Define the new word.

1. poly + dactyl = someone who has ____________.

2. sclero + derma = a condition involving ____________.

3. peri + cardial = something that is ____________.

4. The retrolingual region of the mouth is ____________.

A. under the tongue
B. behind the tongue
C. on top of the tongue
D. to the right of the tongue

5. What would an antithrombin drug be likely to do?

A. Regulate the heartbeat
B. Close up wounds
C. Block cholesterol
D. Break up clots

Answers

1. many fingers. *Poly* = many, and *dactyl* = finger, so *polydactyl* means "multi-fingered."
2. hard skin. *Scler/o* = hard, and *derm/o* = skin, so *scleroderma* is a condition that hardens the skin.
3. around the heart. *Peri* = around, and *cardi/o* = heart, so *pericardial* means "around the heart."
4. B. *Retro* is a prefix that means "behind."
5. D. *Anti-* is "against," and *thromb* means "clot."

CHAPTER 4

Grammar

CONTENTS

This module of the A2 test assesses communication skills. Grammar, punctuation, and spelling represent the building blocks of written communication. If English is not your first language, you can benefit from a review of these skills. Even if English *is* your first language, you may still wish to skim this chapter to get a sense of the key skills covered on the A2 test and to make sure that your skills are adequate.

PARTS OF SPEECH

Parts of speech are the basic grammatical categories into which words are classified according to their functions within a sentence. There are eight main parts of speech in English:

- **Nouns:** Words that name people, places, things, or ideas.

  Examples: *dog, table, love*

  *__Proper nouns__ refer to *specific* people, places, things, or ideas, and are always capitalized.

  Examples: *Aaron, the Declaration of Independence, the Chicago Museum of Science and Industry, President Kennedy, the Taj Mahal*
- **Pronouns:** Words that are used in place of nouns, to avoid repetition.

  Examples: *I, she, we, it, they*

- **Verbs:** Words that describe actions or states of being.
  Examples: *run, jump, is, has*
- **Adjectives:** Words that modify or describe nouns or pronouns.
  Examples: *pink, short, wide, confused*
- **Adverbs:** Words that modify or describe verbs, adjectives, or other adverbs.
  Examples: *quickly, very, often, easily*
- **Prepositions:** Words that show the relationship between a noun or pronoun and other words in a sentence.
  Examples: *in, on, for, with*
- **Conjunctions:** Words that join words, phrases, or clauses.
  Examples: *and, but, or, because*
- **Interjections:** Words that express strong feelings or emotions.
  Examples: *oh, wow, ouch, hey*

Test Yourself

For questions 1–3, identify the part of speech of the underlined word.

1. I could not understand why Cassie ate the last slice of pie without sharing. _______________

2. Emma Lee tiptoed very quietly into the living room. __________

3. The beautiful doll belongs to Jenna. _______________

4. Which word in the following sentence is a verb?

Molly became very ill after lunch.

A. Molly
B. Became
C. Ill
D. Lunch

5. What part of speech is the word *his* in the sentence below?

You need to give William his medicine right before bedtime.

A. Adverb
B. Preposition
C. Conjunction
D. Pronoun

Answers

1. Preposition. *Without* is a preposition beginning the prepositional phrase *without sharing*.
2. Adverb. *Very* is an adverb that modifies the adverb *quietly*.
3. Adjective. *Beautiful* is an adjective that modifies the noun *doll*.
4. B. The verb *became* expresses Jenna's state of being.
5. D. *His* is a possessive pronoun indicating that the medicine belongs to William.

SUBJECT-VERB AGREEMENT

Nouns and pronouns may be **singular**, referring to one person, place, thing, or idea. They may be **plural**, referring to more than one person, place, thing, or idea. In standard English, verbs agree with subjects in number. Singular subjects require singular verbs, and plural subjects require plural verbs.

- My supervisor reviews my work with me weekly. (singular)
- My supervisors review my work with me weekly. (plural)
- Everyone enjoys his lectures on surgical innovations. (singular)
- We enjoy his lectures on surgical innovations. (plural)

Do not become confused by words that come between a subject and verb.

- Recording songs with my friends is often hilarious. (singular)
- The tracks of the truck still show in the muddy ground. (plural)

In the case of multiple subjects, the verb depends on the conjunction used. Use a plural verb with subjects joined with *and.*

- Catherine and she work together on Mondays. (plural)

When subjects are joined with *or, either/or, nor,* or *neither/nor,* the verb should agree with the nearest subject.

- Neither the residents nor Catherine works on weekends. (singular)

The pronouns *I* and *you* take a plural verb, even when *you* is singular.

- I never believe a word in that so-called journal.
- You read far too many pseudo-scientific articles.

Certain indefinite pronouns may cause trouble. Be sure that you know which pronouns are singular and which are plural. A few may be either, depending upon context.

Indefinite Pronouns

Singular	anybody, anyone, anything, each, either, everybody, everyone, everything, neither, nobody, no one, nothing, one, somebody, someone, something
Plural	both, few, many, several
Either	all, any, most, none, some

WHY DO I NEED THIS?
Using standard English in the workplace is expected and preferred and makes you look professional.

- Everybody is going to the party. (singular)
- Several are going to the party. (plural)

Test Yourself

For questions 1–8, circle the correct form of the verb in parentheses.

1. You (prepare/prepares) a meal for your roommates every Saturday.

2. Either Jill or her brothers (fix/fixes) the sink each time it leaks.

3. Living with roommates (is/are) challenging but fun.

4. We (have been reviewing/has been reviewing) the files.

5. Deena and he (intend/intends) to visit in May.

6. Everybody (find/finds) that report impossible to read.

7. Few (has/have) completed the project yet.

8. Neither the doctor nor her assistant (need/needs) new scrubs.

9. Select the phrase that will make the following sentence grammatically correct.

Once the experiment ends, Professor Martin ___________.

A. request an explanation
B. requests an explanation
C. are requesting an explanation
D. have requested an explanation

10. Select the word that makes the following sentence grammatically correct.

    Anyone with sense and reason ____________ the fallacy in that argument.

    A. recognize
    B. recognizes
    C. have recognized
    D. are recognizing

Answers

1. prepare. *You* always takes a plural verb.
2. fix. The verb must match the closer subject, *brothers*.
3. is. The subject is *living*, not *roommates*.
4. have been reviewing. *We* takes a plural verb.
5. intend. Two singular subjects joined with *and* equate to one plural subject.
6. finds. *Everybody* is singular.
7. have. *Few* is plural.
8. needs. The subject closer to the verb dictates the verb in a *neither/nor* construction.
9. B. The subject *Professor Martin* requires a singular verb.
10. B. The subject *anyone* requires a singular verb.

PRONOUNS

Pronouns take the place of nouns in a sentence. They have gender, and they also have case.

Pronoun Case

Personal pronouns come in three cases. They may be subjects, objects, or possessive words. (See Table 4.1.) In addition, the pronoun *who* is a subject pronoun. The pronoun *whom* is an object pronoun.

Table 4.1 Pronoun Cases

Subject	Object	Possessive
I	me	my, mine
you	you	your, yours
he, she, it	him, her, it	his, her, hers, its
we	us	our, ours
they	them	their, theirs
who	whom	whose

Use subject pronouns as sentence subjects or after a linking verb.

- He and I always read to the patients in the children's ward.
- The best volunteers in the hospital are they.
- Who worked the most hours in the month of August?

Use object pronouns as direct objects, indirect objects, or the objects of prepositions.

- The event celebrated him and us. (direct object)
- The director presented me with a plaque. (indirect object)
- To whom was that speech delivered? (object of a preposition)

Person pronouns *my, your, his, her, its, our,* and *their* come before a noun. The other possessive pronouns stand alone.

- That is my lab coat.
- That lab coat is mine.

Notice that *no* possessive pronoun takes an apostrophe!

Pronoun-Antecedent Agreement

The **antecedent** of a pronoun is the noun or pronoun it replaces or renames. Pronouns must agree with their antecedents in number and gender.

- Victoria presented her results in a seminar on Friday.
- He asked Darla to remind him about the lecture.
- Everyone should try to control his or her temper.

Antecedents joined by *and* require a plural pronoun.

- Song Lee and Jasper scowled because they disagreed.

Singular antecedents joined by *or, either/or, nor,* or *neither/nor* require a singular pronoun.

- Neither Vito nor Ralph remembered his notebook.

Test Yourself

For questions 1–3, circle the correct case of the pronoun in parentheses.

1. Farouk and (I/me) attended the concert in Plymouth.

2. The car lost (it/its) tailpipe along the highway.

3. Can you guess (who/whom) ended up fixing it?

4. Which word is best to substitute for the underlined words in the following sentence?

   We knocked on the door to get Rick's and Justin's attention.

   A. his
   B. they
   C. their
   D. theirs

5. Which sentence is grammatically correct?

   A. Anita helped him to submit his credentials.
   B. Anita helped himself to submit his credentials.
   C. Anita helped him to submit its credentials.
   D. Anita helped he to submit his credentials.

Answers

1. I. This calls for a subject pronoun.
2. its. The possessive form is *its*.
3. who. The construction of the sentence is such that "who ended up fixing it" is its own clause with a subject (*who*) and verb.
4. C. The antecedent is joined by *and*, so it requires a plural possessive pronoun. Since the pronoun precedes a noun, it must be *their*, not *theirs* (choice D).
5. A. *Him* is the indirect object, and the possessive *his* matches the antecedent.

MISPLACED MODIFIERS

To make meaning clear, modifying phrases and clauses should appear as close as possible to the words they modify. Sometimes that requires moving words around. Sometimes it requires a rewrite.

- **Wrong:** At the age of two, my father taught me how to box. (Who was two years old? It's not clear.)
- **Right:** When I was two, my father taught me how to box.
- **Wrong:** The house belongs to my uncle that has a cupola. (Who or what has a cupola? It's not clear.)
- **Right:** The house that has a cupola belongs to my uncle.

Test Yourself

1. Underline the phrase that is misplaced in the sentence below.

We watched our team play game 7 on our new TV.

2. Rewrite the sentence to avoid the misplaced modifier.

After eating breakfast, the bus took us to school.

____

____

3. Rewrite the sentence to avoid the misplaced modifier.

With great excitement, the clowns were watched by the children.

____

____

4. Which sentence is grammatically correct?

A. The garments that I had washed by hand rested on my bed.
B. The garments rested on my bed that I had washed by hand.
C. Having washed by hand, the garments rested on my bed.
D. The garments on my bed rested that I had washed by hand.

5. Which sentence is the clearest?

A. Inside the microwave I saw that the soup had spilled.
B. The soup had spilled, I saw, inside the microwave.
C. I saw that the soup had spilled inside the microwave.
D. The soup that I saw had spilled inside the microwave.

Answers

1. on our new TV. The team did not play on top of the TV.
2. Possible answer: After eating breakfast, we went to school on the bus.
3. Possible answer: With great excitement, the children watched the clowns.
4. A. I washed the garments by hand, not my bed (choice B). The other choices are convoluted.
5. C. The soup was in the microwave; I was not (choice A). The other choices are convoluted.

SENTENCES

A sentence states a complete idea and is composed of at least one subject and one verb. Communicating in complete sentences is rare in these days of instant messaging and texts, but it remains a critical part of formal writing.

Run-ons

A run-on sentence typically consists of two or more sentences that lack internal punctuation. A **comma splice** is two or more sentences connected only by a comma. You may correct run-on sentences by breaking the sentences into correctly punctuated parts. You may often correct comma splices by replacing the comma with a semicolon or by adding a conjunction (*and*, *but*, or *or*).

- **Run-on sentence:** When I finished my shift I returned to the apartment it was as cold as an icebox the heat had switched off.
- **Correct:** When I finished my shift, I returned to the apartment. It was as cold as an icebox; the heat had switched off.
- **Comma splice:** I called up the landlord, I had to leave a message, he was not at home.
- **Correct:** I called up the landlord, but I had to leave a message; he was not at home.

Fragments

Fragments are parts of sentences written as sentences. They may be prepositional phrases, items in a series, dependent clauses, or simply subjects without predicates or predicates without subjects. They may require revised punctuation, or they may need additional words to complete them.

- **Fragment:** Trying to understand how anyone could like kale.
- **Correct:** I am trying to understand how anyone could like kale.
- **Fragment:** Our busy but productive day at the library.
- **Correct:** Our busy but productive day at the library meant that we finished our report early.

Organization

Syntax is the way in which we organize words, phrases, and clauses to form sentences. Most sentences in English conform to an SVO word order: The subject precedes the verb, which precedes the object, as in this example:

- The anesthesiologist replaced his gloves.

S V O

Independent clauses and dependent clauses are the building blocks of sentences in English grammar.

An **independent clause** is a group of words that contains a subject and a predicate and expresses a complete thought. It can stand alone as a sentence. For example, *I like to read books* is an independent clause because it contains a subject (*I*) and a predicate (*like to read*) and expresses a complete thought.

A **dependent clause**, on the other hand, is a group of words that contains a subject and a predicate but does not express a complete thought. It depends on an independent clause to form a complete sentence. For example, *because I like to read books* is a dependent clause because it contains a subject (*I*) and a predicate (*like to read*), but it does not express a complete thought. It needs an independent clause to form a complete sentence, such as *I have a good vocabulary because I like to read books.* Dependent clauses are often introduced by subordinating conjunctions, such as *because*, *although*, *if*, or *while*.

Understanding the difference between independent and dependent clauses is important for constructing clear and grammatically correct sentences.

There are four types of sentence structures:

A **simple sentence** contains one independent clause and expresses a complete thought.

- Anna Belle loves pizza.

In a **compound sentence**, two such independent clauses are joined using a semicolon or a comma plus a conjunction.

- The anesthesiologist replaced his gloves, and he discarded the old ones.

A **complex sentence** contains a dependent clause—a group of words, containing a subject and verb, that does not express a complete thought—attached to an independent clause.

- The anesthesiologist replaced his gloves because they were torn.

Finally, a **compound-complex** sentence contains more than one independent clause plus at least one dependent clause.

- The anesthesiologist replaced his gloves because they were torn, and he discarded the old ones.

In a sentence that is in **active voice**, the subject is clearly performing the action of the sentence.

- The receptionist called my name.

In a sentence that is in **passive voice**, the object of the action becomes the subject of the sentence.

- My name was called by the receptionist.

Active voice is usually clearer and more concise than passive voice.

Occasionally, changing passive voice to active voice requires the addition of a subject, as in this example:

- **Passive:** Her purse was stolen.
- **Active:** Someone stole her purse.

End Punctuation

Every sentence ends with a punctuation mark. The mark used depends upon the type of sentence. (See Table 4.2.)

Table 4.2 Sentences and End Punctuation

Type of Sentence	Punctuation Mark	Example
Declarative (statement)	period	Maria is studying for her exam.
Interrogative (question)	question mark	When will she take the test?
Imperative (command)	period	Read this schedule of test dates.
Exclamatory (exclamation)	exclamation point	What a lot of choices she has!

Test Yourself

1. Revise this run-on sentence to make it correct.

I'm not sure how to get there luckily my car has GPS.

____

2. Revise this passive voice sentence to make it active.

Our choices were marked on our ballots.

____

3. Which of the following is a complex sentence?

A. Vicki wanted to go to a movie, but Bruce wanted to go for a hike.
B. If you eat your dinner too quickly, you may get an upset stomach, and you will not be able to have dessert.
C. Jack didn't want to drive all the way to the mall on the other side of town.
D. My husband did the dishes while I folded the laundry.

4. Which sentence is grammatically correct?

A. The sandwiches she made were eaten by us.
B. We ate the sandwiches she made.
C. She made the sandwiches of which we ate.
D. She made the sandwiches we ate them.

5. What punctuation is needed in the following sentence to make it correct?

   Could you please inform the doctor of our grave concerns

   A. Period
   B. Comma
   C. Question mark
   D. Exclamation point

Answers

1. I'm not sure how to get there. Luckily, my car has GPS. OR I'm not sure how to get there; luckily, my car has GPS.
2. We marked our choices on our ballots. This is an example of a passive sentence that requires an added subject.
3. D. This sentence contains one independent clause and one dependent clause.
4. B. Choice A is passive voice, and choices C and D are ungrammatical.
5. C. Although this is similar to a command, it is framed in the form of a question.

COMMAS

Commas are not only the most common punctuation mark outside of the period, but they are also the most frequently misused. The rules are simple, but there are a lot of them.

In a Series

Use commas to separate items in a series. If you use the Oxford comma rule, the number of commas will equal the number of items minus one.

- I purchased a planner, note cards, and a stapler.
- The students gossiped, chatted, texted, and laughed.
- That is a well-stocked, economical, convenient store.

In Direct Address

Use a comma or commas to set off words used in direct address.

- Dr. Martinez, have you met our visiting lecturer?
- The new technique, Joe, is something you should master.

Between Independent Clauses

Use a comma to separate independent clauses joined by a conjunction in a compound sentence.

- That book was not in the library, but I found it online.
- We can work in the lab today, or we can enjoy the sunshine.
- This topic is especially difficult, and the test is next week.

After Words, Phrases, and Clauses

Use a comma after an introductory word, participial phrase, long or combined prepositional phrase, or adverb clause.

- No, I'm afraid that she cannot attend the event on Tuesday.
- Consumed by work, she will be in the office all day.
- At this time of year, the agency is especially busy.
- Until she completes the inventory, she will be unavailable.

With Nonessential Elements

Use commas to set off nonessential clauses, nonessential participial phrases, interrupting elements, or parenthetical asides.

- My friend Ellen, who comes from Chicago, is visiting.
- Ellen, hoping to find a new job, is sleeping on my couch.
- Her sister, my best friend from childhood, works overseas.
- Generally speaking, Ellen is proving to be a good guest.

Test Yourself

For sentences 1–3, add commas where they belong.

1. The liquid in the flask turned pink red and purple as I swirled it.

2. After I performed the experiment I carefully wrote up my notes.

3. Honestly the results were not thrilling but I recorded what I saw.

4. Which sentence is *not* punctuated correctly?

A. Dolores, did you remember the handouts?
B. Ken designed them and had them printed.
C. We should put them up on campus I think.
D. By the end of the week, let's have them all posted.

5. What punctuation is needed in the following sentence to make it correct?

Before completing the course everyone will write a research paper.

A. Period
B. Comma
C. Semicolon
D. Apostrophe

Answers

1. The liquid in the flask turned pink, red, and purple as I swirled it. Commas separate the three adjectives in the series.
2. After I performed the experiment, I carefully wrote up my notes. A comma belongs after the introductory clause.
3. Honestly, the results were not thrilling, but I recorded what I saw. This sentence starts with a parenthetical element but also includes two independent clauses separated by a conjunction.
4. C. *I think* is a parenthetical element that should be set off by a comma.
5. B. The comma belongs after the introductory phrase *before completing the course.*

SEMICOLONS AND COLONS

Some writers go out of their way to avoid semicolons, but this punctuation mark can be very useful. Writers rarely use colons, but when they do, they should use them correctly.

Semicolons

Use a semicolon to separate independent clauses in a compound sentence when the clauses are not joined by conjunctions.

- Kyra wandered all over the city; its history delighted her.

Use a semicolon to join independent clauses joined by transition words such as *for example, nevertheless,* or *therefore.* (Use a comma after the transition word.)

- She had never been abroad; nevertheless, she felt at ease.

Use a semicolon between items in a series when the items contain commas.

- On her tour were visitors from San Jose, California; Reno, Nevada; and Salt Lake City, Utah.

Colons

Use a colon to clarify items in a list or a formal statement or quote.

- You should take the following courses this year: one anatomy class, one psychology class, and a chemistry lab.
- My adviser had this to say: "Organic chemistry makes or breaks students."

Use a colon between the hour and minute in time, between chapter and verse in Bible passages, and after the salutation in a business letter.

- 3:15
- Proverbs 17:22
- Dear Doctor Jessup:

Test Yourself

For sentences 1–4, add punctuation where it belongs.

1. I want to remind you of the following adage Practice makes perfect.

2. We practiced this for weeks therefore we should perform it flawlessly.

3. Use these colors for the autumn costumes gold, red, and auburn.

4. Our audience included people from Paris France Kyoto Japan and Nairobi Kenya.

5. What punctuation is needed in the following sentence to make it correct?

   Our presentation went well even our rivals praised us.

   A. Period
   B. Colon
   C. Comma
   D. Semicolon

Answers

1. I want to remind you of the following adage: Practice makes perfect. OR I want to remind you of the following adage: "Practice makes perfect." The words *the following* are a clue that you should use a colon. The quotation marks are not necessary but may be used.
2. We practiced this for weeks; therefore, we should perform it flawlessly. A semicolon divides the clauses, and a comma follows the transition word.
3. Use these colors for the autumn costumes: gold, red, and auburn. A colon should introduce the list.
4. Our audience included people from Paris, France; Kyoto, Japan; and Nairobi, Kenya. Commas separate city from country, and semicolons separate items in a series that already feature commas.
5. D. The semicolon should divide the two independent clauses between *well* and *even.*

APOSTROPHES

Apostrophes are small but mighty. They make the difference between *well* and *we'll*, or between *kings* and *king's*. Apostrophes are used to represent missing letters, and they are used in possessive forms of nouns.

With Possessives

A possessive noun shows ownership. Use an apostrophe plus *s* to form the possessive case of a singular noun.

- Is that Myra's backpack?
- She took my father's advice.

Use only an apostrophe to form the possessive case of a plural noun that ends in *s*.

- We followed the Smiths' car to town.
- Jack bought five dollars' worth of gas.

Use an apostrophe plus *s* to form the possessive case of a plural noun that does not end in *s*.

- The children's trip to the zoo went well.
- They admired the deer's various antlers.

Use an apostrophe plus *s* to form the possessive case of indefinite pronouns (but *never* of personal pronouns).

- **Correct**: Everyone's reports are finished.
- **Incorrect**: Has the professor read your's yet? (Use *yours*.)

With Contractions

A contraction is a shortened form of a word or group of words. Use an apostrophe to show where letters have been left out.

Some Examples of Contractions

is + not = isn't	you + are = you're	it + is = it's
I + am = I'm	he + would = he'd	we + are = we're
they + had = they'd	should + not = shouldn't	you + have = you've
will + not = won't	can + not = can't	who + is = who's

Test Yourself

For sentences 1–4, add punctuation where it belongs.

1. Wed enjoyed our trip to Beatrices college.

2. Ive noticed many students bicycles along the path.

3. Hes a huge fan of this universitys football team.

4. Wasnt the lecture about childrens diseases excellent?

5. Which sentence contains an error in punctuation?

   A. The buildings were covered with ivy.
   B. Our campus was showing off its beauty.
   C. I wonder if shes seen the auditorium.
   D. Whose name is on the athletic building?

Answers

1. We'd enjoyed our trip to Beatrice's college. The first apostrophe is in a contraction meaning "we had." The second is in a singular possessive noun.
2. I've noticed many students' bicycles along the path. The first apostrophe is in a contraction meaning "I have." The second is in a plural possessive noun.
3. He's a huge fan of this university's football team. One apostrophe is in the contraction that means "he is," and the other shows possession.
4. Wasn't the lecture about children's diseases excellent? The first apostrophe replaces the *o* in a contraction meaning "was not." The second shows possession for a plural noun that does not end in *s*.
5. C. *She's* is a contraction of *she has* and requires an apostrophe. In choice A, *were* is a verb, not a contraction. In choices B and D, *its* and *whose* are possessive pronouns, not contractions.

TROUBLESOME WORD PAIRS

Certain words are frequently confused. If you can keep the meanings and spellings of the following pairs separate, your writing will benefit. Some of the pairs are **homophones**, meaning that they sound alike but mean different things. Others are just close in appearance and cause readers and writers difficulty. (See Table 4.3.)

Table 4.3 Troublesome Word Pairs

Word	Meaning	Sentence
advice	guidance	The counselor gave me good *advice*.
advise	to guide	Did he *advise* you to work harder?
affect	to influence	Does adding water *affect* the results?
effect	consequence	What was the *effect* of adding water?
aural	involving the ear	*Aural* anatomy governs hearing aid size.
oral	involving the mouth	The *oral* dosage is 500 mg a day.
capital	seat of government; money	What is the *capital* of Montana?
capitol	statehouse	The *capitol* was lit up at night.
censor	to suppress communication	Why did they *censor* that documentary?
censure	to criticize	The review seems to *censure* the director.
complement	to complete and improve	The beets *complement* the bitter greens.
compliment	to praise	Please *compliment* her on her cooking.
defuse	to calm, neutralize	I tried to *defuse* their quarrel.
diffuse	to scatter	His anger seems to *diffuse* in all directions.
discreet	tactful; inconspicuous	Be *discreet* about the discoveries we have made.
discrete	separate, distinct	The compound is made up of *discrete* molecules.
forbear	refrain	Please *forbear* from touching the china.
forebear	ancestor	The china was passed down from a *forebear* of my husband's.
foreword	preface	My aunt wrote the *foreword* to that book.
forward	advancing	She is moving *forward* in her career.
imply	suggest	What does his study *imply* to you?
infer	conclude	What can you *infer* from his study?
its	belonging to it	A leopard cannot change *its* spots.
it's	it is	*It's* stuck with the spots it has.
prescribe	recommend	He may *prescribe* herbs for that rash.
proscribe	forbid	Some religions *proscribe* the use of drugs.
principal	primary; school leader	The *principal* role of a *principal* is to hire and support good teachers.
principle	rule, belief	Good teaching is the *principle* on which our school is based.
stationary	motionless	Dad bought me that *stationary* bike.
stationery	writing paper	I wrote Dad a thank-you note on my best *stationery*.

Table 4.3 Troublesome Word Pairs (*Continued*)

Word	Meaning	Sentence
their	belonging to them	What is *their* final destination?
they're	they are	*They're* going to enjoy the trip.
to	toward	Are you heading *to* the concert?
too	also	We are going that way, *too*!
tortuous	complex, twisted	The plot of the movie was *tortuous* and farfetched.
torturous	painful	Sitting in those dreadful seats was a *torturous* experience.
your	belonging to you	Did you use *your* ski tickets yet?
you're	you are	*You're* waiting for better weather.

Test Yourself

For questions 1–4, circle the correct word in parentheses.

1. The case keeps my jewelry in (discreet/discrete) compartments.
2. I do not mean to (imply/infer) that your apartment is messy.
3. Do not let his rudeness (affect/effect) your mood.
4. What was the (principal/principle) intention of this author?
5. Select the word in the following sentence that is *not* used correctly.

   I want to compliment you for prescribing that we move forward with the plan; your advise was excellent.

   A. compliment
   B. prescribing
   C. forward
   D. advise

Answers

1. discrete. The case keeps the jewelry separated.
2. imply. A speaker or writer implies; a listener or reader infers.
3. affect. *Affect* means "to influence."
4. principal. The correct word describes the author's primary, or most important, intention.
5. D. *Advise* is a verb; the correct word here would be *advice*.

SPELLING RULES

Spelling is mostly a matter of memorization. However, as difficult as English is, and as many exceptions as there are to every rule, there *are* some spelling rules worth remembering. Table 4.4 shows a few.

Table 4.4 A Few Spelling Rules

Rule	Examples	Exceptions
Do not change the spelling of the base word when adding suffixes *-ness* or *-ly*.	stubbornness, usually	words of more than one syllable that end in *y*: *emptiness, busily*
Drop the final *e* before a suffix that begins with a vowel.	famous, lovable	words that might be confusing without the *e*: *dyeing*
Change *y* to *i* in words ending in *y* preceded by a consonant if the suffix begins with any letter but *i*.	buried, craziness	some one-syllable words: *shyly, flyable*
When using *all* as a prefix, drop the final *l*.	almost, already	hyphenated adjectives: *all-seeing*
Double the final consonant before a suffix that starts with a vowel if the base word has one syllable or is accented on the last syllable and ends in a single consonant preceded by a vowel.	banned, occurrence	
Form the plural of nouns ending in *o* preceded by a vowel by adding *-s*.	patios, radios	
Form the plural of nouns ending in *o* preceded by a consonant by adding *-es*.	tomatoes, volcanoes	words that come from Spanish or Italian: *avocados, pianos*
If the root word is mostly intact, its adjective-forming ending is usually *-able* rather than *-ible*.	breakable vs. horrible, believable vs. tangible	
If a word is formed from a verb that ends in *-y, -ear, -ate,* or *-ure,* use the suffix *-ance*.	variance, appearance, ambulance, insurance	

Nouns with *-ance* and *-ence* endings are tricky enough that it's worth memorizing a chart of both.

Words Ending in *-ance*

absorbance, abundance, acceptance, acquaintance, admittance, allowance, annoyance, ascendance, avoidance, conveyance, defiance, deliverance, disturbance, dominance, encumbrance, endurance, exorbitance, grievance, guidance, ignorance, importance, inheritance, insurance, intolerance, maintenance, observance, performance, perseverance, radiance, relevance, reliance, resemblance, resistance, resonance, severance, significance, surveillance, sustenance, temperance, tolerance, utterance, vengeance, vigilance

Words Ending in *-ence*

abhorrence, absence, abstinence, adherence, adolescence, ambivalence, belligerence, benevolence, coalescence, coherence, competence, concurrence, conference, congruence, consistence, convalescence, correspondence, decadence, dependence, deterrence, difference, effervescence, equivalence, emergence, existence, fluorescence, incidence, interference, magnificence, negligence, occurrence, permanence, persistence, prevalence, recurrence, reminiscence, reverence, transcendence, vehemence, virulence

In addition, there are scores of spelling demons that everyone seems to misspell. A few that you might need to use in your medical career appear below.

WHY DO I NEED THIS?

Medical reports must be precise. A misspelled word might be misinterpreted.

Health-Related Spelling Demons

A ache, acute, anxious, apparatus, appetite, arthritis, asthma

B balance, bandage, beneficial, benign, breathe, bruise, bury

C cemetery, compatible, conscious, contagious, cough, cyst

D dependent, develop, diarrhea, disappear, discipline, disease

E effect, eligible, environment, equipment, exercise, exhausted, exhibit

F familiar, fatal, forward, fulfill

G gases, gauge, guidance

H height, hospital

I imaginary, immunization, independent, individual, injury

J judgment

K knowledge

L	laboratory, leisure, license, literature
M	maintenance, malignant, maneuver, medicine, muscle
N	nausea, necessary, noticeable, numerous
O	occurrence, often, opinion, ordinary, original
P	parallel, paralysis, particular, permanent, personnel, perspiration, physical, poisonous, preference, preparation, prescription, procedure
Q	quantity
R	receive, recommend, referred, relief, representative, residency, rhythm
S	safety, satisfactory, schedule, science, seizure, separate, serious, similar, stomach, strength, substantial, sufficient, summary, susceptible
T	technique, temperature, tendency, tendon, thorough, transferred
U	unnecessary, urine, usually
V	vacant, vacuum, victim, visible
W	waive, water, weigh, whether, wounded

Test Yourself

For questions 1–4, circle the correct spelling in parentheses.

1. Her (abhorence/abhorrence/abhorrance) of beets makes me laugh.
2. I replaced beets with (potatos/potatoes/potattoes) in this recipe.
3. When will you be (allegable/eligible/illegable) to take the exam?
4. Steadfast (persistance/persistence/persistense) is a good quality in a nurse.
5. Which word is *not* spelled correctly in the context of the following sentence?

   Is this treatment compatable with the medicine he is already taking?

   A. treatment
   B. compatable
   C. medicine
   D. already

Answers

1. abhorrence. This word follows the "double the final consonant" rule and takes the *-ence* suffix ending.
2. potatoes. This follows the same rule as *tomatoes* and *volcanoes*.
3. eligible. *Illegible* is a word, but it does not fit the context.
4. persistence. This is one of those *-ance*/*-ence* words that must simply be memorized.
5. B. *Compatible* ends *-ible* instead of *-able*. Its root word is not intact, indicating that *-ible* is the more likely suffix.

CHAPTER 5

Basic Math Skills

CONTENTS

Most nursing programs will require the math module of the A2 test. Basic math skills are a prerequisite for most of the science courses you may take in nursing school, and they are used on the job as well, whether to measure medication, calculate temperature, or devise a budget. Some A2 tests require you occasionally to work out a problem and write the answer rather than choosing from multiple-choice responses.

COMPUTATION WITH WHOLE NUMBERS

There are a variety of number systems, but the ones we use most are the **binary system** (where all numbers are expressed using a combination of 0 and 1—this is the system on which computing is based) and our **decimal system**, where place value corresponds to powers of 10. In our decimal system, whole numbers are any of the positive integers plus zero—0, 1, 2, 3, and so on.

Addition

When you add whole numbers, you must keep the place value of the addends aligned in order to get the correct sum. (See Figure 5.1.)

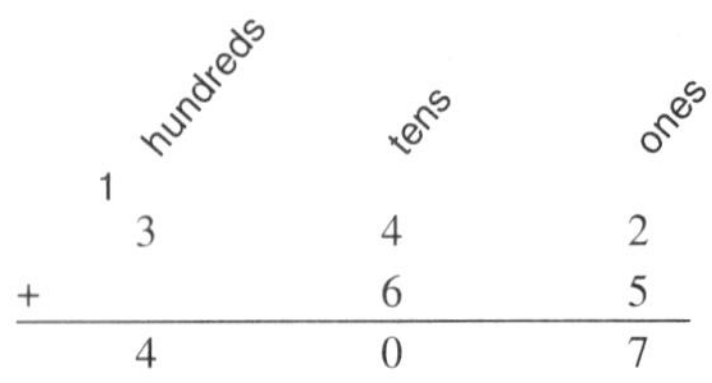

Figure 5.1 Addition

You can help yourself by estimating answers. You know that adding 65 to 342 will get you a number that is greater than 342, but not greater than 442. Just knowing that much will help you to narrow your possibilities on a multiple-choice test. You also know that the ones digit will be 2 + 5, or 7.

In word problems, words that signal the need to add include *altogether, both, in all,* and *total.*

Subtraction

As with addition, subtraction of whole numbers is a matter of keeping digits in the correct place value and knowing basic subtraction facts. (See Figure 5.2.)

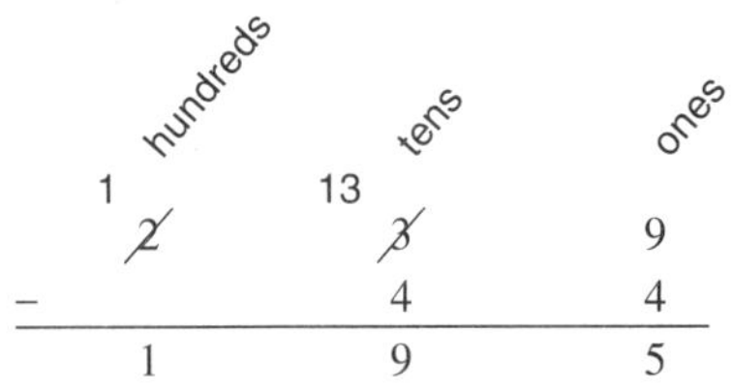

Figure 5.2 Subtraction

Again, estimating and knowing the ones digit of your answer can help you choose among possibilities on a multiple-choice test.

In word problems, words that signal the need to subtract include *less, how many more, difference,* and *how many left.*

Multiplication

When you multiply whole numbers, your answer will always be greater than either of the factors in the multiplication. Looking for patterns can help you choose the correct answer.

$3 \times 4 = 12 \qquad 3 \times 40 = 120 \qquad 3 \times 400 = 1{,}200$

In word problems, words that signal the need to multiply include *every, doubled, times,* and *at this rate.*

Division

When you divide whole numbers, your answer will always be less than the dividend (the number being divided). Use whatever method you learned in school to divide whole numbers. This example shows long division:

$$\begin{array}{r} 2 \\ 3\overline{)720} \end{array} \qquad \begin{array}{r} 2 \\ 3\overline{)720} \\ \underline{-6} \\ 1 \end{array} \qquad \begin{array}{r} 2 \\ 3\overline{)720} \\ \underline{6} \\ 12 \end{array} \qquad \begin{array}{r} 24 \\ 3\overline{)720} \\ \underline{6} \\ 12 \\ \underline{-12} \\ 0 \end{array} \qquad \begin{array}{r} 240 \\ 3\overline{)720} \end{array}$$

In word problems, words that signal the need to divide include *each, shared evenly,* and *into groups.*

Test Yourself

1. Yolanda is preparing snacks for 21 children in the day-care center. She separates mini-pretzels so that they may be shared evenly among the children. If she starts with a bag of 100 mini-pretzels, how many will each child receive? How many will be left over?

____

2. 43 + 44 + 45 + 46 + 47 = ____________

3. Divide: 4,230 ÷ 15 =

A. 24
B. 282
C. 302
D. 506

4. Multiply: 12 × 42 =

A. 404
B. 424
C. 454
D. 504

5. Solve: (2 + 5)(14 + 10) =

A. 31
B. 78
C. 168
D. 1,400

Answers

1. 4, with 16 left over. If each child received 5, that would be 21 × 5 = 105 mini-pretzels—5 more than are in the bag. If each receives 4, that is 21 × 4 = 84 mini-pretzels. The total in the bag, 100, minus 84 used = 16 left over.

2. 225. You can estimate to see that the answer will be between 200 (40 × 5) and 250 (50 × 5).
3. B. All of the ones digits in the answer choices are plausible, so you need to use estimation skills or long division. Estimating can tell you that 15 × 200 = 3,000, so choice A is not even close. 15 × 100 = 1,500, and 3,000 + 1,500 = 4,500, which is a little larger than the given dividend. So you know that your answer will be between 200 and (200 + 100). The only answer that fits is choice B, 282.
4. D. You know that 12 × 40 = 480, so the answer must be greater than that.
5. C. Add first, then multiply. 7 × 24 = 168.

DECIMALS

Decimals are numbers that have a fractional part separated from the integer part by a decimal point. Computing with decimals is exactly like computing with whole numbers, with one critical exception: You must know where to place the decimal point in the sum, difference, product, or quotient.

Addition

As you do when you add whole numbers, you must keep the place value of the addends aligned. Imagine 65.3 + 7.54 = ? (See Figure 5.3.)

	tens	ones		tenths	hundredths
	1				
	6	5	.	3	
+		7	.	5	4
	7	2	.	8	4

Figure 5.3 Addition of Decimals

If a sum is presented horizontally, use common sense and estimation to determine the size of the sum.

$$42.3 + 2.88 \approx 42 + 3 \qquad 902.99 + 4{,}001.0001 \approx 900 + 4{,}000$$

Subtraction

Sometimes you will subtract a decimal with hundredths or thousandths from a decimal with tenths. Simply place zeroes in the missing slots and subtract the way you normally would. Imagine 27.4 – 4.26 = ? (See Figure 5.4.)

	tens	ones		tenths	hundredths
				3	10
	2	7	.	~~4~~	(~~0~~)
−		4	.	2	6
	2	3	.	1	4

Figure 5.4 Subtraction of Decimals

Multiplication

There is an easy trick to getting the decimal point right when multiplying decimals. Add the number of places to the right of the decimal point in the factors. That's how many places to the right of the decimal point you will see in the product.

$0.5 \times 0.5 = 0.25 \qquad 0.14 \times 0.14 = 0.0196$

The exception comes when the final digit or digits are zeroes. Typically, we leave those zeroes off when we write a decimal number.

$0.5 \times 0.2 = 0.10 = 0.1 \qquad 0.14 \times 0.15 = 0.0210 = 0.021$

Division

If you use long division to solve division of decimals, start by placing the decimal point for the quotient directly above the decimal point in the dividend. That will help you to orient your answer and keep the place values where they belong.

$$
\begin{array}{r} . \\ 5\overline{)14.5} \end{array}
\qquad
\begin{array}{r} 2. \\ 5\overline{)14.5} \end{array}
\qquad
\begin{array}{r} 2. \\ 5\overline{)14.5} \\ \underline{-10} \\ 4 \end{array}
\qquad
\begin{array}{r} 2.9 \\ 5\overline{)14.5} \\ \underline{10} \\ 45 \\ \underline{-45} \\ 0 \end{array}
$$

You can check your placement by multiplying quotient by divisor and seeing whether adding the number of places to the right of the decimal point in the factors equals the number of places to the right of the decimal point in the product.

Problems with Money

Computing with money is the same as computing with decimals. It is important to place the decimal point correctly, keeping in mind that money is written with no more than two places to the right of the decimal point. You may need to round off an answer accordingly.

$0.26 \div 5 = 0.052 \qquad \$0.26 \div 5 \approx \$0.05$

As with any problem that involves a system of measurement, you must read carefully to know what unit to use or whether to round your answer.

To the nearest dollar . . . To the nearest ten cents . . .

Test Yourself

1. Multiply: $0.45 \times 0.15 =$ ___________

2. Add: $4.25 + 42.5 + 0.425 =$ ___________

3. Subtract: $4.5 - 3.25 =$ ___________

4. Divide: $3.4 \div 2 =$ ___________

5. Jake cut three 1.25-foot pieces of wire from a 10-foot roll. How much wire was left on the roll?

   A. 8.75 ft
   B. 7.25 ft
   C. 6.25 ft
   D. 3.75 ft

6. Erlene paid $4.55 for coffee and $1.49 for a biscuit. To the nearest 10 cents, what did she spend in all? ___________

7. Elba Dean made $15.10 an hour for 35 hours of work last week. How much was her gross pay for the week? ___________

8. Robert's weekly take-home pay is $892.29. Of that, he puts aside one-third for his rent and utilities and spends $105 on groceries. How much is left of his weekly pay?

   A. $787.29
   B. $649.86
   C. $489.86
   D. $402.43

Answers

1. 0.0675. Each of the factors has two digits to the right of the decimal point, meaning that the product should have $2 + 2 = 4$ digits to the right of the decimal point.
2. 47.175. Add the thousandths first and work toward the left.
3. 1.25. Think 4.50 instead of 4.5, and subtract, keeping the decimal points aligned.

4. 1.7. The number 34 divided by 2 would equal 17, so moving the decimal point to the left in the dividend, as in 3.4, means the decimal point moves to the left in the quotient as well.
5. C. Multiply $1.25 \times 3 = 3.75$ to find how much wire Jake cut. Subtract that from 10 to find how much is left:
   $10 - 3.75 = 6.25$
6. $6.00. Adding the two amounts gives you $6.04, which is $6.00 to the nearest 10 cents.
7. $528.50. Multiply $15.10 by 35 to find the gross pay before taxes.
8. C. Divide the take-home pay by 3 to get $297.43 and subtract that from the whole to get $594.86. Then subtract another $105.

FRACTIONS

A fraction represents part of a whole. Its **numerator** represents the number of equal parts, and its **denominator** represents the number of parts that make up the whole. For example, the fraction 2/3 means "2 equal parts out of 3 equal parts."

Addition

When you add fractions, you add numerators because you are adding the number of equal parts.

$2/5 + 1/5 = 3/5$

The only difficulty comes when the denominators differ. In that case, you must find the **lowest common denominator**, so that you are adding the same sized equal parts.

$2/5 + 1/8 = 16/40 + 5/40 = 21/40$

To add **mixed numbers** that contain a whole number and a fraction, convert the mixed number to an **improper fraction** using these steps:

1. Multiply the whole number by the fraction's denominator.
2. Add the product to the numerator.
3. Use that sum as the new numerator.

$3\ 3/8 + 1/2 = 27/8 + 1/2 = 27/8 + 4/8 = 31/8$

Then express the final sum as a mixed number again using these steps:

1. Divide the numerator by the denominator.
2. Record the whole number.
3. Write the remainder as the numerator of the new fraction.

$31/8 = 3\ 7/8$

Subtraction

Subtraction of fractions and mixed numbers follows the same rules as addition. You subtract only the numerators.

5/6 – 1/6 = 4/6   1/3 – 1/6 = 6/18 – 3/18 = 3/18

Express a fraction in lowest terms by dividing the numerator and denominator by the same **greatest common factor**.

4/6 ÷ 2/2 = 2/3   3/18 ÷ 3/3 = 1/6

Multiplication

When you multiply fractions, you multiply numerator by numerator and denominator by denominator. You do not need to find the lowest common denominator when you multiply fractions. You can understand multiplication of fractions better if you visualize the fractions as pieces of a pie.

1/3 × 1/2 means "What is one-third of one-half?"

1/3 × 1/2 = 1/6   One-third of one-half is one-sixth.

Division

When you divide a fraction by a fraction, you are asking, "How many of this second fraction fit into that first fraction?"

1/2 ÷ 1/4 means "How many one-fourths fit into one-half?" just as

8 ÷ 2 means "How many 2s fit into 8?"

You divide fractions by multiplying the dividend by the **reciprocal** of the divisor.

1/2 ÷ 1/4 = 1/2 × 4/1 = 4/2 = 2, just as

8 ÷ 2 = 8 × 1/2 = 8/2 = 4.

Here are some examples.

3/5 ÷ 1/5 = 3/5 × 5 = 15/5 = 3

(How many one-fifths fit into three-fifths? Three.)

2/7 ÷ 3/8 = 2/7 × 8/3 = 16/21

Test Yourself

1. Multiply and simplify: 1 1/2 × 15/16 = ___________

2. Add and simplify: 2/3 + 2/9 + 2/27 = ___________

3. Multiply and simplify: 2(4/5 × 4/5) = ___________

4. Divide and simplify: 3/8 ÷ 1/24 = ___________

5. Subtract and simplify: 13/18 – 1/3 =

   A. 23/54
   B. 5/6
   C. 7/18
   D. 1/6

Answers

1. 1 13/32. Convert the mixed number to an improper fraction (3/2) and multiply numerators and denominators:
   3/2 × 15/16 = 45/32
   Simplify by dividing the numerator by the denominator and writing the remainder as the new numerator:
   45 ÷ 32 = 1 13/32
2. 26/27. Give each fraction the same denominator:
   18/27 + 6/27 + 2/27 = 26/27.
3. 1 7/25. Multiply within the parentheses to get 16/25. Then double that. 32/25 = 1 7/25.
4. 9. Dividing by 1/24 is the same as multiplying by 24:
   3/8 × 24 = 72/8 = 9
5. C. The lowest common denominator is 18. 1/3 = 6 /18. Subtracting gives you:
   13/18 – 6/18 = 7/18, which is in lowest terms.

PERCENTS

Percent means *for every 100*. We use percents often in our everyday lives to calculate interest, discounts, taxes, and tips. A percent is similar to a fraction or a decimal because it shows us part of a whole, but for percents, the whole is 100. 20% means 20 out of 100.

You can convert a percent into a fraction by dividing the percent by 100. You can convert a percent into a decimal number by multiplying the percent by

100 (which is the same as moving the decimal point two places to the left.) You can express 80% as a fraction, $\frac{80}{100}$, or a decimal, 0.80.

To solve most percentage problems, convert the percentage in the problem back to a decimal. Then solve as you would solve any problem that involved computation with decimals.

If you want to find 32% of 60, convert 32% to a decimal and then multiply it by 60:

$$0.32 \times 60 = 19.2$$

Test Yourself

1. Convert 36% to a decimal. ___________

2. Convert 8% to a fraction in lowest terms. ___________

3. What is 2% of 5?

A. 0.1
B. 2
C. 2.5
D. 10

4. What is 30% of 930?

A. 265
B. 279
C. 305
D. 310

5. What is 18% of 450?

A. 40
B. 65
C. 81
D. 105

Answers

1. 0.36. Think: $36\% = \frac{36}{100} = 0.36$.

2. $\frac{2}{25}$. The greatest common factor for $\frac{8}{100}$ is 4. Dividing the numerator and denominator by 4 yields $\frac{2}{25}$.

3. A. Think: $2\% = \frac{2}{100} = 0.02$. Multiply that by 5: $0.02 \times 5 = 0.1$.

4. B. Be careful. 30% does not equal $\frac{1}{3}$. $\frac{30}{100} = 0.3$. Multiply that by 930: $0.3 \times 930 = 279$.

5. C. Think: $18\% = \frac{18}{100} = 0.18$. Multiply that by 450: $0.18 \times 450 = 81$.

CONVERTING AMONG FRACTIONS, DECIMALS, AND PERCENTAGES

Fractions, decimals, and percentages are all ways of representing parts of a whole. Sometimes measurements or amounts are expressed in one way but must be used in another. For that reason, it's important to know how to convert fractions to decimals, decimals to percentages, and so on.

Expressing Fractions as Decimals

Decimals are expressed as tenths, hundredths, thousandths, and so on. Some fractions are easy to convert; for example, 1/10 = 0.1 and 3/100 = 0.03.

All other fractions can be converted to decimals simply by dividing the numerator by the denominator.

7/8 = 7 ÷ 8 = 0.875   44/55 = 44 ÷ 55 = 0.8

Table 5.1 shows some common conversions.

Table 5.1 Fraction to Decimal Conversions

Fraction	Decimal
1/2	0.5
1/4	0.25
1/5	0.2
1/8	0.125
3/4	0.75
3/8	0.375
5/8	0.625
7/8	0.875

Expressing Decimals as Fractions

The only difficult part about converting decimals to fractions is remembering to express the fraction in lowest terms.

0.45 = 45/100 = 9/20   1.6 = 1 6/10 = 1 3/5

Expressing Fractions as Percent

A percentage is the amount per hundred. For that reason, any fraction that you wish to express as a percentage must end up with a denominator of 100.

Some examples are easy:

1/10 = 10/100 = 10%   4/5 = 8/10 = 80/100 = 80%

In other cases, you must divide the numerator by the denominator and multiply the resulting decimal by 100.

$3/8 = 3 \div 8 = 0.375 \qquad 0.375 \times 100 = 37.5\%$

$1/40 = 0.025 \qquad 0.025 \times 100 = 2.5\%$

Expressing Decimals as Percent

A decimal is already in tenths, hundredths, thousandths, and so on. All you need to do to a decimal is to move the decimal point two spaces to the right, which is where it lands when you multiply a decimal by 100.

$0.39 = 39\% \qquad 1.45 = 145\% \qquad 0.058 = 5.8\%$

Test Yourself

1. Express 0.2555 as a percentage. ____________

2. Express $\frac{24}{25}$ as a decimal. ____________

3. Express 0.64 as a fraction in lowest terms. ____________

4. Express $\frac{1}{5}$ as a percent. ____________

5. A group of three friends is dividing up their dinner bill. If the total bill is $42.96, what is each person's third?

   A. $12.89
   B. $14.32
   C. $39.96
   D. $128.88

Answers

1. 25.55%. Think: $0.2555 \times 100 = 25.55$.

2. 0.96. Think: $\frac{24}{25} = 24 \div 25 = 0.96$.

3. $\frac{16}{25}$. Think: $0.64 = \frac{64}{100} = \frac{16}{25}$.

4. 20%. Think: $\frac{1}{5} = 0.2; 0.2 \times 100 = 20\%$

5. B. Think: $\frac{1}{3} \times 42.96 = 42.96 \div 3 = 14.32$.

RATIOS AND PROPORTIONS

Many of the problems you will encounter on the A2 test will involve ratios. Every time you compare values, sizes, or amounts, you are using ratios.

A **ratio** expresses the relationship between two quantities in terms of a fraction, where the numerator represents the first quantity, and the denominator represents the second quantity.

For example, if there are 10 red balls and 20 green balls, the ratio of red balls to green balls is $\frac{10}{20}$, which simplifies to $\frac{1}{2}$. Percents are a type of ratio that shows how many of something per 100. A ratio is different from a fraction, which shows how many parts there are out of the total number of parts. Ratios show parts to parts rather than parts to whole.

There are several different ways to express a ratio. The most common way to write a ratio is with a colon in between the two values, like this, 2:3. For example, if there is a ratio of two women to three men in a group, this can be written as:

- 2:3
- 2 to 3
- ratio of $\frac{2}{3}$ (also read as *two to three*)

Notice that the last option looks a lot like a fraction. A ratio is **not** a fraction though, so if you see a ratio expressed this way, the question will say that it is a ratio. Also notice that none of those options tell you the actual number of women or men in the group. None of them tell you the total number of people in the group, though you can say that there are five total parts to the ratio (two parts women and three parts men). Here are things you can say:

- the ratio of women to men is 2:3
- the ratio of men to women is 3:2
- the ratio of women to the group total is 2:5
- the ratio of men to the group total is 3:5

You can see that the order you list the two values makes a big difference, so read questions carefully.

A **proportion** is an equation that states that two ratios are equal. It can be written as: $\frac{a}{b} = \frac{c}{d}$ where a, b, c, and d are numbers. This equation can also be expressed as a cross-multiplication:

$$a \times d = b \times c$$

When working with proportions, you can use this equation to find unknown values. For example, if you know that $\frac{a}{b} = \frac{3}{4}$, and you know that $a = 15$, you can use the proportion to find b:

Substitute 15 for a: $\frac{15}{b} = \frac{3}{4}$

Cross multiply: $15 \times 4 = 3b$; $60 = 3b$

Solve for b by dividing both sides of the equation by 3: $\frac{60}{3} = \frac{3b}{3}$; $20 = b$

The proportion is: $\frac{15}{20} = \frac{3}{4}$

Proportions are used in many real-life situations, such as scaling up recipes or calculating the size of objects in an image.

Scale

One specific use of ratios is in **scale drawings**. In a scale drawing, a large object is drawn in miniature, with each measurement precisely a fraction of the original.

For example, in a building blueprint with a scale of 1:24, 1 inch on the drawing might equal 24 inches (2 feet) in the actual building. Building blueprints often contain ratios with different units; for example, 1″:1′ (one inch is equivalent to one foot).

A map is one type of scale drawing. A scale of miles somewhere on the map indicates the ratio that is being used. On a road map, the scale might be 1″:10 miles. On the map of a state, it might be 1″:100 miles. If a river on the state map appears to be about 1 3/4 inches long, you can assume that in real life, it is about 175 miles long.

Solving Problems with Ratios

A **rate** is one kind of ratio that is used to compare quantities. Miles per hour is an example of a rate.

35 miles per hour = 35 mi/h, or 35:1

In the example above, 35/1 is the **unit rate**, because it is in lowest terms. You can use this unit rate to solve a problem such as the one below.

Danishka traveled 175 miles, averaging 35 miles per hour. If she did not stop along the way, how long did Danishka's trip take?

Solve this by setting up a proportion.

$\frac{35}{1} = \frac{175}{x}$

Cross-multiply: $\frac{35}{1} \times \frac{175}{x}$

$35x = 175$

$x = 5$ hours

Rates can apply to such things as batting averages or money spent on an item. In a problem involving money, you often need to find the **unit price** before solving:

Paul paid \$11.52 for seeds priced at 3 packets for \$2.88. How many packets of seeds did he buy?

Start by setting up a proportion to find the unit price. Think: If 3 cost \$2.88, how much does 1 cost?

$$\frac{3}{2.88} = \frac{1}{x}$$
$$3x = 2.88$$
$$x = 0.96$$

Once you know that 1 packet of seeds costs \$0.96, you can divide that into \$11.52 to find the answer.

\$11.52 ÷ \$0.96 = 5 packets

Test Yourself

1. Write the ratio "two out of five" in two forms. ___________

2. If the scale of a plan is 1″:1′, what is the length in feet and inches of an object that appears on the plan as 3.75 inches long?

____

3. If pens are 6 for \$5.94, what is the unit price? ___________

4. The ratio of students to RAs in one dorm is 24:1. Which of the following is a possible actual number of students and RAs in the dorm?

A. 125:5
B. 192:8
C. 207:9
D. 312:12

5. A party planner figures on 3 liters of punch for every 10 guests. How much punch should she provide for a party of 85?

A. 12.5
B. 23
C. 25.5
D. 26

6. If there are 16 boys and 17 girls in a classroom, what is the ratio of girls to the total number of students?

A. 16:33
B. 17:33
C. 16:17
D. 33:17

7. The ratio of adults to children at a party is 6:1. If there are 7 children, how many adults are there? ___________

8. How many total people are at the party? ___________

9. Lemonade is made with a ratio of 1 part lemon juice, 5 parts water, and 1 part sugar. If Marisa has only $\frac{1}{2}$ cup lemon juice, how much sugar will she need?
   A. $\frac{1}{2}$ cup
   B. $\frac{2}{3}$ cup
   C. 1 cup
   D. $1\frac{1}{2}$ cup

10. In a school with a 24:1 student/teacher ratio, if there are 480 students, how many teachers are there? ___________

Answers

1. 2:5, 2/5. Ratios may be written using a colon or fraction bar.
2. 3 feet 9 inches. If 1 inch represents 1 foot, 3.75 inches represent 3.75 feet.
3. \$0.99. Divide the total cost by the number of pens: \$5.94 ÷ 6 = \$0.99.
4. B. Reduce the fraction in each answer choice until you find one equal to $\frac{24}{1}$. For choice B: $\frac{192}{8} = \frac{24}{1}$.
5. C. Think: $\frac{3}{10} = \frac{x}{85}$; $3 \times 85 = 10x$; $255 = 10x$; $25.5 = x$.
6. B. First, find the total: 16 boys + 17 girls = 33 students. The ratio of girls to total is 17:33.
7. 42. Think: $\frac{6}{1} = \frac{x}{7}$; $42 = x$
8. 49. 42 adults plus 7 children = 49 people.
9. A. The ratio calls for 1 part lemon juice, but if she uses only $\frac{1}{2}$ cup, then she will need to divide the other quantities in half as well. She will need $\frac{1}{2}$ cup sugar and $2\frac{1}{2}$ cups water.
10. 20. Think: $\frac{24}{1} = \frac{480}{x}$; $24x = 480$; $x = 20$

SOLVING PROBLEMS USING ALGEBRA

Algebraic equations contain at least one unknown variable. This unknown variable is represented by a letter, such as *x* or *y*. The A2 test will not require you to know algebra, but you may often wish to use algebra to solve certain kinds of problems, so here is a quick review.

Basic Algebra

To solve an algebraic equation, isolate the variable x on one side of the equation. In the case below, first subtract the number 4 from both sides:

$$2x + 4 = 8$$

$$2x + 4 - 4 = 8 - 4$$

$$2x + 0 = 4$$

$$2x = 4$$

Subtracting 4 from both sides leaves only the term $2x$ on the left side of the equation. Now, divide both sides by 2 to isolate the variable x:

$$2x = 4$$

$$\frac{2x}{2} = \frac{4}{2}$$

$$x = 2$$

The value of x is 2.

Using Algebra in Percentage Problems

Suppose you know that 15 percent of your class got an A on the latest exam. You also know that 6 students received an A. You can determine the total number of students in the class by using algebra.

Think:

$15\%x = 6$, where x = the number of students in the class

Solve for x by isolating x on one side of the equation. In this case, you must divide both sides by 15% to isolate x.

$x = 6 \div 0.15$ (Remember that a percent may be expressed as a decimal.)

$x = 40$

There are 40 students in the class.

Using Algebra in Ratio Problems

Suppose you know that a train averages 125 km/h. It is embarking on a nonstop journey of 4.5 hours. How many kilometers will it travel?

Think:

125 km/h = x km/4.5 h

For ratios and proportions, you may cross-multiply to determine the answer:

$$\frac{125}{1} \times \frac{x}{4.5}$$

$x = 125 \times 4.5$

$x = 562.5$ km

Test Yourself

1. Solve for x: $3x + 1 = 13$ ________________

2. Solve for x: $24/x = 1/5$ ________________

3. Solve for x: $4x - 12 = 12$ ________________

4. $12 - x/4 = 8$

Solve the equation. Which of the following is correct?

A. $x = 6$
B. $x = 8$
C. $x = 12$
D. $x = 16$

5. Cassandra's height is 3 inches greater than twice her baby brother's height, which is 26 inches.

Which algebraic equation best represents the statement above?

A. $x = 3x + 26$
B. $x = 2(26) + 3$
C. $26 = 2x + 3$
D. $x = 3(26) + 2$

Answers

1. 4. Isolate x by subtracting 1 from both sides: $3x = 12$, so $x = 4$.
2. 120. Cross-multiply: $24 \times 5 = x$, so $x = 120$.
3. 6. Isolate x by adding 12 to both sides: $4x = 24$, so $x = 6$.
4. D. First subtract 12 from both sides: $-x/4 = 8 - 12$, so $-x/4 = -4$. Then multiply both sides by -4 to solve for x: $x = 16$.
5. B. Cassandra's height is twice her brother's height plus 3 inches, so it is $2(26) + 3$.

TIME AND ROMAN NUMERALS

Occasional questions in the Basic Math Skills section of the A2 test will deal with military time or Roman numerals.

Military Time

Standard, or civilian, clocks are on a 12-hour cycle. Military clocks are on a 24-hour cycle. (See Table 5.2.)

Table 5.2 Standard to Military Time Conversions

Standard Time	Military Time	Standard Time	Military Time
12:00 A.M.	0000	12:00 P.M.	1200
1:00 A.M.	0100	1:00 P.M.	1300
2:00 A.M.	0200	2:00 P.M.	1400
3:00 A.M.	0300	3:00 P.M.	1500
4:00 A.M.	0400	4:00 P.M.	1600
5:00 A.M.	0500	5:00 P.M.	1700
6:00 A.M.	0600	6:00 P.M.	1800
7:00 A.M.	0700	7:00 P.M.	1900
8:00 A.M.	0800	8:00 P.M.	2000
9:00 A.M.	0900	9:00 P.M.	2100
10:00 A.M.	1000	10:00 P.M.	2200
11:00 A.M.	1100	11:00 P.M.	2300

So a standard time of 4:30 A.M. would equate to a military time of 0430, and a standard time of 4:30 P.M. would equate to 1630 in military time.

> WHY DO I NEED THIS?
>
> *Most medical facilities use military time! It avoids confusion on medical charts.*

Roman Numerals

As you might guess, the Roman numeral system originated in ancient Rome. Unlike the Arabic system we use today, it is based on seven symbols, with other numbers formed by combining symbols and adding or subtracting values. (See Table 5.3.)

Table 5.3 Roman to Arabic Numeral Conversions

Roman	Arabic
I	1
V	5
X	10
L	50
C	100
D	500
M	1,000

So, for example, the Arabic number 4 is written IV (V minus I), whereas 6 is written VI (V plus I). The number 900 is written CM (M minus C), whereas 1,100 is written MC (M plus C). Only I, X, or C may be added or subtracted, and each may be subtracted only once.

WHY DO I NEED THIS?

The apothecary system, featuring Roman numerals, is still used to label some medications.

Converting from Arabic to Roman

Break down the Arabic number into a combination of 1s, 5s, 10s, 50s, 100s, 500s, and 1,000s.

23 = 10 + 10 + 1 + 1 + 1 = XXIII

405 = 500 – 100 + 5 = CDV

1,260 = 1,000 + 100 + 100 + 50 + 10 = MCCLX

Converting from Roman to Arabic

Assign an Arabic value to each letter and calculate the total.

XL = 10 50. Because the X precedes the L, subtract it: 50 – 10 = 40.

VII = 5 1 1. Because the I's follow the V, add them: 5 + 1 + 1 = 7

MCIX = 1,000 100 1 10. First subtract I from X: 10 – 1 = 9. Then add: 1,000 + 100 + 9 = 1,109.

Test Yourself

For questions 1–4, write a standard time for each military time.

1. 2130 __________

2. 1645 __________

3. 1310 __________

4. 1815 __________

5. Nurse Preston gave the patient his last dose of antibiotics at 10:45 p.m. What would that be in military time? __________

6. Write the number 145 in Roman numerals: __________

7. Write the number DCIV in Arabic numerals: __________

8. Write the number 3,003 in Roman numerals: __________

9. Which of the following is LXIV in Arabic numerals?

A. 44
B. 64
C. 66
D. 514

10. Which of the following is the date 2018 in Roman numerals?

A. MCXIIIB
B. MDDIIXXC
C. MMXXIID
D. MMXVIII

Answers

1. 9:30 P.M.
2. 4:45 P.M.
3. 1:10 P.M.
4. 6:15 P.M.
5. 2245. Standard time 10:00 p.m. would be 2200, so 10:45 p.m. is 2245.
6. CXLV. C = 100, XL = 40, and V = 5.
7. 604. D = 500, C = 100, and IV = 4.

8. MMMIII. M = 1,000, and I = 1.
9. B. L = 50, X = 10, and IV = 4.
10. D. MM = 2,000. X = 10. VIII = 8.

MEASUREMENT CONVERSION

More than most jobs, nursing requires accurate measurement using a variety of units of measure.

Standard System

The customary system of measurement, which we also refer to as the standard system, has a long history but is now largely confined to the United States. Table 5.4 includes some typical units in this system.

Table 5.4 Standard Units of Measure

Length	Weight	Capacity
12 in = 1 ft	16 oz = 1 lb	8 oz = 1 cup
3 ft = 1 yd	2,000 lb = 1 ton	2 cups = 1 pt
5,280 ft = 1 mi		2 pt = 1 qt
1,760 yd = 1 mi		4 qt = 1 gal

Metric System

The metric system is a decimal system (based on tens), which makes it easier to use. It is based on a French system developed in the late 1600s. (See Table 5.5.)

Table 5.5 Metric Units of Measure

Length	Weight	Capacity
10 mm = 1 cm	1,000 mg = 1 g	1,000 mL = 1 L
100 cm = 1 m	1,000 g = 1 kg	
1,000 m = 1 km		

Converting Within the Standard System

Once you have memorized the equivalences shown in Tables 5.4 and 5.5, converting within the system is mostly a matter of computation.

If 3 ft = 1 yd, 6 ft = 2 yd, and 24 ft = 8 yd.

If 16 oz = 1 lb, 32 oz = 2 lb, and 50 oz = 3.125 lb.

If 8 oz = 1 cup and 2 cups = 1 pt, then 16 oz = 1 pt.

It may be helpful for standard volumes to picture this graphic:

The graphic shows that a gallon is made up of 4 quarts, each quart is made up of two pints, and each pint is made up of two cups. It's easy to see that there are 4 quarts, 8 pints, and 16 cups in a gallon.

Converting Within the Metric System

Again, converting within the metric system is a matter of computation. However, because the metric system is a decimal system, most conversions are just a matter of moving a decimal point.

1 mm = 0.1 cm	10 mm = 1 cm	100 mm = 10 cm
5 kg = 5,000 g	0.5 kg = 500 g	0.05 kg = 50 g
4,200 mL = 4.2 L	420 mL = 0.42 L	42 mL = 0.042 L

Be sure that you know the following metric prefixes:

Table 5.6 Metric Prefixes

kilo-	thousand
hecto-	hundred
deca-	ten
deci-	one tenth (divide by 10)
centi-	one hundredth (divide by 100)
milli-	one thousandth (divide by 1,000)

It may be helpful to memorize a mnemonic for these prefixes: "King Henry died drinking chocolate milk."

Converting Between Standard and Metric

Because there may be times when conversion is necessary from one system to another, it is worth memorizing these basic conversions. (See Table 5.7.)

At the very least, you should know the relative sizes of inches and centimeters, feet and meters, and kilograms and pounds.

Table 5.7 Standard to Metric Conversions

Length	Weight	Capacity
1 in = 2.54 cm	1 kg ≈ 2.2 lb	1 oz ≈ 29.6 mL
1 m ≈ 3.28 ft	1 ton ≈ 907 kg	1.06 qt ≈ 1 L
1 m ≈ 1.09 yd		1 gal ≈ 3.79 L
1 mi ≈ 1.6 km		

Temperature Conversions

In the English system, temperature is measured on the Fahrenheit scale. In the metric system, temperature is measured on the Celsius scale. You will need to know how to convert temperature measurements from one scale to the other. Some common temperatures are shown in Table 5.8.

Table 5.8 Celsius to Fahrenheit Conversions

	Celsius	Fahrenheit
Absolute zero	–273.15	–459.67
Parity	–40	–40
Freezing point	0	32
Body temperature	37	98.6
Boiling point	100	212

To get a rough approximation of Celsius temperature from a Fahrenheit measurement, subtract 30 and then divide by 2. For an exact conversion, the formula is $C = (F - 32) \times \frac{5}{9}$.

Test Yourself

1. How many liters are there in 1,500 milliliters?____________

2. How many ounces are there in 2 quarts? ____________

3. How many grams are there in 20 kilograms? ____________

4. How many feet are there in 5 miles? ____________

5. To the nearest inch, how many inches long is a meterstick?

   A. 39
   B. 25
   C. 15
   D. 10

Answers

1. 1.5. The ratio of liter to milliliter is 1,000:1.
2. 64. There are 8 ounces in a cup, 16 in a pint, and 32 in a quart.
3. 20,000. A kilogram equals 1,000 grams.
4. 26,400. If there are 5,280 feet in a mile, there are $5{,}280 \times 5 =$ 26,400 feet in 5 miles.
5. A. A meter stick is 100 centimeters long, or 1/0.0254 inches long. Dividing yields around 39.37 inches.

CHAPTER 6

Biology

CONTENTS

Biology is likely to be a required module on the A2 test you take. The test covers just the basics of biology, so if you have taken college-level courses, you will be a step ahead.

SCIENTIFIC METHOD

The scientific method is a process for scientific exploration and experimentation. Typically, it begins with observations and the formulation of questions. The process might look like Figure 6.1.

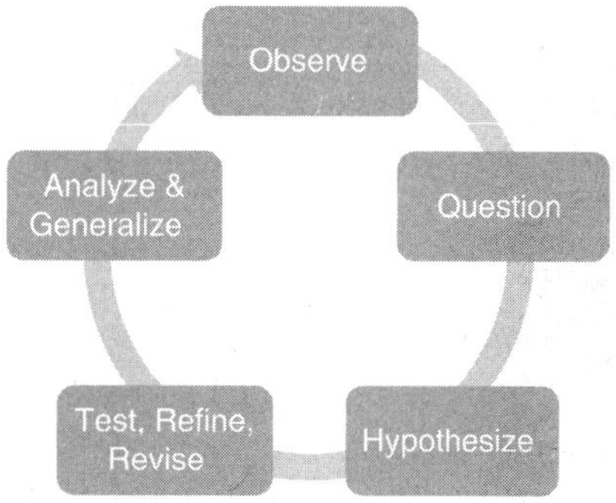

Figure 6.1 The Scientific Method

WHY DO I NEED THIS?

The nursing process, from assessment to evaluation, is one form of scientific method.

In the testing, or experimental, phase of the process, scientists look for causal relationships. They determine variables that will help them to answer their question.

- **Independent variable:** This is what changes to answer the question. If the question is "What kind of plant food helps plants grow taller?," the independent variable is the kinds of plant food.
- **Dependent variable:** This is what responds to the independent variable. For the question above, the dependent variable is the height of the plants.
- **Constant:** These remain the same in all cases so that you can see the true causal relationship of the independent variable on the dependent variable. Constants for the question above might include type of soil, amount of light, and amount of water.
- **Controlled variable:** This is the standard of comparison in an experiment. If your question were, "What kind of plant food helps plants grow taller?," your control might include a plant that was not given any plant food at all.

Two kinds of reasoning may apply to a given experiment. When a scientist formulates a hypothesis and then tests it, moving from a general statement to specific observations, that process is called **deductive reasoning**. When a scientist starts with specific observations and creates a generalization or theory to explain them, that process is called **inductive reasoning**.

An experiment is **reliable** if it is consistent and repeatable. If one scientist repeats the experiment many times with similar results, the test is reliable. If many different scientists perform the same experiment and achieve the same results, the test is reliable.

An experiment is **valid** if it measures what it is supposed to measure. If controls and constants are maintained, methodology is sound, instruments are appropriately sensitive, and the results may be applied or generalized beyond the single study, the test may be valid. The more measurements that are made, and the greater the size of the subject population, the more valid an experiment is likely to be.

Test Yourself

1. Once a scientist develops a question about observations, he or she formulates a ____________.

2. What kind of reasoning does Figure 6.2 illustrate? ____________

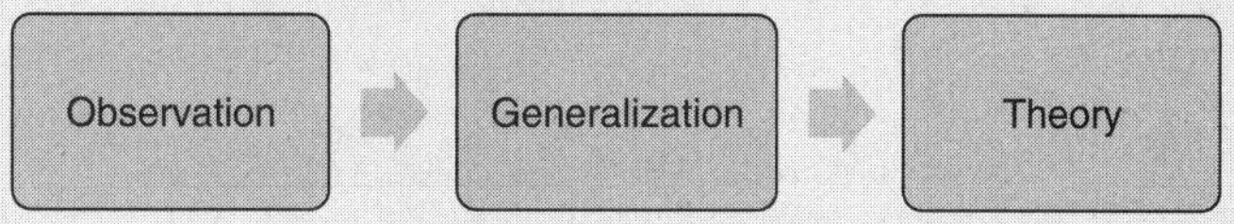

Figure 6.2 One Form of Reasoning

3. If a study's results are repeatable, the study is ____________.

4. If a study measures what it claims to measure, the study is ____________.

5. A vet student is testing the question: "Which brand of dog food best promotes a shiny coat?" What might be a reasonable constant?

   A. Dog breed
   B. Brand of food
   C. Warmth of room
   D. Dryness of food

Answers

1. hypothesis. Look back at the graphic to see the order of the process.
2. inductive. Deductive reasoning would start with a theory.
3. reliable. A reliable study can be replicated in other labs.
4. valid. A valid study has a large sample size and is carefully controlled.
5. A. The student would not want to compare coats across breeds, because the variations might mask the causal relationship being tested.

TAXONOMY

In biology, taxonomy is the branch of science that classifies organisms. Figure 6.3 shows the classification strata from most general at the bottom to most specific at the top.

For example, imagine a common house mouse. In order, from domain to species, the house mouse is classified Eukarya, Animalia, Chordata, Mammalia, Rodentia, Muridae, *Mus*, *musculus*. Its common Latin name, also known as its binomial name, is simply *Mus musculus*.

Scientists compare species in a variety of ways. They may look at their structures. Vertebrates, for example, have **closed transport**, or closed circulatory systems, with blood carried within vessels and pumped by a heart. Certain invertebrates, such as mollusks and arthropods, have **open transport**, or open circulatory systems, with a heart that pumps blood into open body cavities.

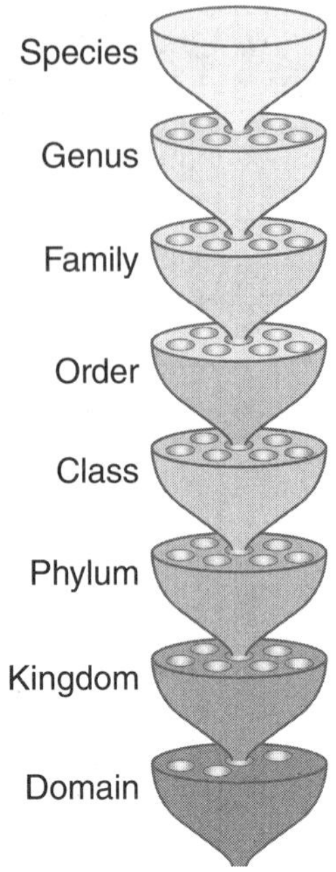

Figure 6.3 Classification Levels

There are a number of other ways to classify living organisms. For example, the energy pyramid looks at whether organisms are **producers** (acquiring energy from the sun and not feeding on other organisms) or **consumers** (acquiring energy from other organisms). Consumers are further divided, as in Figure 6.4.

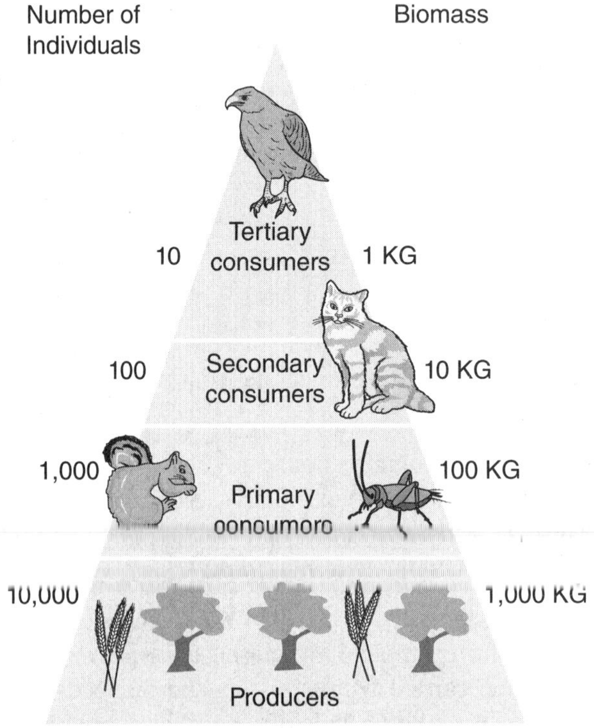

Figure 6.4 Energy Pyramid

Within the plant kingdom, plants are often divided into spore-producing plants such as mosses and ferns, and seed-producing plants. Seed-producing plants are further divided into **gymnosperms** (with naked seeds, such as pine trees) and **angiosperms** (flowering plants with enclosed seeds, such as apple trees).

Test Yourself

1. A wolf's binomial name is *Canis lupus*. Its __________ is *Canis,* and its __________ is *lupus.*

2. Which major classification lies between class and family? __________

For question 3, circle the correct answer in parentheses.

3. A shark is a (primary/secondary/tertiary) consumer.

4. Which of these animals is a primary consumer?

   A. Cow
   B. Dog
   C. Cat
   D. Snake

5. Which of the following trees is a gymnosperm?

   A. Oak
   B. Cherry
   C. Date palm
   D. White pine

Answers

1. genus, species. The binomial name features the genus and species.
2. order. In a house mouse, the order is Rodentia.
3. tertiary. Sharks are at the top of the undersea food chain.
4. A. Cows are vegetarians, consuming only producers; the other animals eat some form of meat.
5. D. Conifers of all kinds are gymnosperms.

MOLECULES

A molecule is a bonded group of atoms. Two or more like or unlike atoms may bind together to form a molecule. If the atoms are unlike, the molecule is called a **compound**. O_2 is a molecule, and so is H_2O. But only the latter is a compound.

Molecules may be **polar**, with positive charges grouped on one side and negative charges on the other. H_2O is one such molecule. Molecules may be **nonpolar**, with electrons distributed more symmetrically. CO_2 is nonpolar. Polar and nonpolar molecules do not mix well together to form solutions.

Organic compounds are the ingredients that make up living organisms. All organic compounds contain a carbon atom. There are four classes of organic compounds: carbohydrates, lipids, proteins, and nucleic acids.

Carbohydrates

Carbohydrate compounds contain only carbon, hydrogen, and oxygen. Typically, there are two hydrogen atoms and one oxygen atom for each carbon atom in a carbohydrate compound. (See Table 6.1.)

Table 6.1 Types of Carbohydrates

Type	Components	Examples
monosaccharide (simple sugar)	$(CH_2O)_3$, $(CH_2O)_5$, or $(CH_2O)_6$	glucose, fructose, ribose
disaccharide	2 simple sugars minus a molecule of water	sucrose, maltose, lactose
polysaccharide	multiple simple sugars arranged in chains	cellulose, starch, glycogen

Lipids

Lipids, like carbohydrates, are primarily carbon, hydrogen, and oxygen, but they have much less oxygen than carbohydrates do and are insoluble in water. (See Table 6.2.)

Table 6.2 Types of Lipids

Type	Components	Examples
fats	glycerol (an alcohol), 3 fatty acids	saturated fat (butter, coconut oil), polyunsaturated fat (sunflower oil)
waxes	long-chain alcohol, 1 fatty acid	beeswax, earwax, cutin
phospholipids	phosphate group, glycerol, 2 fatty acids	lecithin, sphingomyelin, cephalin
steroids	fused carbon rings, 0 fatty acids	cholesterol, estrogen, cortisone

Proteins

Proteins are made up of carbon, hydrogen, oxygen, and nitrogen, bonded to form compounds called **amino acids**. Like all organic acids, they contain the COOH group, but in addition, they have an amino group, NH_2. Both bond to the same carbon atom in the compound.

Condensation reactions between the COOH groups and the NH_2 groups bond amino acids together to form chains. The bonds are known as **peptide bonds**, and the chains are **polypeptide chains**. The chains coil and fold in different patterns, and these patterns suggest one way to classify proteins. (See Table 6.3.)

Table 6.3 Types of Proteins

Pattern	Examples
linear	collagen, keratin, fibrin
globular	enzymes, blood proteins, hormones

Nucleic Acids

These building blocks of genetic material are made up of carbon, hydrogen, oxygen, nitrogen, and phosphorus. More specifically, each **nucleotide** that comprises nucleic acid contains a $(CH_2O)_5$ (pentose) sugar, one or more phosphate groups, and one of five nitrogenous bases. In RNA, the sugar is ribose. In DNA, the sugar is deoxyribose. The possible bases are adenine, cytosine, guanine, thymine, and uracil.

More about nucleic acids appears later in this chapter.

Test Yourself

For questions 1–3, circle the correct answer in parentheses.

1. All organic compounds contain one or more atoms of (carbon/oxygen/nitrogen).

2. One example of a polysaccharide might be (ribose/starch/sucrose).

3. Unlike proteins, nucleic acids contain (hydrogen/nitrogen/phosphorus).

4. Which substance is a compound?

A. Hydrogen gas
B. Ozone
C. Sodium chloride
D. Gold

5. Which is true about enzymes?

A. They are made from proteins.
B. They contain no nitrogen.
C. They are insoluble in water.
D. They make up RNA and DNA.

Answers

1. carbon. This is the definition of an organic compound.
2. starch. Starch is composed of glucose monomers (subunits) joined in a chain.
3. phosphorus. The phosphate groups in nucleotides form bonds with the carbon in sugar. A phosphate group is a polyatomic ion.
4. C. A compound is made up of atoms from two or more elements. Hydrogen gas (H_2) is entirely hydrogen. Ozone (O_3) is entirely oxygen. Gold (Au) is a single element. Sodium chloride (NaCl) is sodium and chlorine.
5. A. Enzymes are proteins with a globular structure. Because they are proteins, they do contain nitrogen, making choice B incorrect.

WATER

Water is a very important and unique substance, with many physical and chemical properties that make it essential for life on Earth.

Physical Properties

- Water is a liquid at room temperature, which means it can flow and take on the shape of its container.
- It is transparent, meaning that light can pass through it.
- It has a high boiling point and melting point compared to other substances of similar size and weight, which means it can exist in all three states of matter (solid, liquid, and gas) under normal conditions.
- It has a high **surface tension**, which allows small insects and other objects to float on its surface.
- **Cohesiveness** allows water to travel through tiny capillaries, and cohesiveness creates surface tension on the surface of a body of water.
- **Adhesiveness** allows water to stick to other molecules and dissolve them, making it known as the "universal solvent."
- **Capillary action** is the ability of water (or any liquid) to flow upward against the force of gravity in narrow spaces, such as in thin tubes or narrow gaps in porous materials. This occurs due to the combined effects of adhesion and cohesion. As water molecules are attracted to the walls of the narrow tube, they form a concave shape at the edges of the water surface. This shape creates a surface tension that pulls the water up the tube or through the narrow gaps in the material, against the force of gravity. Capillary action is important for many natural processes, such as the movement of water from the roots to the leaves of plants and the movement of water through soil and other porous materials

Chemical Properties

- Water is a very good solvent; it can dissolve many substances such as salts, sugars, and acids.
- It is a neutral substance with a pH of 7.

- It is a polar molecule, meaning it has a slightly positive end and a slightly negative end. This polarity allows it to form hydrogen bonds with other water molecules and with other polar molecules, making it an important part of many chemical reactions.
- The **polarity** of water allows it to exhibit both cohesive and adhesive properties.
- H_2O is a covalent compound because oxygen and hydrogen are nonmetals. It has 8 total valence electrons (6 from oxygen and 1 from each hydrogen). Breaking the bonds requires a lot of energy, so water has a very high specific heat and heat of vaporization. The molar mass of water is 18.02 g/mol.
- The high specific heat of water allows it to absorb a lot of heat energy without changing temperature very much. This property helps to regulate the temperature of the Earth's surface and protect living organisms from sudden changes in temperature.
- Water also has a unique property called **osmosis**, which is a specific type of diffusion in which water moves passively through a semipermeable membrane to equalize water concentration on both sides of the membrane. This is how water moves through cell walls in the body.

Test Yourself

1. Which of the following properties is *not* responsible for water's capillary action?

A) adhesion
B) density
C) cohesion
D) surface tension

2. Why are droplets of water spherical?

A) Because of the high surface tension of water
B) Because water is an inorganic molecule
C) Because water is an excellent solvent
D) Because of water's high heat of vaporization

3. Which property of water allows water to stick to the sides of a straw?

A. Solubility
B. Surface tension
C. Adhesion
D. Cohesion

4. H_2O is an example of which typc of bond?

A. ionic bond
B. hydrogen bond
C. metallic
D. polar covalent

5. The ingredients in a mixture are shown in the chart below. Circle the name of the substance that is the solvent.

Substance	Chemical Formula	Amount
salt	NaCl	10.0 g
glucose	$C_6H_{12}O_6$	10.0 g
water	H_2O	100.0 g

Answers

1. B. Capillary action is a combination of adhesion, cohesion, and surface tension.
2. A. Surface tension pulls the water molecules at the surface of the droplet equally in all directions, creating a symmetrical, rounded shape.
3. C. Adhesion is the attraction between water and other molecules. Water exhibits adhesion when its attraction to another substance is greater than the water's attraction to itself (cohesion).
4. D. H_2O (water) is an example of a polar covalent bond because the hydrogen atoms are not evenly distributed around the oxygen atom.
5. Water. Salt and glucose will dissolve in the water, so salt and glucose are solutes and water is the solvent.

CELLS

A cell is the smallest structural and functional unit of an organism. With the exception of viruses, all living organisms are composed of cells. Cells range in size from the tiniest of bacteria to the relatively enormous egg of an ostrich.

Parts of a Cell

All cells contain a cell membrane, cytoplasm, and DNA. Cells may be **prokaryotic**, in which case they lack a nucleus or other internal, walled-off structures. They may be **eukaryotic**, housing a nucleus and other organelles.

Bacteria are one domain of prokaryotic cells. They come in four basic shapes—spherical (cocci), rod-shaped (bacilli), spiral-shaped (spirochete), and comma-shaped (vibrio). No matter the shape, all contain the same basic structures.

Animal cells differ from plant cells in certain structures. Figure 6.5 illustrates parts of an animal cell.

- **Centriole:** Made of microtubules, this small organelle aids in cell division.
- **Cytoplasm:** This fluid fills the cell, provides its shape, and contains molecules that break down waste and aid in metabolism.

- **Golgi body:** This organelle stores, sorts, processes, and releases products from the endoplasmic reticulum.
- **Lysosome:** This digests excess materials from the cytoplasm, using a variety of enzymes to break down molecules.
- **Microtubule:** This structure aids with transport and motility, including movement of chromosomes during mitosis.
- **Mitochondrion:** Through cellular respiration, this organelle breaks down nutrients to produce energy.
- **Nucleus:** This organelle stores the cell's genetic material and coordinates cellular activity from protein synthesis to reproduction.
- **Nucleolus:** A small structure in the nucleus, this body makes ribosomal RNA (rRNA), a key element in the construction of proteins.

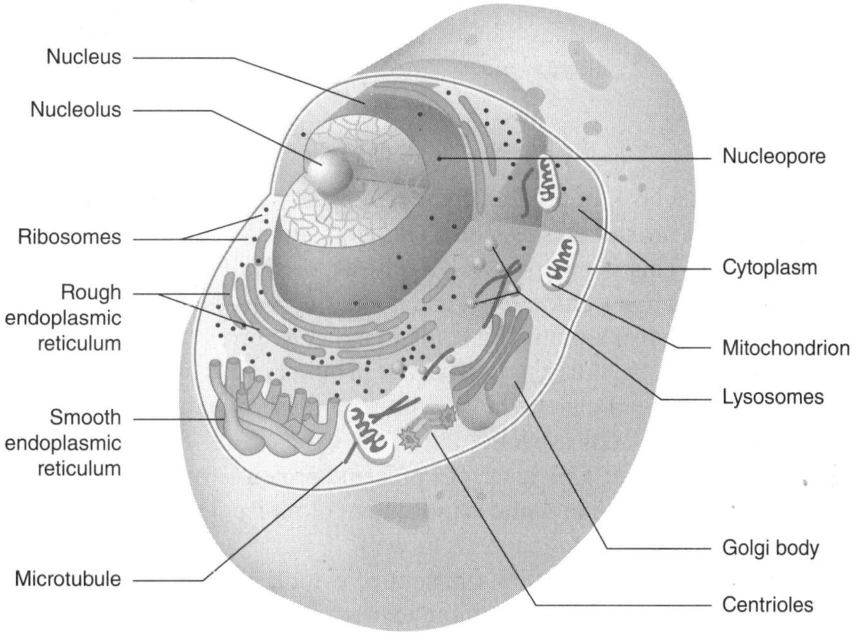

Figure 6.5 Animal Cell

- **Nucleopore:** The nuclear membrane is strong and protective, but these small holes help to channel nucleic acids and proteins in and out as needed.
- **Ribosome:** This mix of RNA and proteins is the site of protein synthesis and may float free or attach to the endoplasmic reticulum.
- **Rough endoplasmic reticulum:** This network of tubes is dotted with ribosomes and aids in protein production and transport.
- **Smooth endoplasmic reticulum:** Lacking ribosomes, this smooth network of tubes helps to produce and metabolize fats and steroid hormones.

Plant cells have a few parts that animal cells lack. On the other hand, they do not have lysosomes, and most plant cells lack centrioles as well. (See Figure 6.6.)

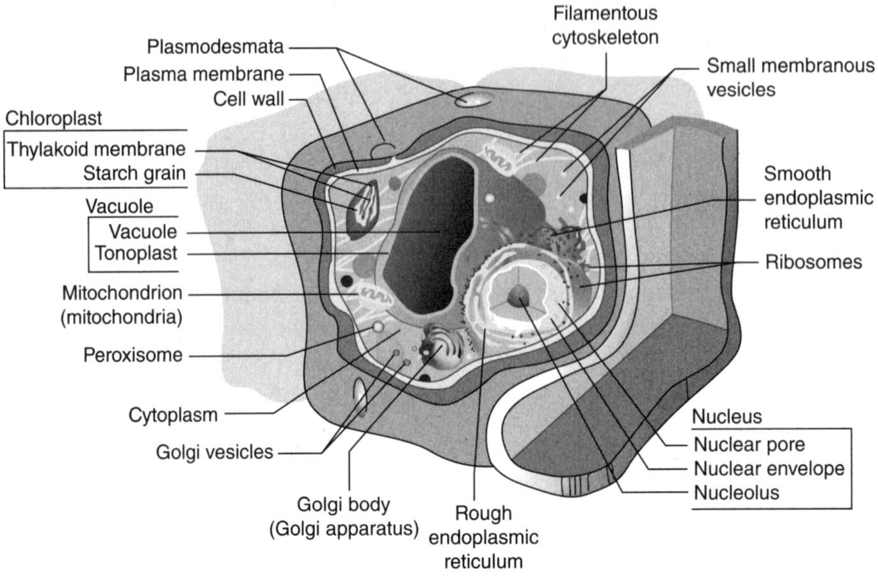

Figure 6.6 Plant Cell

- **Cell wall:** This layer of polysaccharides supports and protects the cell. It is found in most prokaryotes as well as in fungi and plants.
- **Chloroplast:** This is one of several plastids, or small organelles, in plant cells only. It contains chlorophyll and is the site of photosynthesis.
- **Filamentous cytoskeleton:** This protein structure gives the cell shape and aids in movement and transport. It exists in animal cells as well.
- **Peroxisome:** This organelle helps with a number of metabolic functions. It exists in animal cells as well.
- **Plasma membrane:** This layer of lipids and proteins forms the boundary of a cell or vacuole and regulates movement of molecules in and out of the cytoplasm. It exists in animal cells as well.
- **Plasmodesmata:** This narrow filament of cytoplasm connects plant cells and allows for transport and communication.
- **Vacuole:** This large organelle contains and stores water, enzymes, and waste products. It is found in all plant and fungal cells as well as in some animal and prokaryote cells.

Transport

Molecules of water, oxygen, and nutrients are always moving into a cell, and waste products are always moving out.

When molecules move from areas of high concentration to areas of low concentration, no energy is required. That movement is called **passive transport**. (See Table 6.1.)

Table 6.4 Types of Passive Transport

Type	Definition	Example
diffusion	movement of molecules from region of high concentration to region of low concentration	oxygen from blood cells to muscles
facilitated diffusion	diffusion of larger molecules across a membrane using carrier proteins	movement of glucose using permease proteins
osmosis	movement of molecules through a semipermeable membrane from dilute solution to concentrated solution	absorption of water by the small intestine
filtration	movement of molecules and water across a membrane using cardiovascular pressure	waste products filtered out of blood into tubules of the kidney to be eliminated in urine

When molecules move from areas of low concentration to areas of high concentration, chemical energy is required, usually from the high-energy molecule known as ATP (adenosine triphosphate). That movement is called **active transport**. (See Table 6.5.)

Table 6.5 Types of Active Transport

Type	Definition	Example
sodium-potassium pump	pumping of sodium and potassium ions in opposite directions across a membrane using chemical energy	maintenance of electrical charge in nerve or muscle cells
exocytosis	expelling of molecules out of a cell using chemical energy	secretion of enzymes
endocytosis	engulfing of molecules by a cell using chemical energy	leucocytes consuming bacteria

Tonicity

Tonicity is the relationship between the concentrations of solutes on either side of a membrane. A cell may have one of three different relationships to its surroundings:

- **Isotonic:** The concentration of solutes is the same; there is no net movement of water between the cell and its environment.
- **Hypertonic:** The concentration outside the cell is greater than inside the cell; water leaves the cell via osmosis, and the cell shrinks.

- **Hypotonic:** The concentration inside the cell is greater than outside the cell; water moves into the cell via osmosis, and the cell swells or bursts. (See Figure 6.7.)

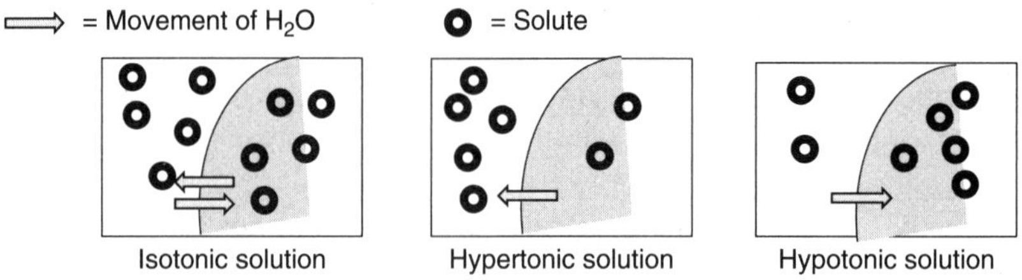

Figure 6.7 Solutions

WHY DO I NEED THIS?

Understanding tonicity is critical to knowing how to regulate IV fluids.

Test Yourself

1. A cell that lacks a nucleus is ___________.

2. What is the site for protein synthesis in a cell? ___________

3. Which structure does *not* appear in a plant cell?

A. Endoplasmic reticulum
B. Mitochondria
C. Lysosome
D. Vacuole

4. When a woodstove door is opened, smoke wafts through a room. What sort of transport does this represent?

A. Diffusion
B. Osmosis
C. Filtration
D. Active transport

5. A cell that is 90 percent water floats in a solution that is 98 percent water. What is the tonicity of the solution?
   A. Isotonic
   B. Hypertonic
   C. Hypotonic
   D. The answer cannot be determined from the information given.

Answers

1. prokaryotic. Examples include single-celled organisms such as bacteria.
2. ribosome. This structure, found both in prokaryotes and eukaryotes, synthesizes polypeptides and proteins.
3. C. Plant cells get rid of cell waste differently from animal cells. Some of the work done by lysosomes in animal cells is done by vacuoles in plant cells.
4. A. Diffusion is the movement of a substance from higher to lower concentration. It does not involve solvents and solutions, as osmosis would (choice B).
5. C. There is more water in the solution than in the cell, meaning that the concentration of solutes is higher in the cell than outside it.

METABOLISM

Metabolism refers to all the chemical reactions that occur within an organism to maintain life. It is the process by which living organisms convert food and other substances into energy and the building blocks necessary for growth, repair, and reproduction.

There are two types of metabolic reactions: **catabolic** and **anabolic**.

- Catabolic reactions involve breaking down large molecules into smaller ones, which releases energy that can be used for cellular processes. Cellular respiration is an example of a catabolic reaction.
- Anabolic reactions involve building up small molecules into larger ones, which requires energy. Photosynthesis is an example of an anabolic reaction.

In the human body, we refer to the **basal metabolic rate** (BMR) as the amount of energy your body needs to carry out its basic functions while at rest, such as breathing, circulating blood, and maintaining body temperature. Metabolism is a complex process that involves many different pathways and enzymes, and it is influenced by a variety of factors such as genetics, diet, exercise, and environmental conditions. Disruptions in metabolism can lead to various disorders, such as metabolic syndrome, diabetes, and obesity.

Cellular Respiration

Cells derive energy via cellular respiration, which breaks down glucose.

$$C_6H_{12}O_6 + 6O_2 \rightarrow 6CO_2 + 6H_2O + \text{energy}$$

In this formula, glucose plus oxygen yields carbon dioxide, water, and energy in the form of heat and ATPs. The process has three main steps, with most of the action taking place in the mitochondria of the cell.

1. The first step in cellular respiration is the breaking down of glucose, or **glycolysis**. In an anaerobic process, carbon in glucose breaks into two three-carbon strands called **pyruvates**. The net gain of ATPs in this step is 2 ATPs. A small amount of NADH (nicotinamide adenine dinucleotide) is also made. Glycolysis takes place in the cytoplasm.
2. The second step in cellular respiration is the **Krebs cycle** (or citric acid cycle), which is aerobic—it requires oxygen. The net gain of ATPs in this step is 2 ATPs. NADH and $FADH_2$ (flavin adenine dinucleotide) are byproducts of this step. The Krebs cycle takes place in the matrix of the mitochondria.
3. The final step in cellular respiration is the **electron transport chain**, which is also aerobic. Hydrogen electrons are transported via NADH down a chain. This step produces most of the ATPs in cellular respiration—as many as 34 in all. The electron transport chain takes place on the cristae of the mitochondria.

If no oxygen exists, the byproducts of glycolysis may instead go through the process of **fermentation**, producing either alcohol or lactic acid and releasing carbon dioxide.

Test Yourself

1. Which step in cellular respiration is anaerobic? ____________

2. Which step in cellular respiration generates the most energy? ____________

3. Cellular respiration breaks glucose into energy, water, and ____________.

4. Where does most cellular respiration take place?

A. Lungs/gills
B. Chloroplast
C. Ribosome
D. Mitochondria

5. What happens to glucose during glycolysis?

   A. It splits into molecules of pyruvic acid.
   B. It joins with molecules of citric acid.
   C. It bonds with oxygen to release ATPs.
   D. It loses hydrogen to the electron transport chain.

Answers

1. glycolysis. Steps 2 and 3 require oxygen, or else fermentation may take place.
2. the electron transport chain. The final step results in the most ATPs by far.
3. carbon dioxide (CO_2). Check the equation above to confirm.
4. D. The mitochondria handle respiration and energy production for the cell.
5. A. The carbon in glucose breaks into two pyruvates.

Photosynthesis

Plants and some bacteria and protists use the process of photosynthesis to convert light energy into chemical energy that can provide fuel for the organism's growth, movement, and other metabolic work.

$$6CO_2 + 6H_2O + \text{photons} \rightarrow C_6H_{12}O_6 + 6O_2$$

In this formula, six molecules of water combine with six molecules of carbon dioxide, and with the assistance of light, they produce one molecule of sugar plus six molecules of oxygen. The process has two steps:

1. In **light-dependent reactions**, energy from the sun is absorbed by **chlorophyll** and converted to energy in the form of ATP and NADPH (which is a reduced form of NADH).
2. In **light-independent reactions**, also known as the **Calvin cycle**, energy from ATP and NADPH fixes (converts inorganic molecules to organic compounds) CO_2 to form carbohydrates.

In plants, this process takes place in the chloroplasts in the leaves. (See Figure 6.8.)

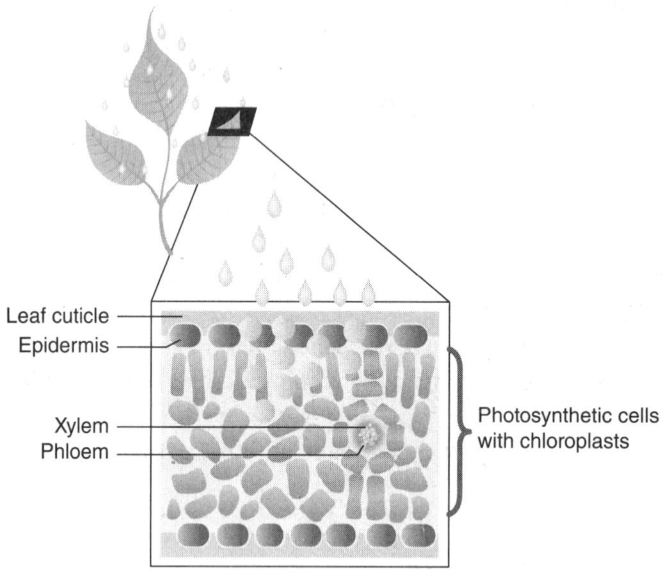

Figure 6.8 Cross-Section of a Leaf

In flowering plants, photosynthesis is a key factor in providing the energy to reproduce. The **stamen** contains the male pollen in its **anther**. Pollen lands on the **stigma** and proceeds down the **style** to the **ovary**. (See Figure 6.9.)

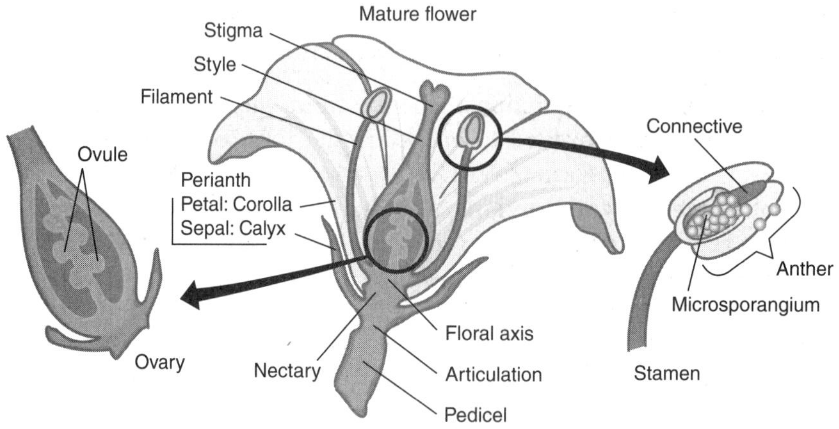

Figure 6.9 Parts of a Flowering Plant

Test Yourself

1. In which step of photosynthesis is glucose produced? ____________

2. Where does photosynthesis take place in plants? ____________

3. The products of photosynthesis include a carbohydrate and ____________.

For question 4, circle the correct answer in parentheses.

4. The anther of a plant contains (glucose/nectar/pollen).

5. Which is a female organ in a plant?

   A. Stamen
   B. Anther
   C. Sepal
   D. Style

Answers

1. Calvin cycle. The first step produces energy; the second step uses energy to make a carbohydrate, in this case, glucose.
2. chloroplasts (leaves). Sunlight on the leaves starts the process.
3. oxygen. Check the equation above to confirm.
4. pollen. The anther is the part of the stamen where the male pollen is produced.
5. D. Choices A and B are male organs, and choice C is not affiliated with reproduction.

CELLULAR REPRODUCTION

Cellular reproduction allows a parent cell to pass on genetic information to daughter cells through a process of cell division.

Binary Fission

Prokaryotes, such as bacteria, reproduce using binary fission. The cell replicates its genetic material, grows larger, and then divides into two similarly sized daughter cells through the process called **cytokinesis**.

Mitosis

Like binary fission, mitosis is a form of **asexual reproduction**, in that it produces daughter cells that are genetically identical to the parent cell. Mitosis is preceded by **interphase**, during which the cell grows, duplicates its chromosomes, and grows some more. (See Figure 6.10.)

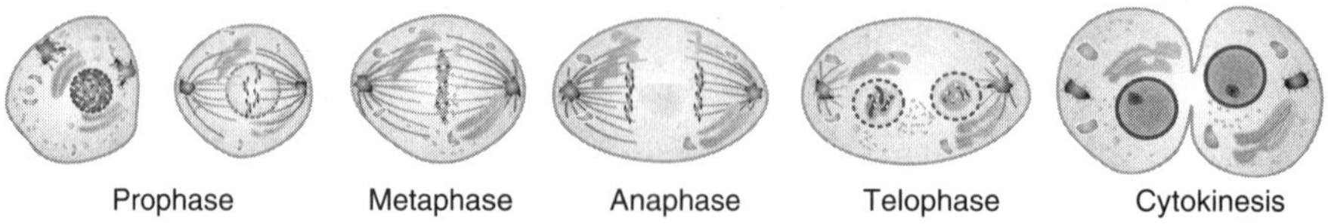

Figure 6.10 Phases of Mitosis

1. **Prophase:** The duplicated chromosomes condense, the nuclear membrane breaks down, and a **spindle** apparatus forms at each end (pole) of the cell.
2. **Metaphase:** Condensed chromosomes line up and attach to the spindle.
3. **Anaphase:** Chromosomes separate into sister **chromatids,** which migrate toward opposite ends of the spindle.
4. **Telophase:** The spindle breaks down, and nuclear membranes form around each new set of chromosomes, preparing for cytokinesis, which results in daughter cells.

Meiosis

Whereas mitosis generates cells used for growth or regeneration, meiosis is the form of cellular division that generates cells used for **sexual reproduction**, the cells called **gametes**. Mitosis produces two **diploid** daughter cells that are copies of the parent cell. Meiosis produces four **haploid** cells—each contains half the chromosomes of the parent cell. (See Figure 6.11.)

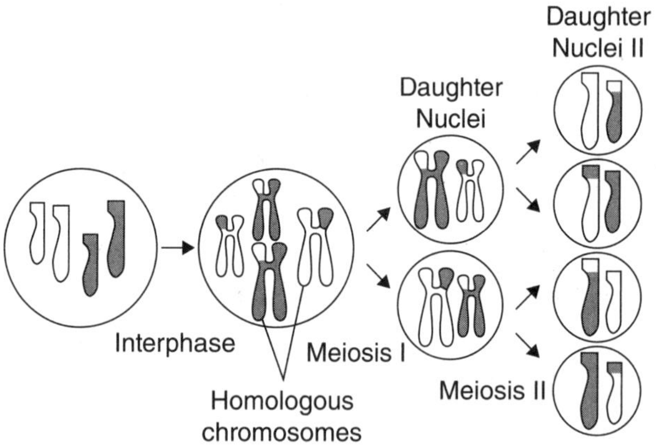

Figure 6.11 Phases of Meiosis

The process begins with **meiosis I**.

1. **Prophase I:** The duplicated chromosomes condense, and pair up, aligning with their partners and forming **tetrads** of four chromatids each. Homologous chromosomes may trade (**recombine**) parts in the process called **crossing over**. The nuclear membrane breaks down.

2. **Metaphase I:** Tetrads align, with centromeres of homologous chromosomes facing opposite ends of the cell.
3. **Anaphase I:** Chromosomes migrate to opposite ends of the cell, with sister chromatids remaining together.
4. **Telophase I:** Each end of the cell ends up with a haploid number of sister chromatids that are not identical. Nuclear membranes re-form around the new sets of chromosomes in preparation for cytokinesis.

The process may continue with **meiosis II**, which bears many similarities to mitosis.

1. **Prophase II:** Chromosomes condense, the nuclear membrane breaks down, and a spindle apparatus forms at each pole of the haploid cell.
2. **Metaphase II:** Condensed chromosomes line up and attach to the spindle.
3. **Anaphase II:** Chromosomes separate into sister chromatids, which migrate toward opposite ends of the spindle.
4. **Telophase II:** The spindle breaks down, and nuclear membranes form around each new set of chromosomes, preparing for cytokinesis, which results in daughter cells.

The end result of meiosis I and II, then, is the production of four daughter cells containing one chromatid apiece. In human reproduction, these might be four sperm cells, or they might be one functional egg cell and **polar bodies**, cells that do not develop into ova. Some invertebrates and occasionally some snakes or fish may reproduce via **parthenogenesis**, in which the animal clones itself using a polar body and bypasses fertilization entirely.

Test Yourself

For questions 1–3, circle the correct answer in parentheses.

1. In mitosis, the chromosomes line up during (prophase/metaphase).

2. In meiosis, recombination takes place in (prophase I/prophase II).

3. In meiosis II, nuclear membranes form in (anaphase II/telophase II).

4. How many daughter cells exist at the end of meiosis I and II?

____

5. Which is one key difference between asexual and sexual reproduction?
   A. In asexual reproduction, chromosomes are not involved.
   B. In asexual reproduction, cytokinesis occurs at the end of the process.
   C. In sexual reproduction, daughter cells are not identical to parent cells.
   D. In sexual reproduction, the end result may be daughter cells or son cells.

Answers

1. metaphase. In prophase, the spindle forms; in metaphase, chromosomes line up along it.
2. prophase I. As the chromosomes form tetrads in this phase, crossing over and exchanging of genetic material may occur.
3. telophase II. The membranes form around the new sets of chromosomes in preparation for cytokinesis.
4. four. Meiosis I results in two haploid cells, which proceed to divide again in meiosis II, creating four haploid daughter cells that become sperm or egg cells.
5. C. Daughter cells are reproductions of parent cells in fission or in mitosis. In meiosis, the resulting cells are haploid, and recombination makes them unique. Choice B is true of either form of reproduction; choices A and D are true of neither.

GENETICS

Genetics is the study of **heredity**, the inheritance of traits from a parent. The science began with observations of physical traits of plants by an Austrian monk, Gregor Mendel. Mendel's plant-breeding experiments led him to posit the existence of invisible factors that caused certain traits to be **dominant** or **recessive**. By the 1900s the invisible factors were called **genes**, but it would take some time before scientists understood how they worked.

WHY DO I NEED THIS?

Genomic medicine is becoming an important new way to individualize treatment.

Punnett Squares

An English geneticist, Reginald Punnett, devised a visual way to map and predict inheritance of physical traits, or **phenotypes**. A phenotype is a combination of **alleles**, forms of genes that are inherited from parents. It may be expressed as a **genotype**, a description of the dominant and recessive traits inherited.

This Punnett square shows the connection of genotype to phenotype. Here, the dominant trait is purple flowers. The recessive trait is white flowers. (See Figure 6.12.)

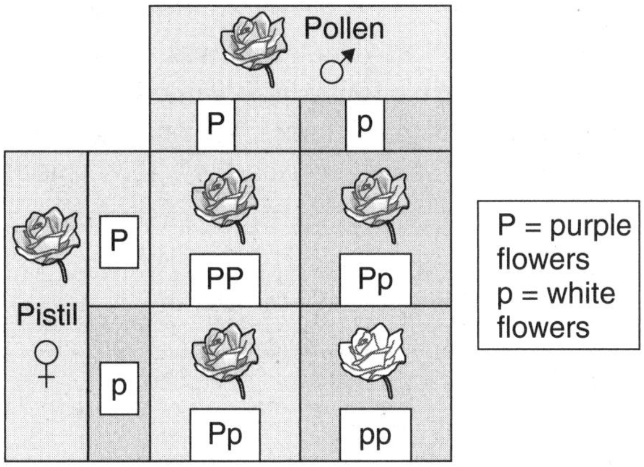

Figure 6.12 Punnett Square

In the square, male pollen from a flower with **heterozygous** (having one each of two alleles) traits for purple flowers (Pp) pollinates the pistil of another flower with heterozygous traits for purple flowers (Pp). The resulting offspring have one of three possible genotypes. One (1/4 of the square) is **homozygous** (having two of the same allele) dominant for purple flowers (PP). One (1/4 of the square) is homozygous recessive for white flowers (pp). Two (1/2 of the square) are heterozygous dominant for purple flowers (Pp). So in any four offspring, you would predict that three will have purple flowers and one will have white flowers. An offspring with purple flowers may have the homozygous dominant genotype (PP) or the heterozygous genotype (Pp). There is no way to tell without doing more experimenting.

Sometimes, a recessive gene represents a certain disease that is only expressed when the offspring's genotype is homozygous recessive; for example, dd. If the offspring's genotype is heterozygous, Dd, we say that the offspring is a **carrier** of that disease. The disease may not be expressed, but it may be passed down, or inherited.

A **sex-linked** trait is one that is carried only by a male or a female parent. In humans, men usually have XY chromosomes, whereas women have XX. Only men, then, can inherit Y-linked traits, but either men or women may inherit X-linked traits.

DNA

Although scientists recognized that a molecule of inheritance existed, it took decades of experimentation in the early to mid-twentieth century to determine just what that molecule was and how it worked. The components of the molecule were isolated by Phoebus Levene in 1929:

- Adenine (A)
- Cytosine (C)
- Guanine (G)
- Thymine (T)
- Sugar (deoxyribose)
- Phosphate

Levene determined that the DNA molecule was composed of a series of nucleotides linked together in the following order: phosphate-sugar-base. Not until the Rosalind Franklin–inspired James Watson and Francis Crick model in 1953 did scientists understand precisely how those pieces fit together. (See Figure 6.13.)

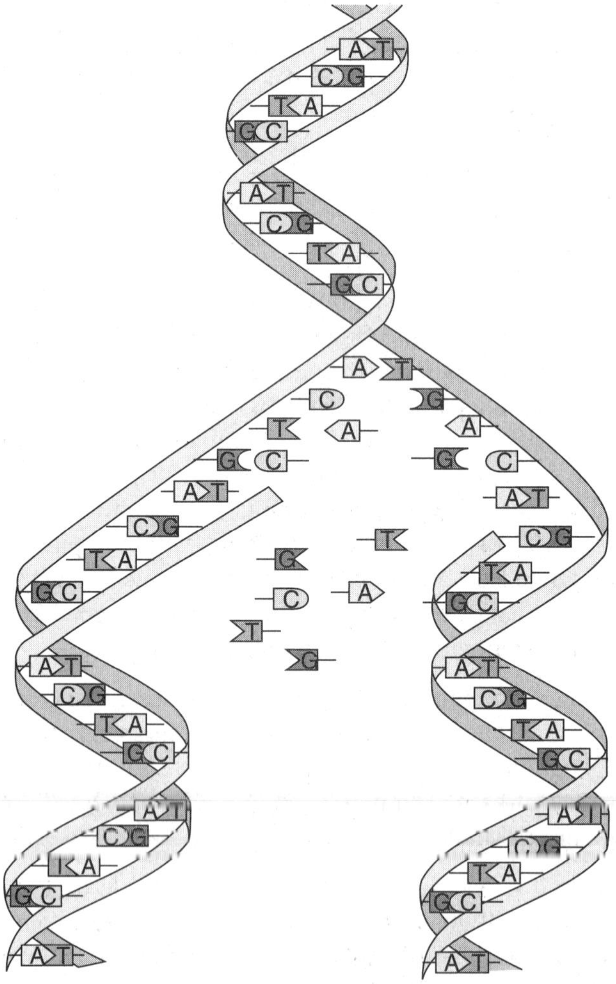

Figure 6.13 DNA Replication

The Rosalind Franklin–inspired Watson-Crick model envisions DNA as a spiraling helix, or ladder, with bases aligning to form the steps. Adenine pairs with thymine, and cytosine pairs with guanine. When DNA replicates, the helix unwinds, and some of the steps split apart. Enzymes called **DNA polymerases** bind along the single strands, read the nucleotides, and find and position complementary nucleotides until a complete copy is formed.

The genetic code in DNA tells the cell how to build a protein. DNA never leaves the nucleus of a cell. Instead, it locates and copies the gene to make the given protein into a messenger called **mRNA**. This messenger RNA can travel out of the nucleus to the ribosomes where proteins are made. This process of copying is called **transcription**.

Unlike DNA, RNA is single-stranded, and its sugar is ribose instead of dioxyribose. In the process of transcription, all thymine bases in DNA change to uracil bases in RNA.

The ribosome reads the mRNA message three nucleotides at a time (in groups called **codons**) and uses transfer RNA (**tRNA**) to locate appropriate amino acids based on those codons. The finished chain of amino acids is the protein. This process of reading and constructing is called **translation**.

Test Yourself

1. Name all the possible genotypes in a cross between a male with genotype Zz and a female with genotype zz. ___________

2. Name three ways in which RNA differs from DNA in structure. ____

3. Which base pairs with thymine in DNA? ___________

4. A codon is a group of three ___________.

5. A woman carries the gene for colorblindness on one of her X-chromosomes. If her husband does not have the gene, what ratio of their offspring is predicted to be colorblind?

   A. 0 female : 1 male
   B. 1 female : 0 male
   C. 1 female : 2 male
   D. 1 female : 1 male

Answers

1. Zz and zz. Try a Punnett square if it helps you to visualize the cross. You should end up with two Zz genotypes and two zz genotypes.
2. single-stranded, uracil instead of thymine, ribose instead of dioxyribose. Reread the paragraphs on RNA if necessary.
3. adenine. The base guanine pairs with cytosine.
4. nucleotides. In translation, groups called codons are read by the ribosome, which uses tRNA to locate amino acids to match the message in the codons.
5. A. Only a boy will manifest the disorder, and only a boy who inherits the recessive X instead of the dominant X. In a Punnett square, you would expect to see XX, XX^c, XY, and X^cY. Only the last would have the disorder, although the second female offspring would be a carrier like her mother.

CHAPTER 7

Chemistry

CONTENTS

The study of matter, the chemistry of the human body, the chemical structure of pharmaceuticals—all of these are fundamental concepts that are important for medical professionals. Your nursing program may not require this module, but it is sure to require some coursework in chemistry. Some of the topics in this chapter might just as easily fit under Physics, but they have typically been tested in the Chemistry module of the A2 test.

STATES OF MATTER

Matter is a term for anything that has mass and occupies space. On Earth, there are a few physical forms in which matter may appear. **Extensive properties** of matter are those that depend on the amount of matter being considered; they include mass and volume. **Intensive properties** of matter do not vary based on the amount of matter; they include color, luster, conductivity, and hardness. The main states of matter are described below.

Solid

Solids hold their shape. Their atoms are in a fixed arrangement and tend not to move easily. Solids may be a single element. For example, graphite and diamonds are both solid forms of carbon. Both forms have distinct patterns of atoms called **crystals**. The two different patterns are called **allotropes** of carbon. Many other elements have different allotropes in the solid state; they include tin (gray, white, and rhombic); arsenic (yellow, gray, and black); boron (brown powder and hard black), and phosphorus (white, red, violet, and black).

Solids may also be compounds. Ice is a solid form of H_2O. Solids may be mixtures of multiple compounds. Sand is one example of this; it may be composed of silica, calcium carbonate, and a variety of other materials.

Liquid

Liquids do not hold their shape, but they do retain their volume and density. A liquid flows to conform to the shape of its container. Its molecules are said to slide, but they do not move entirely freely. There are only two elements that are found naturally in liquid form at room temperature—mercury and bromine. Many compounds (such as H_2O) exist as liquids at room temperature, and molecules may dissolve in a liquid to form a solution.

Gas

Gas has no definite shape or volume, and its density may vary. Its atoms are separate; they bounce around and collide frequently. Gas expands or contracts to fit its container. The relationships among the properties of gases are defined in a series of scientific laws. (See Table 7.1.)

Table 7.1 Gas Laws

Law	Relationship
Boyle's Law	When temperature is constant, the pressure and volume of a gas have an inverse relationship.
Charles' Law	The volume of gas at a constant pressure is directly proportional to the Kelvin temperature.
Gay-Lussac's Law	The pressure of gas at a constant volume is directly proportional to the Kelvin temperature.
Avogadro's Law	When temperature and pressure are constant, equal volumes of different gases contain an equal number of molecules.

As with solids and liquids, a gas may be an element (He) or a compound (CO_2). Several elements have gaseous allotropes; for example, ozone is an allotrope of oxygen.

Nitrogen and oxygen are the most common gases on Earth. Oxygen and carbon dioxide are the most common gases in the human body.

Plasma

Plasma is similar to a gas, but it is primarily formed from free electrons and ions that are charged in low pressures or high temperatures. Plasmas have a definite mass, but they change volume and density easily and have extremely high energy. Examples of plasmas include the dancing lights of an aurora borealis and the glow of a neon sign.

Phase Changes

Matter may be converted from one state to another, usually by means of temperature, pressure, or both. In a neon sign, neon exists as a gas until a switch is flipped, and the energy from electricity energizes the atoms to create neon plasma. All phase changes require some form of energy. The chemical structure of the matter does not alter as the matter changes phase. (See Table 7.2.)

Table 7.2 Phase Changes

Process	Transformation	Example
freezing	from liquid to solid at freezing point	water to ice
melting	from solid to liquid at melting point	ice to water
condensation	from gas to liquid at condensation point	water vapor to rain
vaporization	from liquid to gas at boiling point	water to steam
sublimation	from solid to gas without a liquid phase	dry ice
deposition	from gas to solid without a liquid phase	frost crystals

As pressure increases, the temperature needed for phase changes increases as well. This may relate to air pressure—at higher altitudes with less air pressure, water boils at a lower temperature. It may relate to the pressure of an external force—in a pressure cooker, water boils at a higher temperature, reducing cooking time.

The **water cycle** is a good example of phase changes. Heat from the sun causes water to evaporate, changing from liquid to gas and rising into the air to form clouds. As it cools, the water vapor condenses, turning back into liquid. It returns to the Earth in liquid form as precipitation. (See Figure 7.1.)

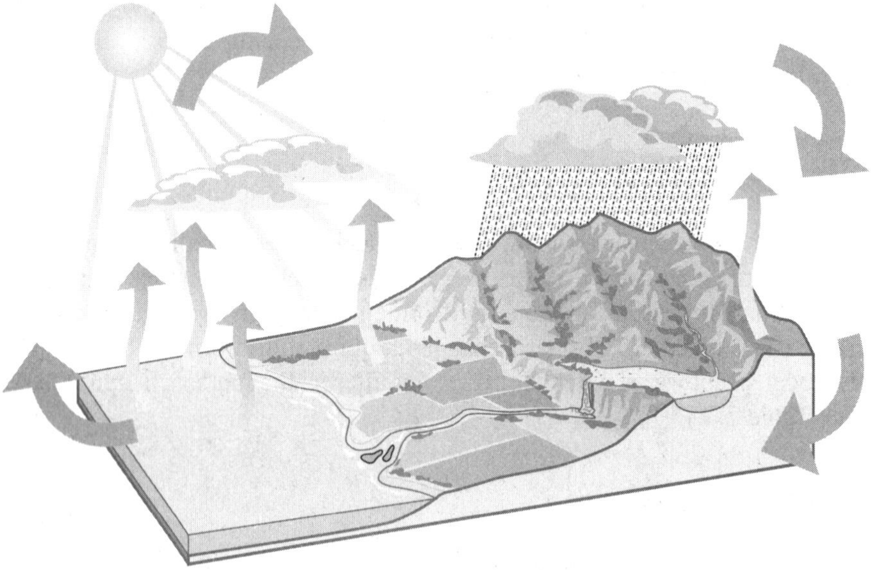

Figure 7.1 The Water Cycle

Temperature, Pressure, and Solubility

In addition to affecting phase changes, changes in temperature and pressure have specific effects on certain properties of matter. One of the most important of these properties is **solubility**, the ability of matter to dissolve in a solvent.

- A gas at room temperature tends to become less soluble with increased temperature.
- A solid at room temperature tends to become more soluble with increased temperature.
- Liquids and solids have little change in solubility with changes in pressure.
- Gases increase in solubility with increases in pressure.

Test Yourself

1. The process by which gas turns to liquid is known as ____________.

2. According to Gay-Lussac's Law, the ____________ of gas at a constant volume is directly proportional to the ____________.

For questions 3–4, circle the correct answer in parentheses.

3. A phase change from liquid to gas is called (deposition/condensation/vaporization).

4. A gas at room temperature becomes (more/less) soluble as the temperature rises.

5. A glass of carbonated fizzy water was left on a table and went flat. What happened to the carbon dioxide in the water?

   A. It evaporated.
   B. It lost solubility.
   C. It sublimed.
   D. It changed density.

Answers

1. condensation. Steam on a mirror or drops of water on a cold soda can are examples of this.
2. pressure, Kelvin temperature. The gas laws are all related, but you may simply have to memorize their names.
3. vaporization. Review the chart of phase changes to confirm.
4. less. Solids become more soluble, but gases become less soluble at increased temperatures.
5. B. An increase in temperature can lead to the loss of solubility of a gas in liquid. As the gas separated from the liquid, it was released into the air.

ATOMIC STRUCTURE

Matter is made up of atoms. Chemical reactions occur when parts of an atom are transferred or shared. Reactivity, mass, and radioactivity all depend on the structure of a given atom.

Physical Structure

The most important subatomic particles that make up every atom are **protons**, **neutrons**, and **electrons**. (See Figure 7.2.)

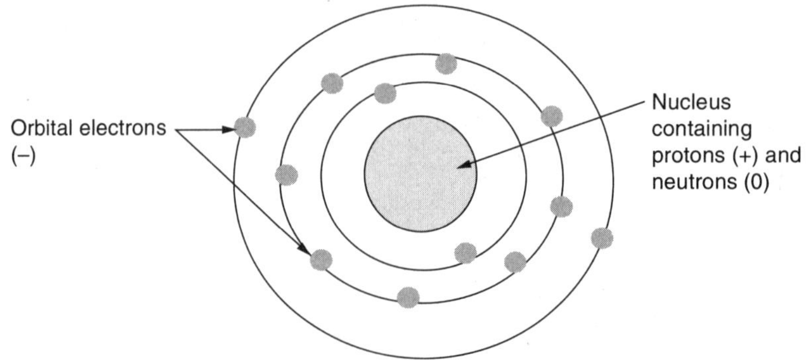

Figure 7.2 Atomic Structure

Protons and neutrons cluster in the nucleus of the atom. Protons have a positive charge. That charge is countered by the negative charge of the much smaller electrons in orbit around the nucleus. Electrons remain in their shells, or orbitals, unless the atom bonds with another atom, losing or gaining electrons as it does so.

If an atom loses or gains electrons, it becomes an **ion**. Losing electrons forms a **cation**, with a positive charge. Gaining electrons forms an **anion**, with a negative charge.

Atomic Number and Mass

The atomic number of an element tells you the number of protons in that atom. For example, carbon has six protons, so its atomic number is 6. If the atom has a neutral charge and is not an ion, the number of electrons will equal the atom's atomic number.

Because electrons are so tiny, most of an atom's mass is in its nucleus. The mass number of an atom is its number of protons plus its number of neutrons. All atoms of a given element have the same number of protons. However, the number of neutrons can vary. Atoms with different numbers of neutrons also have different mass numbers. These atoms are called **isotopes** of each other.

Since there are varying numbers of neutrons in any given group of atoms of an element, scientists take an average when they calculate the atomic mass. For example, carbon has three isotopes. Instead of being exactly 12 (6 protons plus the same number of neutrons), the atomic mass of carbon is usually listed as slightly greater than 12, at 12.0107. This is because of the relative abundances of the C-12, C-13, and C-14 isotopes that exist.

Periodic Table

The periodic table of the elements organizes all existing elements on a grid. Each row on the table is called a **period**, and all of the elements within a period have their electrons in the same principal energy level. Period 1 elements have their electrons in just one principal energy level. Period 7 elements have seven principal energy levels. (See Figure 7.3.)

Group→ ↓Period	1	2	3	4	5	6	7	8	9	10	11	12	13	14	15	16	17	18
1	1 H																	2 He
2	3 Li	4 Be											5 B	6 C	7 N	8 O	9 F	10 Ne
3	11 Na	12 Mg											13 Al	14 Si	15 P	16 S	17 Cl	18 Ar
4	19 K	20 Ca	21 Sc	22 Ti	23 V	24 Cr	25 Mn	26 Fe	27 Co	28 Ni	29 Cu	30 Zn	31 Ga	32 Ge	33 As	34 Se	35 Br	36 Kr
5	37 Rb	38 Sr	39 Y	40 Zr	41 Nb	42 Mo	43 Tc	44 Ru	45 Rh	46 Pd	47 Ag	48 Cd	49 In	50 Sn	51 Sb	52 Te	53 I	54 Xe
6	55 Cs	56 Ba	* 71 Lu	72 Hf	73 Ta	74 W	75 Re	76 Os	77 Ir	78 Pt	79 Au	80 Hg	81 Tl	82 Pb	83 Bi	84 Po	85 At	86 Rn
7	87 Fr	88 Ra	** 103 Lr	104 Rf	105 Db	106 Sg	107 Bh	108 Hs	109 Mt	110 Ds	111 Rg	112 Cn	113 Uut	114 Fl	115 Uup	116 Lv	117 Uus	118 Uuo

*	57 La	58 Ce	59 Pr	60 Nd	61 Pm	62 Sm	63 Eu	64 Gd	65 Tb	66 Dy	67 Ho	68 Er	69 Tm	70 Yb
**	89 Ac	90 Th	91 Pa	92 U	93 Np	94 Pu	95 Am	96 Cm	97 Bk	98 Cf	99 Es	100 Fm	101 Md	102 No

Figure 7.3 Periodic Table of Elements

Each column in the table is called a **group**. Elements within a group have the same electron configurations and tend to behave similarly. Sometimes groups are referred to by group names. For example, group 1 is the highly reactive alkali metals. Group 2 is the alkaline earth metals. Group 17 is the halogens. Group 18 is the relatively stable noble gases, known for their lack of reactivity, low boiling points, and lack of flammability.

On the table, metals are divided from nonmetals by a zigzag line that starts to the left of carbon and continues to the left of phosphorus, selenium, iodine, and radon. Elements to the left of that zigzag are metals, metalloids, or semimetals. Elements to the right are nonmetals. (See Table 7.3.)

Table 7.3 Characteristics of Metals and Nonmetals

Metals	Nonmetals
lustrous	dull
good conductors of heat and electricity	poor conductors of heat and electricity
malleable	brittle
usually solid at room temperature	may be solid, liquid, or gas at room temperature
usually have 1–3 electrons in outer shell; lose electrons easily	usually have 4–8 electrons in outer shell; gain or share electrons easily

Test Yourself

Use the periodic table to answer questions 1–3.

1. How many electrons are in a neutral atom of vanadium (V)? ____________
2. Which element would have an atomic mass approximately twice that of carbon? ____________
3. What is the name of the group that contains chlorine (Cl)? ____________
4. Which of the following elements is an alkali metal?
   A. Calcium (Ca)
   B. Caesium (Cs)
   C. Scandium (Sc)
   D. Tungsten (W)
5. What is true of an cation of coppesr (Cu)?
   A. Its atomic mass is now greater as a cation.
   B. It contains fewer electrons than an atom of copper.
   C. It is less stable as an ion.
   D. It has more electrons than an atom of zinc (Zn).

Answers

1. 23. The atomic number of vanadium is 23, meaning that it has 23 protons. If it is neutral, it also has 23 electrons.
2. magnesium. Carbon's atomic mass is approximately equal to twice its atomic number, 6. Magnesium's atomic number is 12, and its atomic mass is just a bit higher than 24.
3. halogens. Chlorine is in group 17.
4. B. Alkali metals are in group 1.
5. B. Because a cation is formed by losing electrons, it will have fewer electrons than the original metal atom.

ELECTRON CONFIGURATIONS

Electron configurations describe the arrangement of electrons around the nucleus of an atom. Understanding configurations helps you to understand how different atoms may bond.

Usually, we refer to four energy levels of electrons. S sublevels are spherical; thus, they are labeled *s*. S orbitals can hold two electrons. The three p orbitals can hold six in all. The five d orbitals can hold 10. The seven f orbitals can hold 14. The **valence electrons** of an element are those electrons in its outermost electron shell.

Consider hydrogen, which has atomic number 1. It has one proton, and in its neutral state, one electron. The electron configuration notation for hydrogen is:

$1s^1$

The first 1 is the energy level—also the period where the element is found on the periodic table. The s represents the orbital. The superscript 1 represents the number of electrons in that orbital.

Now consider lithium, with atomic number 3. Lithium's three electrons are one too many for a single s orbital to hold; an s orbital can hold only two electrons in all. Lithium's notation is:

$1s^2\ 2s^1$

In other words, lithium fills the first orbital with two electrons and starts a second s orbital (the 2 represents its period on the periodic table), placing the third electron in that orbital. Adding the superscripts helps you check: $2 + 1 = 3$. Lithium has three electrons.

There are a number of ways to determine the electron configuration of an element, and many shortcuts to use for elements with a large number of electrons. For your purposes on the A2 test, you should consider memorizing this list, which shows the order of filling the orbitals:

1s 2s 2p 3s 3p 4s 3d 4p 5s 4d 5p 6s 4f 5d 6p 7s 5f 6d 7p

Alternatively, use this traditional diagram, starting always with 1s and following the arrows to complete the sublevels. (See Figure 7.4.)

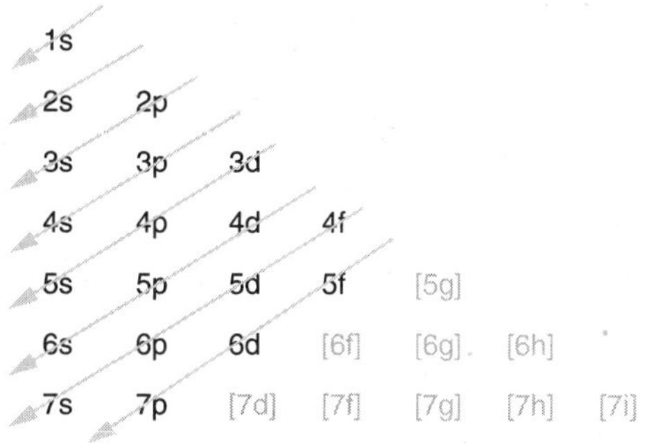

Figure 7.4 Filling Orbitals

Looking at this diagram should tell you at a glance that the electron configuration notation for oxygen, with atomic number 8, must be:

$1s^2\ 2s^2\ 2p^4$

The first energy level holds two electrons, the second holds two, and the third (because it is p level, which can hold up to six in all) holds the remaining four electrons in oxygen.

The electron configuration for aluminum, with atomic number 13, is:

$1s^2\ 2s^2\ 2p^6\ 3s^2\ 3p^1$

Test Yourself

Use the periodic table to answer questions 1–5.

1. How many electrons are in a neutral atom of boron? ___________
2. How many of boron's electrons are in the p orbital? ___________
3. What is the electronic configuration notation for carbon (C)? ___________
4. Which element has the electron configuration $1s^2\ 2s^2\ 2p^6\ 3s^1$? ___________
5. How many valence electrons are in a neutral atom of nitrogen (N)?
   A. 1
   B. 2
   C. 5
   D. 6

Answers

1. five. You can determine the number of electrons in the neutral atom from the atomic number, which tells how many protons the atom has. In a neutral atom, the number of electrons will equal the number of protons.
2. one. Boron has five electrons, for a configuration of $1s^2\ 2s^2\ 2p^1$.
3. $1s^2\ 2s^2\ 2p^2$. Carbon has six electrons. Two fill the first orbital, two fill the second, and two fit into the third.
4. sodium (Na). Add up the superscripts to find the number of electrons: $2 + 2 + 6 + 1 = 11$. The element with an atomic number of 11 is sodium.
5. C. Nitrogen has seven electrons, but only the outermost principal energy level contains the valence electrons. This is the five electrons in the 2s and 2p orbitals.

CHEMICAL EQUATIONS

A **chemical reaction** is a process that changes the structure and energy content of atoms, ions, or molecules without changing their nuclei. In the process, heat is absorbed or emitted.

Reactions of this sort are represented symbolically as chemical equations. On the left side of the equation are the **reactants**, the substances that initiate the reaction. On the right side are the **products**, the substances that result from the reaction. An arrow separates the two.

To balance a chemical equation, you must ensure that each side of the equation describes the same quantity of each element. Quantities are not changed in a reaction.

One example is the equation for photosynthesis:

$$6CO_2 + 6H_2O \rightarrow C_6H_{12}O_6 + 6O_2$$

Because the product is known to be glucose and oxygen, and glucose is $C_6H_{12}O_6$, it is clear that a single molecule of water won't be enough of a reactant to balance the equation. You need six molecules, as shown with the coefficient 6 in $6H_2O$. $6H_2O$ is equivalent to 12 hydrogen plus 6 oxygen atoms, both of which equate to the number of hydrogen and oxygen atoms in $C_6H_{12}O_6$. To get six atoms of carbon and another six atoms of oxygen, you need the coefficient 6 before the carbon dioxide.

When propane combusts with oxygen, the reaction looks like this:

$$C_3H_8 + 5O_2 \rightarrow 4H_2O + 3CO_2$$

To check the balance, you must make sure that each element is represented equally on both sides of the arrow. There are three carbons on the left and three on the right. There are eight hydrogens on the left and 4×2, or eight on the right. There are 5×2, or 10 oxygens on the left, and there are 4 oxygens plus 6 more oxygens on the right. The equation is balanced.

Test Yourself

Add coefficients to balance the equations in items 1–3.

1. $Zn +$ __________ $HCl \rightarrow ZnCl_2 + H_2$

2. $C_2H_6O + 3O_2 \rightarrow$ __________ $CO_2 +$ __________ H_2O

3. __________ $KOH + H_3PO_4 \rightarrow K_3PO_4 +$ __________ H_2O

4. When balanced, the reaction $SiO_2 + HF \rightarrow SiF_4 + H_2O$ will be

A. $SiO_2 + 4HF \rightarrow SiF_4 + 2H_2O$
B. $SiO_2 + 2HF \rightarrow 2SiF_4 + H_2O$
C. $2SiO_2 + 2HF \rightarrow SiF_4 + 4H_2O$
D. $3SiO_2 + 2HF \rightarrow 3SiF_4 + H_2O$

5. When balanced, the reaction $SnO_2 + H_2 \rightarrow Sn + H_2O$ will be

A. $2SnO_2 + H_2 \rightarrow 2Sn + H_2O$
B. $SnO_2 + 4H_2 \rightarrow Sn + 2H_2O$
C. $SnO_2 + 2H_2 \rightarrow Sn + 2H_2O$
D. $3SnO_2 + 2H_2 \rightarrow 6Sn + 2H_2O$

Answers

1. 2. Because the product shows two atoms of H and two ions of Cl, there must be a coefficient of 2 in front of HCl to balance the equation.
2. 2, 3. The reactant has two carbon atoms, six hydrogen atoms, and seven oxygen atoms.
3. 3, 3. This reaction shows phosphoric acid reacting with potassium hydroxide to produce tripotassium phosphate and water. Coefficients of 3 on both sides give you balanced oxygen, hydrogen, potassium, and phosphorus.
4. A. You may be able to see at a glance that a coefficient of 4HF gives you the correct fluorine. From there, it's a matter of balancing hydrogen and oxygen; the silicon remains as it was.
5. C. Only this equation gives you one tin (Sn), two oxygen, and four hydrogen atoms on either side.

CHEMICAL REACTIONS

Most reactions fit into one of several categories.

Single Replacement

In a single replacement reaction, one element is substituted for another element in a compound.

$$AB + C \rightarrow AC + B$$

An example would be the reaction between zinc and hydrochloric acid, resulting in zinc chloride and hydrogen.

$$Zn + 2HCl \rightarrow ZnCl_2 + H_2$$

Double Replacement

In a double replacement reaction, two compounds exchange components.

$$AB + CD \rightarrow AD + CB$$

When silver nitrate reacts with sodium chloride, the result is a double trade of ions.

$$AgNO_3 + NaCl \rightarrow AgCl + NaNO_3$$

Synthesis

In a synthesis reaction, two reactants combine to make a more complex compound.

$$A + B \rightarrow AB$$

Potassium plus chloride equals potassium chloride in this synthesis reaction:

$$2K + Cl_2 \rightarrow 2KCl$$

Decomposition

In a decomposition reaction, a complex compound splits into elements or simple compounds.

$$AB \rightarrow A + B$$

Heating calcium carbonate breaks it down into calcium oxide and carbon dioxide in this decomposition reaction:

$$CaCO_3 \rightarrow CaO + CO_2$$

Combustion

Combustion reactions always involve oxygen (O_2), and they usually result in the production of heat. Most combustion reactions begin with a hydrocarbon reactant and result in the products carbon dioxide and water. Otherwise, they resemble decomposition reactions.

An example might be the burning of the hydrocarbon ethane:

$$2C_2H_6 + 7O_2 \rightarrow 4CO_2 + 6H_2O$$

Test Yourself

1. Iron and sulfur form iron sulfide. What kind of reaction is this?

   ____

2. Methanol and oxygen form carbon dioxide and water. What kind of reaction is this? ______________________________

3. Ferric dioxide is heated and forms ferric oxide and water. What kind of reaction is this? ______________________________

4. Which of the following is an example of a synthesis reaction?

   A. $H_2CO_3 \rightarrow H_2O + CO_2$
   B. $Na_2S + HCl \rightarrow NaCl + H2S$
   C. $2KBr + Cl_2 \rightarrow 2KCl + Br_2$
   D. $8Fe + S_8 \rightarrow 8FeS$

5. Which of the following is an example of a single replacement reaction?

   A. $2KClO_3 \rightarrow 2KCl + 3O_2$
   B. $Mg + 2HCl \rightarrow MgCl_2 + H_2$
   C. $SO_3 + H_2O \rightarrow H_2SO_4$
   D. $C_3H_8 + 5O_2 \rightarrow 3CO_2 + 4H_2O$

Answers

1. synthesis. Two elements combine to make a compound.
2. combustion. The addition of oxygen creates the products carbon dioxide, water, and heat.
3. decomposition. In this kind of reaction, a compound breaks down into two or more products.
4. D. Iron plus sulfur yield iron sulfide in this simple reaction. Choice A is decomposition of carbonic acid. Choice B is a double replacement reaction in which sodium sulfide and hydrochloric acid produce sodium chloride and hydrogen sulfide. Choice C is a single replacement reaction: Potassium bromide and chlorine gas form potassium chloride.
5. B. Magnesium plus hydrochloric acid yields magnesium chloride plus hydrogen gas. Choice A is decomposition of potassium chlorate. Choice C is the synthesis of hydrogen sulfate. Choice D is combustion of propane.

CHEMICAL BONDS

The force that holds atoms together in molecules is called a chemical bond. Atoms form bonds by sharing or transferring electrons from their outer orbitals. The object is always to achieve stability by completely filling outer orbitals with electrons.

Covalent Bonds

In a covalent bond, two atoms share one or more pairs of electrons. A simple example is fluorine atoms bonding to create F_2. Fluorine has atomic number 9. It has two electrons in its inner 1s orbital and seven in its outer orbital (two in 2s, five in 2p). To achieve stability, it needs eight valence electrons. It can achieve this by setting up a covalent bond with a second fluorine atom. (See Figure 7.5.)

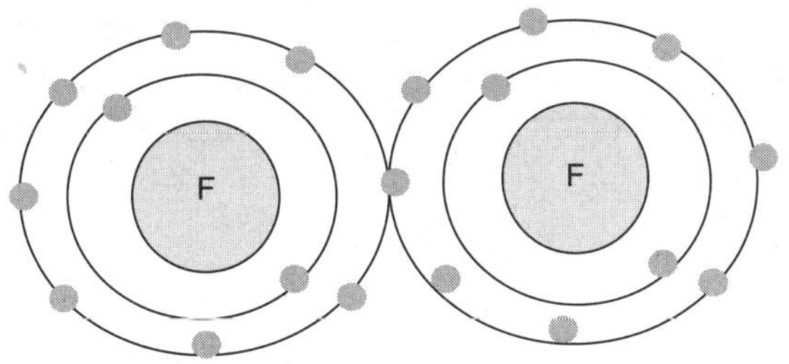

Figure 7.5 Covalent Bonding

The covalent bond creates a molecule, F_2, which is more stable than the original atoms were.

Polar bonds are covalent bonds in which the electrons are not equally distributed. This gives the created molecule a slightly uneven electrical charge, with a slightly positive charge at one end and a slightly negative charge at the other. H_2O is held together by polar covalent bonds.

Ionic Bonds

In ionic bonding, valence electrons are transferred between atoms. A metal loses electrons through **ionization energy**, becoming a cation, and a nonmetal receives those electrons, becoming an anion.

An example is lithium, with one electron in its outer shell, bonding with fluorine, which as above, has seven electrons in its outer shell. Lithium gives up an electron to fluorine, giving lithium a full shell of two electrons and fluorine a full shell of eight electrons. The new compound is lithium fluoride, LiF. (See Figure 7.6.)

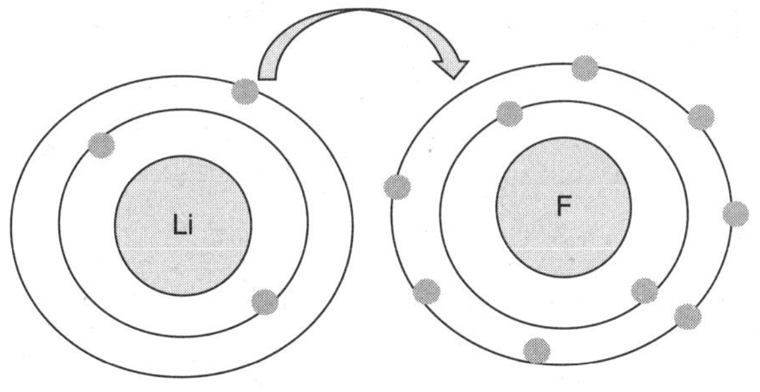

Figure 7.6 Ionic Bonding

Intermolecular Forces

Bonds hold atoms together through intramolecular forces. The forces of attraction and repulsion that keep molecules together are called intermolecular forces. These forces are weaker than the forces that bond atoms. Intermolecular forces allow molecules to group together to form liquids, solids, and solutions.

To understand intermolecular forces, you need to understand **dipoles**, which occur when positive and negative charges in an atom are distributed unevenly. The attraction between positive and negative charges creates the force that connects molecules.

Table 7.4 lists some intermolecular forces.

Table 7.4 Intermolecular Forces from Weakest to Strongest

Force	Attraction
London dispersion	between any two molecules
dipole-dipole/Keesom	between two polar molecules
hydrogen bond	between molecules with O-H, N-H, or F-H bonds
ion-dipole	between an ion and a polar molecule

As force strength increases, the energy required to separate molecules or ions increases, meaning that the melting point or boiling point of the molecules increases as well.

Test Yourself

For items 1–3, circle the correct answers in parentheses.

1. In an ionic bond, a metal (loses/gains) electrons to become (a cation/an anion).

2. Methane has four C-H (covalent/ionic) bonds with electrons shared equally. These bonds are (polar/nonpolar).

3. A polar bond is a(n) (ionic/covalent) bond with (equal/unequal) distribution of electrons.

4. Which intermolecular force is weakest?

A. Dipole-dipole
B. London dispersion
C. Ion-dipole
D. Bonding

5. Which intermolecular force would have the highest boiling point?

A. Dipole-dipole
B. London dispersion
C. Ion-dipole
D. Hydrogen bonding

Answers

1. loses, cation. It is the nonmetal in such a bond that gains electrons.
2. covalent, nonpolar. Because the electrons are shared, the bonds are covalent. Because they are shared equally, they are nonpolar.
3. covalent, unequal. This is the definition of a polar bond.
4. B. London dispersion is weakest, and ion-dipole is strongest.
5. C. This is the strongest of the forces and would require a high boiling point.

REACTION RATES

Some chemical reactions happen almost instantly. Others take years. On the A2 test, you will probably not be asked to calculate reaction time, but you may be asked about the effects of certain conditions upon the rate of reaction.

Reactions only take place when atoms collide. The frequency of those collisions can affect the rate of reaction. (See Table 7.5.)

Table 7.5 Effects upon Reaction Rate

Condition	Effect
temperature	Increased temperature increases reaction rate.
pressure	Increased pressure increases reaction rate.
concentration	Increased concentration increases reaction rate.
surface area	Increased surface area increases reaction rate.

These effects make sense when you think about them. Rising temperature moves atoms faster, so they collide more often. Increased pressure and concentration push atoms together, giving them more chances to collide. (Gases are especially altered under pressure.) Increasing surface area—for example, by pulverizing rock into sand—increases the chances for atoms to collide.

A **catalyst** is a substance that speeds up a reaction without altering its own chemistry. Catalysts do not increase the numbers of atomic collisions, but they do improve their efficiency. For example, the catalytic converter in your car uses platinum or a similar metal as a catalyst to help change hazardous CO into CO_2. Adding a catalyst of phosphoric acid to ethane and water speeds up the making of ethanol.

Enzymes

In biological systems, the specialized proteins called enzymes are important catalysts. They increase the rate of reaction in most of the chemical reactions that take place within a cell. Here are some of the most important enzymes:

- **Proteases** are enzymes that break down proteins into smaller peptides or amino acids. They are important in digestion, protein turnover, and many other biological processes.
- **DNA polymerases** are enzymes that synthesize DNA molecules by adding nucleotides to a growing chain. They are essential for DNA replication and repair.
- **RNA polymerases** are enzymes that synthesize RNA molecules by copying DNA sequences. They are essential for gene expression and regulation.
- **Kinases** are enzymes that add phosphate groups to other molecules, typically proteins, and are important in signal transduction and regulation of cellular processes.
- **Phosphatases** are enzymes that remove phosphate groups from other molecules, typically proteins, and are important in signal termination and regulation of cellular processes.
- **Oxidoreductases** are enzymes that catalyze redox reactions, in which one molecule is oxidized and another is reduced. They are important in energy production, metabolism, and detoxification.
- **Hydrolases** are enzymes that break down molecules by adding water. They are important in digestion, metabolism, and many other biological processes.
- **Ligases** are enzymes that join two molecules together, typically nucleic acids or proteins, and are important in DNA repair, recombination, and synthesis.

Test Yourself

For questions 1–3, circle the correct answer in parentheses.

1. A large pile of iron nails will rust (faster/slower) than a block of iron.

2. If more water is added to two reactants dissolved in a liter of water, their reaction rate will (speed up/slow down).

3. If hydrogen peroxide breaks down into water and oxygen with the addition of manganese dioxide, MnO_2 is being used as a (reactant/catalyst).

4. A home appliance that uses principles of reaction rates is the ___________.

   A. pressure cooker
   B. dishwasher
   C. ceiling fan
   D. blender

5. Which method for increasing reaction rate does not increase atomic collisions?

   A. Raising temperature
   B. Increasing concentration
   C. Multiplying surface area
   D. Adding a catalyst

Answers

1. faster. The greater surface area of the nails gives them more exposure to the oxygen atoms that cause iron to rust.
2. slow down. Reducing the concentration will reduce the rate of reaction.
3. catalyst. Hydrogen peroxide might decompose slowly on its own, but the addition of the catalyst increases the rate of the reaction.
4. A. A pressure cooker uses pressure and heat to speed up the reaction time needed for cooking.
5. D. Choices A, B, and C work by offering more ways for atoms to collide, but choice D works by making such collisions more effective by creating an alternative pathway for the reaction to take place.

MOLARITY

Reaction rate may be thought of as the change in concentration of a reactant over the change in time. It may measure either of two observed events: the rate of disappearance of reactants or the rate of formation of products.

So, in the synthesis reaction $A + B \rightarrow AB$, you might observe one of three things:

$$\text{Rate} = -\frac{\Delta < A >}{\Delta t} \qquad \text{Rate} = -\frac{\Delta < B >}{\Delta t} \qquad \text{Rate} = \frac{\Delta < AB >}{\Delta t}$$

In the first two equations, the change in A and B is negative, since A and B are disappearing, but the rate is always positive.

The units for reaction rate are usually expressed as molarity per second, or M/s. Molarity (M) is the number of **moles** of a solute in 1 liter of solution.

WHY DO I NEED THIS?

Molarity is one way of expressing the strength of a given medicine.

A mole is the amount of a substance that contains as many elemental units as there are atoms in 12 grams of carbon-12. That number, also known as **Avogadro's number**, comes to about 6.02×10^{23}, a very large number indeed.

It is easy to calculate molarity if you are given both the number of moles and the number of liters, as here:

Find the molarity of a solution containing 0.65 mol NaCl in 2 liters of solution.

$M = \text{mols of solute/liters of solution}$

$M = 0.65/2$

$M = 0.325$

It is also possible to calculate molarity if you are given the mass of the solute and the volume of the solution:

Find the molarity of a solution containing 50 grams of KBr in 2 liters.

First, find the gram formula mass of KBr, which is the atomic mass of K ($\approx$ 39 g) plus the atomic mass of Br ($\approx$ 80 g/mol), or $\approx$119 g/mol.

By definition, this equals the mass of KBr in 1 mole of KBr.

Next, find the moles of KBr in 50 grams:

$50 \text{ g KBr} \times 1 \text{ mol KBr}/119 \text{ g KBr} \approx 0.42 \text{ mol}$

Finally, divide moles of solute by liters of solution as you did above:

$M = 0.42/2$

$M = 0.21$

Test Yourself

1. To the nearest whole number, what is the gram formula mass of water? ____________

2. To the nearest whole number, what is the gram formula mass of carbon dioxide? ____________

3. To the nearest hundredth, how many moles of KBr would be in 85 grams of KBr? ____________

4. Find the molarity of a solution containing 0.025 mol KCl in 2 L of water.

A. 0.0125 M
B. 0.125 M
C. 0.8 M
D.80 M

5. Find the molarity of a solution containing 0.15 mol NaCl in 450 mL of solution.

A. 0.33 M
B. 3 M
C. 3.3 M
D. 3,000 M

Answers

1. 18. The atomic mass of hydrogen is around 1, and that of oxygen is around 16, so the gram formula mass of H_2O is around 18.
2. 44. Carbon's atomic mass is around 12, and oxygen's is 16, so the gram formula mass of CO_2 would be 12 plus 32, or around 44 g/mol.
3. 0.71. The gram formula mass is 119 g; divide that into 85 g to get the number of moles.
4. A. The molarity is the concentration of KCl in terms of moles per liter, so divide the moles by 2 liters to get 0.0125 M.
5. A. Convert milliliters to liters (450 mL is 0.450 L) and divide 0.15 mol by 0.45 L to get 0.33.

ACIDS AND BASES

Ionic compounds have positive or negative charges. Their charges determine how they are classified.

Acids

An acid is a water-based liquid compound that forms a positively charged hydrogen ion (H^+) in water. Acids react strongly with active metals. An acid is sour and is often corrosive. Acids in the human body include hydrochloric acid in gastric juices, uric acid in urine, and lactic acid in the muscles.

Bases

A base is a water-based liquid compound that forms a negatively charged hydroxide ion (OH^-) in water. Bases taste bitter and may feel slippery. Common bases include ammonia, baking soda, and anything with a chemical name that ends with the word *hydroxide*.

When acids and bases are mixed, they may react to neutralize each other, creating a salt and water as the product of the reaction. The H^+ and OH^- ions combine to form H_2O.

$HCl + NaOH \rightarrow NaCl + H_2O$: Hydrochloric acid plus sodium hydroxide yields sodium chloride (table salt) and water.

$H_2SO_4 + Ca(OH)_2 \rightarrow CaSO_4 + 2H_2O$: Sulfuric acid plus calcium hydroxide yields calcium sulfate and water.

WHY DO I NEED THIS?

Interpreting and restoring acid-base balance can be a key part of nursing critically ill patients.

The pH Scale

We measure the relative strength of acids and bases using a pH scale. The scale measures hydrogen ion concentration in liquid compounds, using a scale from 0 to 14. The midpoint, pH 7, is neutral. A pH value higher than 7 is basic, and less than 7 is acidic. The higher the value, the more **alkaline**, or basic, the compound is. The lower the score, the more acidic the compound is. (See Figure 7.7.)

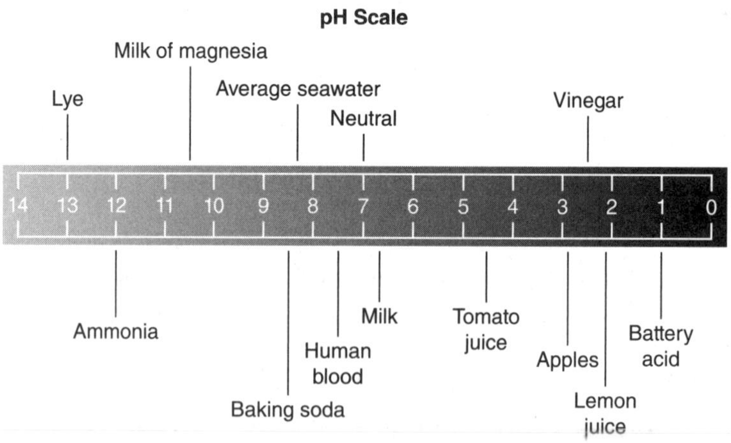

Figure 7.7 pH Scale

A variety of indicators exist to test for acidity and alkalinity. Usually these acid-base indicators change color when added to the compound being tested. (See Table 7.6.)

Table 7.6 Some Acid-Base Indicators

Indicator	Color in Presence of Acid	Color in Presence of Base
alizarin yellow	yellow	red
bromothymol blue	yellow	blue
litmus	red	blue
methyl violet	yellow	blue
phenol red	yellow	red
phenolphthalein	no color	magenta

Test Yourself

1. An acid-base indicator that turns red in the presence of acids is ____________.

2. You would expect a compound ending in *hydroxide* to fall between ____________ and ____________ on the pH scale.

3. In chemistry, another word for *basic* is ____________.

4. Human blood is generally neutral. Which of these might be a normal pH for a blood sample?

A. 5.50
B. 7.40
C. 8.95
D. 9.25

5. Which equation represents a neutralization reaction?

A. $4NH_3 + 5O_2 \rightarrow 4NO + 6H_2O$
B. $C_6H_6 + 15H_2O_2 \rightarrow 6CO_2 + 18H_2O$
C. $Ca(OH)_2 + H_2CO_3 \rightarrow CaCO_3 + 2H_2O$
D. $2ZnS + 3O_2 \rightarrow 2ZnO + 2SO_2$

Answers

1. litmus. Some other indicators turn red in the presence of bases.
2. 7, 14. Hydroxides are bases.
3. alkaline. The word is from the Arabic, and refers to the ashes of the saltwort plant.
4. B. Blood is generally between 7.35 and 7.45. Changes in blood pH usually indicate health problems.
5. C. In choices A, B, and C, one of the products is water, but only choice C represents a base (calcium hydroxide) being added to an acid (carbonic acid) and resulting in a salt (calcium carbonate) plus water.

REDOX REACTIONS

The **oxidation state** of an atom is a hypothetical number assigned to that atom. It corresponds to the number of electrons that the atom loses, gains, or uses when joining other atoms to form compounds. The number may be positive, negative, or zero.

You can find the oxidation state of a compound by adding and subtracting a lot of atomic oxidation numbers, but it's easier to follow some basic rules.

1. In its elemental form, an atom has an oxidation state of 0.
2. In single-atom ions, the oxidation state equals the charge of the ion.
3. Group 1 metals have an oxidation state of +1.
4. Group 2 metals have an oxidation state of +2.
5. In compounds, fluorine has an oxidation state of –1.
6. In compounds, hydrogen has an oxidation state of +1 when bonded to a nonmetal and –1 when bonded to a metal.
7. In compounds, oxygen has an oxidation state of –1 in peroxides and –2 everywhere else.
8. The sum of atomic oxidation numbers is 0 in neutral compounds.

So, in a neutral molecule of CO_2, each oxygen atom has an oxidation number of –2, for a total of –4, meaning that carbon must have an oxidation number of +4 for a sum of 0. In a neutral molecule of NaOH, the oxygen atom is –2, the hydrogen is +1, and sodium (Na) must be +1 as well to achieve a sum of 0.

In an **oxidation-reduction reaction**, or redox reaction, electrons are transferred between ions or molecules. The ion or molecule that gains electrons has been reduced and is called the **oxidizing agent**. The ion or molecule that loses electrons is oxidized and is called the **reducing agent**.

You will almost certainly not need to balance redox reactions on the A2 test, but you should recognize what is happening in a redox reaction like this one:

$$Zn + 2H^+ \rightarrow Zn^{2+} + H_2$$

Zinc, the reducing agent, is oxidized, and its oxidation state increases and changes from 0 to +2. Hydrogen, the oxidizing agent, is reduced, and its oxidation state decreases and changes from +1 to 0.

Test Yourself

1. What is the oxidation state of boron in boron trifluoride (BF_3)? ___________

2. What is the oxidation state of bromide ion in potassium bromide (KBr)? ___________

3. What is the oxidation state of lithium in lithium hydride (LiH)? ___________

4. Which element is reduced in this equation?

$Cr^{+} + Sn^{4+} \rightarrow Cr^{3+} + Sn^{2+}$

A. Cr^{+}
B. Sn^{4+}
C. Cr^{3+}
D. Sn^{2+}

5. A reducing agent reduces other substances and ____________ electrons, ____________ its oxidation state.

A. gains, decreasing
B. gains, increasing
C. loses, decreasing
D. loses, increasing

Answers

1. +3. Fluorine has an oxidation state of –1 in a compound, so F_3 has an oxidation number of –3. For oxidation states in BF_3 to equal 0, boron must have an oxidation state of +3.

2. –1. Potassium is a group 1 metal with an oxidation state of +1, so bromide ion must have an oxidation state of –1.

3. +1. Hydrogen has an oxidation state of –1 when bonded to a metal, so lithium must be +1.

4. B. The reactants are to the left of the arrow. Looking at the products on the right should tell you that chromium is oxidized, while tin is reduced.

5. D. Reducing agents such as CO, Zn, or Fe lose electrons as they reduce other substances, thus increasing their own oxidation states.

RADIOACTIVITY

Radioactivity is one of several topics that bleed over from chemistry into physics, but you are more likely to see it tested in the Chemistry module of the A2 test. Radioactivity results from the decay of an unstable nucleus. The goal of radioactivity is to end up with a stable isotope.

As unstable isotopes decay, they may emit any of three types of radiation. **Alpha particles** are composed of two protons and two neutrons. They are slow and heavy but have a large positive charge (+2). **Beta particles** are fast-moving electrons with a charge of –1. **Gamma rays** are waves with neither mass nor electrical charge. Unlike alpha and beta particles, gamma rays do not change the state of a nucleus, but they do carry energy away from the nucleus.

The **half-life** of a given isotope is the average time it takes for half of the atoms in a sample to decay. For example, the half-life of cobalt-60 is 5.27 years. That means that in 5.27 years, half of a sample of cobalt-60 will have decayed, with the state of the nucleus changing in those decaying atoms. After two half-lives, or 10.54 years, half of the remaining half will have decayed, and so on.

Imagine a sample of 500 atoms with a half-life of two hours. In two hours, you would have 250 atoms from the original sample. In four hours, you would have 125. In six hours, you would have 62.5, and so on. An easy way to think about it is:

- After one half-life: 1/2 sample
- After two half-lives: 1/4 sample
- After three half-lives: 1/8 sample
- After four half-lives: 1/16 sample
- After five half-lives: 1/32 sample

Test Yourself

1. Which form of radiation does not result in a change in the nucleus?

 ____

2. Which form of radiation is composed of rapidly moving electrons?

 ____

3. You have a sample of lawrencium, with a half-life of 4 hours. What fraction of that sample will remain after one 24-hour day?

 ____

4. Polonium has a half-life of 102 years. If you start in the year 2020 with 10 g of polonium, in what year will there be 0.625 g left?

 A. 2122
 B. 2224
 C. 2326
 D. 2428

5. The half-life of Zn-71 is 2.4 minutes. How much Zn-71 is left from a 50-g sample after 12 minutes?

 A. 20.83 g
 B. 12.5 g
 C. 3.125 g
 D. 1.5625 g

Answers

1. gamma rays. These rays represent energy loss without a fundamental change to the nucleus.
2. beta particles. Alpha particles are made up of protons and neutrons.
3. 1/64. 24 hours would equal six half-lives.
4. D. One half-life (102 years) would bring you to 5 g, two (204 years) to 2.5 g, three (306 years) to 1.25 g, and four (408 years) to 0.625 g.
5. D. Twelve minutes would equal five half-lives, so the resulting quantity would be 1/32 (50 g).

CHAPTER 8

Anatomy and Physiology

CONTENTS

Studying anatomy and physiology in nursing school means studying the structure and function of the body and its systems. Knowledge of these systems is fundamental to any study of medicine.

CELLS AND TISSUES

Humans are complex organisms. We are composed of cells that make up **tissues**, which in turn make up **organs**, which in turn make up **systems** of organs that work together to maintain the entire organism and keep us alive and functioning.

Functions of Cells

Critical functions of human body cells include reproduction, energy conversion, and transport. Glandular cells produce hormones or enzymes. Adipose cells store fat. Nerve and muscle cells conduct electrical impulses. Bone and blood cells connect body parts.

A cell's function dictates its actions. For example, skin cells reproduce rapidly. Nerve cells do not. Blood cells move freely. Muscle cells are tightly attached to one another.

Cells in a human embryo begin as **pluripotent stem cells**, meaning that they have the ability to differentiate into any of the variety of cells that make up the human body. As cells divide and the embryo grows, cells migrate to one of the three layers of the embryo. **Endodermal** cells may differentiate into some epithelial cells, the trachea, the bronchi, the bladder, the thyroid, the parathyroid, or the intestines. **Mesodermal** cells may become muscle and bone cells or form the cartilage, veins and arteries, lymphatic system, or dermis. **Ectodermal** cells may differentiate into the skin, hair, lens and cornea, sebaceous glands, or tooth enamel.

Types of Tissues

Cells with a common embryonic origin combine to form tissues in the body. Table 8.1 shows the four categories of tissue with some of their structures and functions.

Table 8.1 Tissue Structures and Functions

Tissue	Structure	Function
epithelial	classified by cell shape: squamous, cuboidal, columnar, or transitional classified by arrangement: simple (single layer of cells) or stratified (multiple layers of cells)	protection (skin); absorption (stomach lining); filtration (kidney); secretion (glands)
connective	loose or dense special connective tissues include cartilage, bone, blood, and lymph	protection (areolar); storage (adipose); connection (ligament); support (bone); transport (blood)
muscle	striated (cardiac or skeletal muscle) or smooth (smooth muscle)	movement (skeletal); blood flow (cardiac); regulation (smooth)
nervous	comprised of nerve cells (neurons) and neuroglia (glia)	transmission (neurons); storage, support, and protection (glia)

Some body structures combine tissue types. For example, the **pleura** that coats the lungs and lines the thorax consists of both epithelial and connective tissue.

Test Yourself

1. Complete the diagram: cells → ____________ → organs → ____________.

2. Connective tissue is classified as loose or ____________; muscle tissue is classified as smooth or ____________.

3. Which type of tissue is classified by shape or arrangement?

____

4. Which of these might form from embryonic ectodermal cells?

   A. Thyroid
   B. Vein
   C. Hair
   D. Bone

5. Where might you find a simple epithelial tissue?

   A. Connecting two bones
   B. Lining a blood vessel
   C. Contracting the heart
   D. Moving iron through the body

Answers

1. tissues, systems. Cells make up tissues. Tissues make up organs. Organs make up systems.
2. dense, striated. Check the chart to see the structural classifications.
3. epithelial. Epithelial cells come in four shapes and two arrangements.
4. C. Ectodermal cells become the outermost layers of the body.
5. B. Simple (single-layer) squamous epithelial cells line the blood vessels. Choices A and D name connective tissue; choice C names cardiac muscle tissue.

BODY PLANES AND DIRECTIONS

The medical world uses anatomical directional terms to describe the locations of structures and systems in the body. The terms may be unfamiliar, but memorizing them will be of critical importance as you study anatomy and physiology.

First, imagine the body sliced into planes, as shown in Figure 8.1.

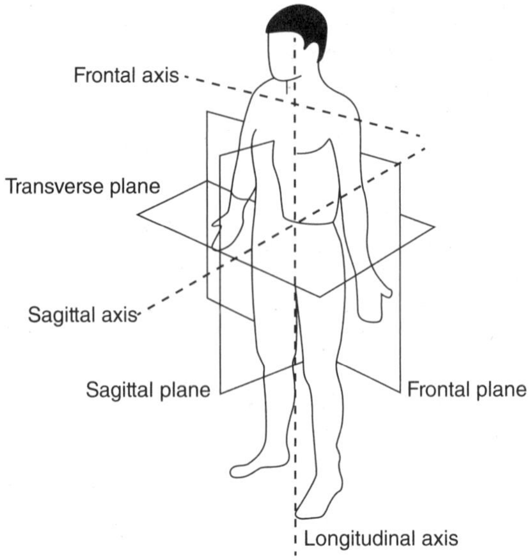

Figure 8.1 Body Planes

Frontal (coronal) plane: divides the body into front and back regions

Sagittal (lateral) plane: divides the body into right and left regions

Transverse plane: divides the body into upper and lower regions

Table 8.2 includes other important directional terms.

Table 8.2 Directional Terms in Anatomy

Word	Meaning
anterior posterior	toward the front toward the back
dorsal ventral	toward the back toward the belly
cranial caudal	toward the head away from the head
superior inferior	above below
lateral medial	away from the midline toward the midline
axial intermediate	around a central axis between two structures
distal proximal	away from the origin toward the origin
prone supine	facedown face up
superficial deep	toward the surface away from the surface
ipsilateral contralateral	on the same side on opposite sides

WHY DO I NEED THIS?

Symptoms and surgeries are described using these terms.

Test Yourself

1. A ___________ plane divides the body into anterior and posterior parts.

2. Which joint is intermediate to the shoulder and wrist? ___________

3. Another term for *prone* might be ___________.

4. Which body part is distal to the knee?

A. Ankle
B. Hip
C. Thigh
D. Elbow

5. On a human face, the eyes are lateral to which body part?

A. Ears
B. Nose
C. Eyelids
D. Cheekbones

Answers

1. frontal or coronal. This plane divides the body vertically into front (anterior) and back (posterior) parts.
2. elbow. On the arm, the elbow is the joint between the shoulder and wrist.
3. face down. Prone is facedown; supine is face up.
4. A. If the body part is distal, it is farther from the point of origin, or attachment.
5. B. The nose is the midline, and the eyes are away from that midline.

INTEGUMENTARY SYSTEM

An integument is a natural covering, such as the shell of an egg or the rind of a grapefruit. The body's integumentary system is aptly named; it is the external covering of the body.

Key Parts

The integumentary system includes the skin, hair, nails, and **exocrine glands**. The skin is the largest organ in the body. It is composed of three layers, the **epidermis**, **dermis**, and **hypodermis**. (See Figure 8.2.)

The epidermis contains specialized cells. **Keratinocytes** form the tough, water-resistant protective layer of the skin. **Melanocytes** produce the pigment **melanin**, which protects the skin from ultraviolet radiation and helps to determine skin color.

Below the layers of epidermis cells lies the dermis, which is thick and strong. It contains nerves, blood vessels, and exocrine glands. Sweat glands, or **sudoriferous glands**, secrete water and sodium chloride to lower the body temperature via evaporation on the surface of the skin. **Sebaceous glands** secrete **sebum**, an oily substance that waterproofs and lubricates the skin. The palms of the hands and soles of the feet lack these sebaceous glands.

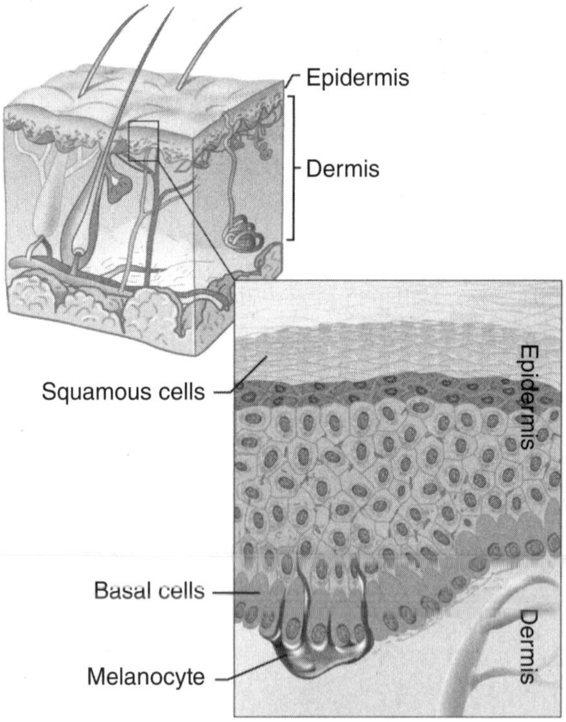

Figure 8.2 The Skin

Finally, **ceruminous glands**, which occur only in the dermis of the ear canal, produce a waxy substance that lubricates the eardrum and keeps dust and particles out of the ear.

The deepest layer is the hypodermis, or **subcutaneous tissue**. It is largely composed of adipose tissue, or fat.

Hair is made up of dead keratinocytes. The **follicle** of each hair extends down into the dermis. Inside the follicle, melanocytes give the hair its color, and new cells are produced, pushing older cells outward. As people age, production of the enzyme that helps manufacture melanin decreases, and the hair turns the grayish color of keratin.

Toenails and fingernails are sheets of keratinocytes. They grow, as hair does, because new cells are constantly being produced in the nail matrix and pushing the old cells outward.

Key Functions

The integumentary system protects underlying tissues from disease, ultraviolet light, and other external damage. The skin regulates body temperature, both through the evaporation of sweat and through regulation of blood flow. Here are some ways in which the integumentary system works with some other systems of the body:

The Integumentary System Works with the . . .

skeletal system	by activating vitamin D to provide calcium for bones
muscular system	by triggering signals that tell the body to shiver to prevent hypothermia
nervous system	by housing sensory receptors that give information about touch
circulatory system	by regulating blood flow to maintain body temperature
lymphatic system	by offering a first line of defense against infection
digestive system	by aiding with the uptake of calcium via vitamin D
reproductive system	by housing sensory receptors that play a role in sexual activity and nursing

Test Yourself

1. Subcutaneous tissue is primarily ____________.
2. Hair, nails, and skin are mostly made of ____________.
3. One purpose of melanin is to protect the skin from ____________.

4. Which system works with the integumentary system to provide information to the brain via touch?
   - A. Skeletal system
   - B. Muscular system
   - C. Nervous system
   - D. Lymphatic system

5. Which is a primary function of the sebaceous gland?
   - A. Lubrication
   - B. Cushioning
   - C. Melanin production
   - D. Temperature regulation

Answers

1. fat or adipose. The hypodermis is a cushiony, protective layer of fat.
2. keratinocytes. These cells are the majority of the cells in hair, nails, and skin.
3. UV rays. Ultraviolet light is damaging to the skin. The more melanin in the skin, the less damage is likely to occur.
4. C. Nerves in the skin provide information via touch.
5. A. Oil from the sebaceous glands lubricates, moisturizes, and waterproofs the skin.

SKELETAL SYSTEM

Adult humans have 206 bones, from 22 in the skull to 26 in each foot. Those bones, the teeth, and three kinds of connective tissue form the skeletal system.

Key Parts

The **axial skeleton** is comprised of the bones of the head and torso. Those are generally classified into six groups: the skull bones, the bones of the middle ear (malleus, incus, and stapes), the hyoid bone in the neck, the rib cage, the sternum, and the spinal column.

The **appendicular skeleton** contains the limbs, the pelvis, and the pectoral girdle (clavicle and scapula).

Figure 8.3 labels many of the important bones in the human body.

Connective tissue is part of the skeletal system. **Tendons** connect muscle to bone. **Ligaments** connect bone to bone. **Cartilage** cushions the ends of bones.

Joints, or **articulations**, form where two or more bones meet and connect. Functionally, joints are classified as immovable (as skull bones are), partly movable (as in the bones of the spine), or freely movable (as in the hip). Table 8.3 shows how joints are classified structurally.

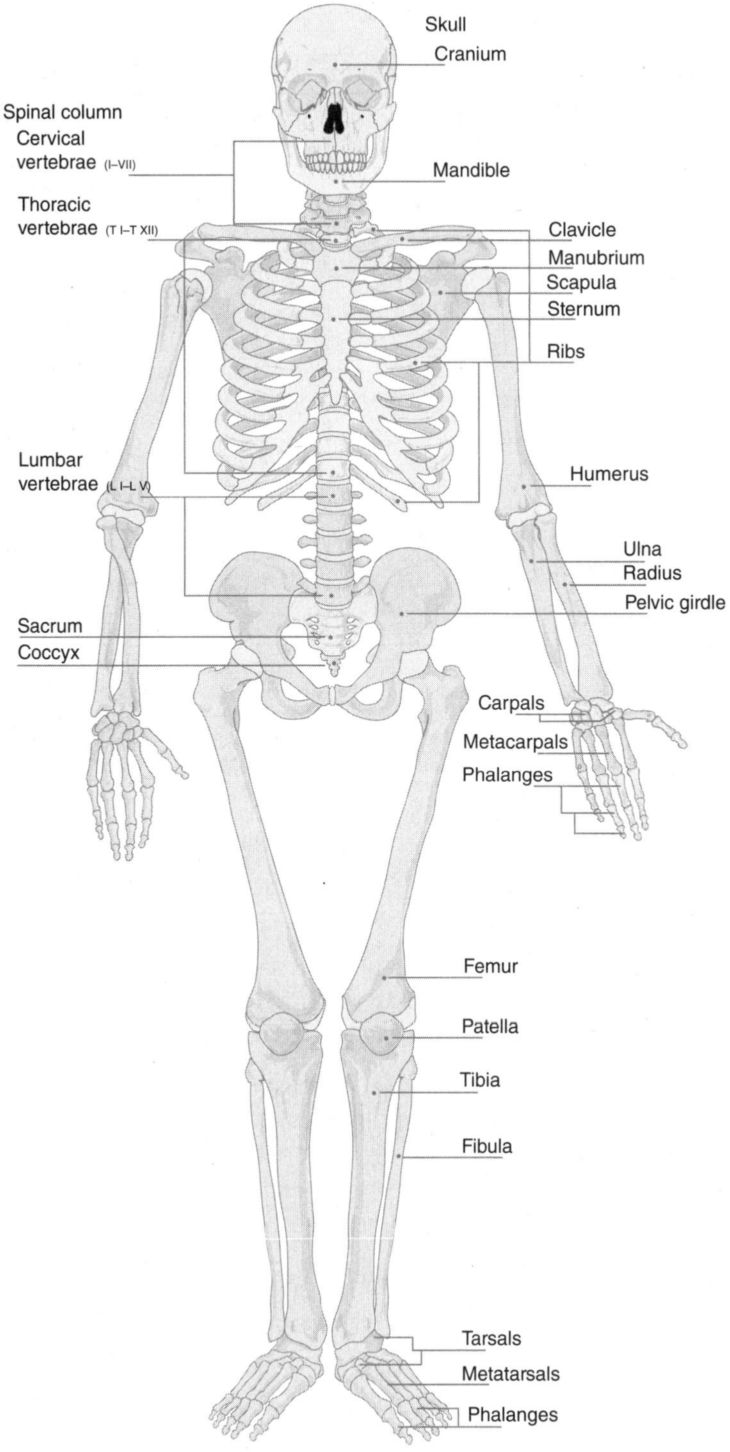

Figure 8.3 The Skeleton

Table 8.3 Structural Types of Joints

Type of Joint	Description	Examples
fibrous	bound together by tough, fibrous ligaments; may be immovable or partly movable	gomphosis: teeth in tooth sockets suture: skull bones syndesmosis: joint between tibia and fibula at the ankle
cartilaginous	connected by cartilage that serves as a shock absorber	symphysis: pubic bones synchondrosis: vertebrae
synovial	filled with synovial fluid; freely movable	ball and socket: shoulder condyloid: wrist gliding/plane: collarbone/shoulder hinge: elbow pivot: first and second vertebrae in neck saddle: base of thumb

Smooth bones that are embedded in muscles or tendons are called **sesamoid** bones. They form tiny parts of the wrist, hands, and feet; and the kneecap is another, much larger example.

Key Functions

The skeletal system provides structural support for the body and protects key organs behind a hard outer shell. It also allows for movement, and bones are an important site of mineral storage and blood cell production.

Bone marrow, the tissue inside bones, is the site both of red blood cell production and of the development of **phagocytes**, cells that protect the body by ingesting pathogens and other invaders. Channels in bone such as the **Volkmann's canals** contain blood vessels and nerves that connect bone to the connective tissue that surrounds the bone.

Here are some ways in which the skeletal system works with some other systems of the body.

The Skeletal System Works with the . . .

integumentary system	by absorbing calcium in a process enhanced by vitamin D from the skin
muscular system	by following the contractions of muscles, allowing the body to move
nervous system	by protecting the spinal cord
circulatory system	by producing red and white blood cells in bone marrow

lymphatic system	by producing the T cells and B cells that fight pathogens
respiratory system	by expanding and contracting to allow for the movement of air
digestive system	by chewing food to start the process of digestion

Test Yourself

For questions 1–3, circle the correct answer or answers in parentheses.

1. (Tendons/Ligaments) connect muscles to bones.

2. Finger joints are (partly movable/freely movable) in function and (cartilaginous/synovial) in structure.

3. Bone marrow produces red blood cells and (phagocytes/growth hormones).

4. Which system works with the skeletal system to assist in the absorption of calcium?

A. Nervous system
B. Respiratory system
C. Circulatory system
D. Integumentary system

5. Which bone is part of the appendicular skeleton?

A. Cranium
B. Sternum
C. Mandible
D. Radius

Answers

1. Tendons. Ligaments connect bones to other bones.
2. freely movable, synovial. Finger joints are an example of hinge joints.
3. phagocytes. In addition to blood cells and platelets, the marrow produces weapons to fight infection.
4. D. The skin takes in vitamin D, which aids in the processing of calcium.
5. D. The radius is part of one of the limbs, which along with the pelvis and pectoral girdle make up the appendicular skeleton.

MUSCULAR SYSTEM

The muscular system controls movement of the body, from the tiniest twitch of an eyelid to the ability to stand, walk, and run. Muscles are composed of fibers that are in turn made up of thick and thin filaments that slide past each other, creating tension and contraction.

Key Parts

Muscles come in three types, as described in the section of this chapter on types of tissues. **Skeletal muscles** are voluntary. Most skeletal muscles move bones. **Smooth muscles** are involuntary. They are found inside organs such as the stomach or inside blood vessels. **Cardiac muscles** are involuntary muscles that pump blood from the heart to the rest of the body.

There are a variety of ways to classify muscles. Some of them are reviewed in Table 8.4.

Table 8.4 Classification of Muscles

Characteristic	Muscles
by size	maximus, minimus, longus, brevis
by shape	deltoid, trapezius, serratus, rhomboid
by origin	biceps (two origins), triceps (three origins), quadriceps (four origins)
by action	abductor: moves bone away from midline adductor: moves bone toward midline flexor: decreases angle of joint extensor: increases angle of joint depressor: moves downward levator: moves upward pronator: turns palm down supinator: turns palm upward sphincter: reduces size of opening tensor: makes rigid rotator: moves bone around its axis

Figure 8.4 shows important muscles in the human body.

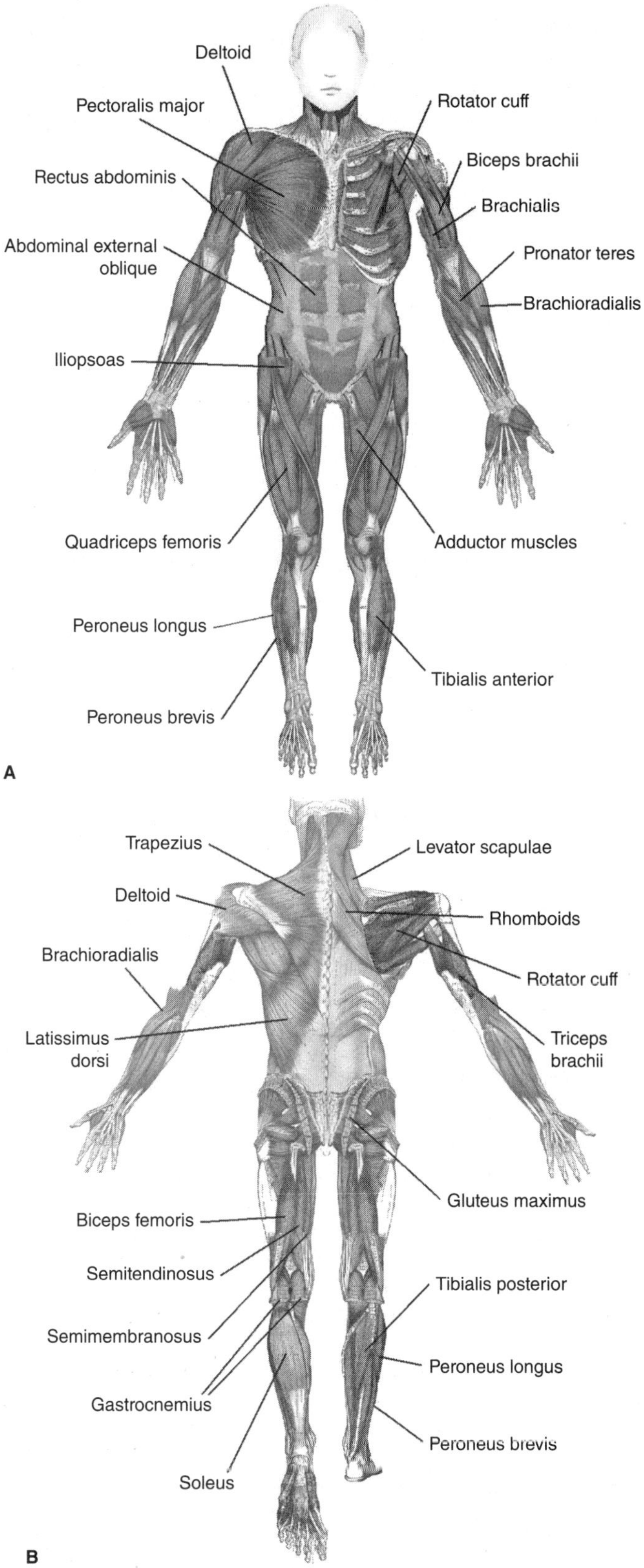

Figure 8.4 The Muscles

Key Functions

The muscular system both controls movement and maintains body posture, position, and joint stability. Muscle contractions also produce heat, which helps to maintain body temperature. Here are some ways in which the muscular system works with some other systems of the body.

The Muscular System Works with the . . .

integumentary system	by moving the facial skin to produce expressions
skeletal system	by moving the bones at the point of articulation (the joint)
nervous system	by housing receptors that tell the brain about body position and movement
circulatory system	by pushing blood through the vessels of the body
lymphatic system	by pushing lymphatic fluid through the vessels of the body
respiratory system	by moving the diaphragm so that the lungs can inflate and deflate
digestive system	by moving food down the esophagus, breaking it up in the stomach, and pushing it through the intestines
urinary system	by controlling the release of urine

Test Yourself

1. The large muscle in the front of the thigh is the ______________.

2. The muscles in the thigh whose job is to pull the leg inward are the ____.

3. The two types of involuntary muscles are ____________ and ____________ muscles.

4. The deltoids are muscles in the ___________________________.

5. Which type of muscle works in conjunction with the lymphatic system?

   A. Skeletal
   B. Cardiac
   C. Smooth
   D. Tensor

Answers

1. quadriceps femoris. Look back at the diagram to see the name of the muscle.
2. adductor muscles. An adductor pulls the bone toward the midline.
3. smooth, cardiac. Skeletal muscles are voluntary.
4. shoulders or upper arms. The deltoids are so named because of their triangular shape.
5. C. Smooth muscle lines the vessels that carry blood and lymph.

NERVOUS SYSTEM

The nervous system is the master coordinator of all the other systems in the body.

Key Parts

The **central nervous system** contains the brain and spinal cord. The **peripheral nervous system** consists of all the nerves that connect the central nervous system to external stimuli. (See Figure 8.5.)

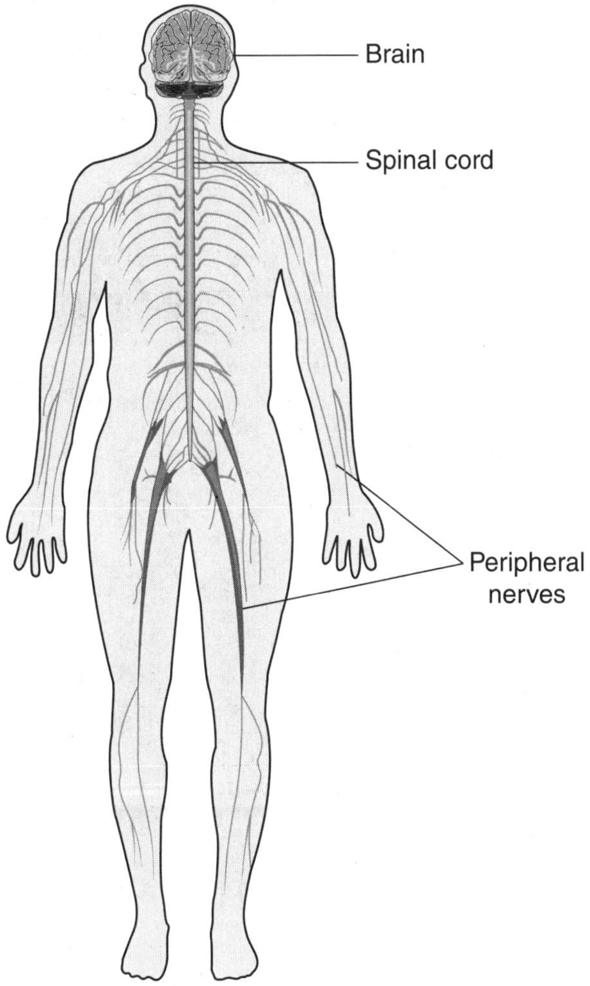

Figure 8.5 The Nervous System

The brain has three main sections. The forebrain consists of the **cerebrum**, **thalamus**, and **hypothalamus**. The midbrain contains the **tegmentum** and **tectum**. The hindbrain contains the **cerebellum**, **medulla**, and **pons**.

The cells that communicate to make the nervous system work are called **neurons**. Each neuron has a nucleus and extensions called **axons** and **dendrites**. (See Figure 8.6.)

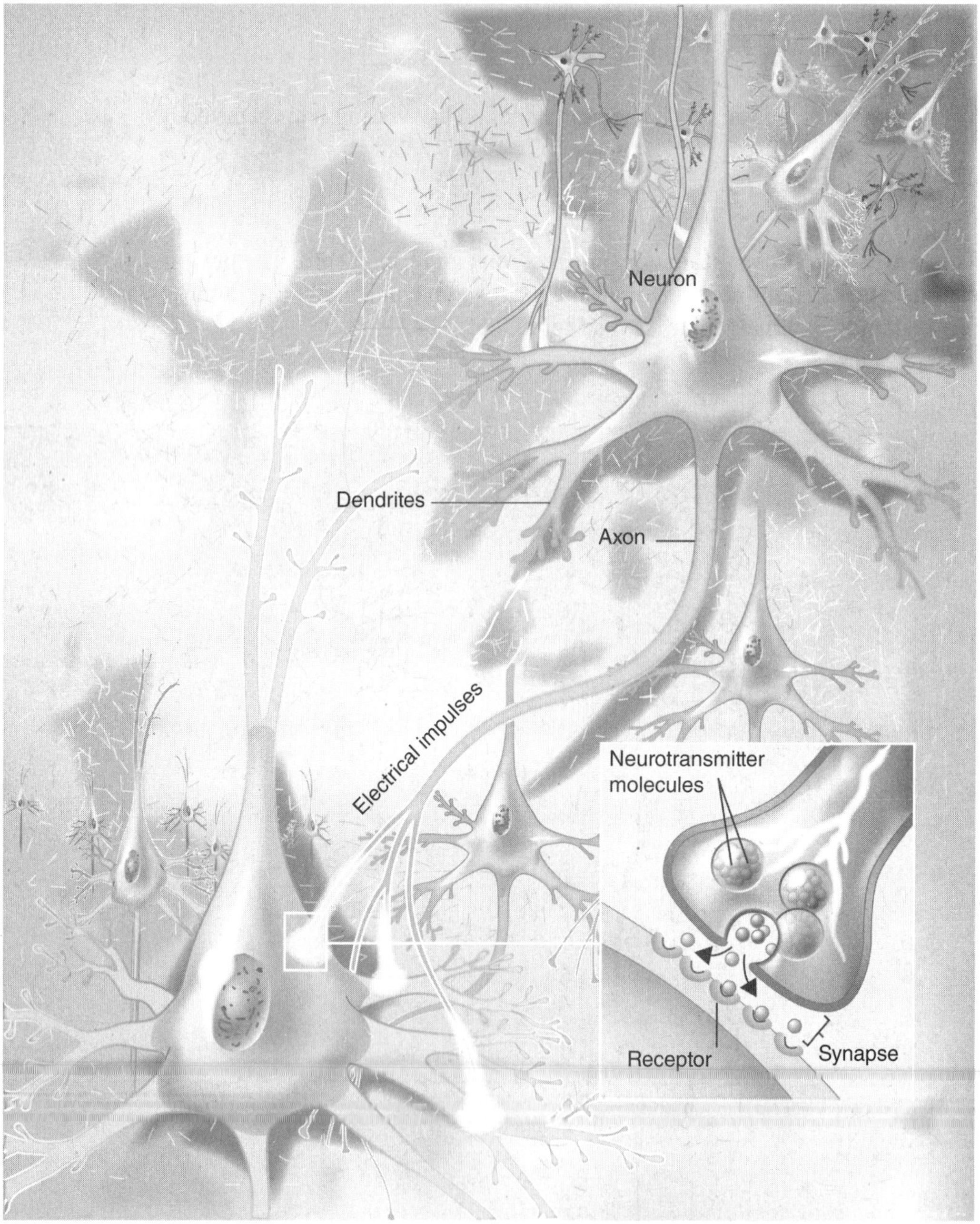

Figure 8.6 Neurons

Neurons communicate with each other by sending and receiving electrical signals. The signals travel down an axon, where they are converted to chemical signals called **neurotransmitters**. These chemical messengers are launched across the space (the **synapse**) between the end of the axon and the tip of the next neuron's dendrite, where they are converted back into electrical signals.

In the human body, **sensory neurons** send information from receptors in the skin or elsewhere toward the central nervous system. **Motor neurons** send information from the central nervous system to muscles or glands. **Interneurons** send information between sensory and motor neurons.

Within the peripheral nervous system, there are two parts. The **somatic nervous system** has motor neurons that control skeletal muscles. The **autonomic nervous system** has motor neurons that control smooth muscles, cardiac muscles, and glands. Within the autonomic nervous system are three branches. The **sympathetic nervous system** helps to maintain homeostasis and stimulates the fight-or-flight response in times of danger. The **parasympathetic nervous system** works to conserve energy by decreasing blood pressure, slowing pulse rate, and preparing the body for digestion. The **enteric nervous system** controls the function of the gastrointestinal system.

Key Functions

Each structure in the brain has its own peculiar functions. Some of those are listed in Table 8.5.

Table 8.5 Brain Structures and Functions

Brain Structure	Functions
cerebrum	
• frontal lobe	controls emotions, judgment, speech, intelligence
• parietal lobe	interprets language, sensory input, spatial perception
• occipital lobe	perceives color, light, movement
• temporal lobe	interprets language, organizes memory
thalamus	senses pain, controls alertness/attention
hypothalamus	regulates hunger, thirst, sleep, sexual response, body temperature
tegmentum	controls eye movement and some basic body movements
tectum	processes information from eyes and ears
cerebellum	controls motor movements, maintains posture and balance
medulla	regulates breathing, digestion, heartbeat
pons	relays messages from cortex to cerebellum

Here are some ways in which the nervous system works with some other systems of the body.

The Nervous System Works with the . . .

integumentary system	by regulating sweat glands and receiving and relaying sensory input
skeletal system	by receiving and relaying information about body position
muscular system	by controlling the contraction of skeletal muscle and regulating reflex actions
endocrine system	by interpreting input about chemical balance and controlling release of hormones via the pituitary glands
circulatory system	by regulating blood pressure and heart rate
respiratory system	by monitoring blood gas levels and respiratory rate
digestive system	by controlling the speed of food movement
urinary system	by regulating the release of urine

Test Yourself

For items 1–3, circle the correct answers in parentheses.

1. The (somatic/autonomic) nervous system controls the digestive tract.

2. Electrical signals are converted to chemical signals in the (axon/dendrite).

3. The hypothalamus controls (body temperature/motor movements).

4. Which part of the brain acts as a pain sensor?

   A. Cerebrum
   B. Thalamus
   C. Medulla
   D. Tectum

5. An injury to the occipital lobe might result in which of the following?

   A. Loss of color recognition
   B. Difficulty with depth perception
   C. Problems with balance or stability
   D. Inability to regulate body temperature

Answers

1. autonomic. The autonomic nervous system controls unconscious bodily functions.
2. axon. The dendrite captures those chemical signals and converts them back to electrical signals.
3. body temperature. The cerebellum controls motor movements.
4. B. The thalamus relays sensory impulses to the cerebral cortex, acting as a sensor for pain, touch, and temperature.
5. A. The occipital lobe controls many aspects of visual perception but can also have an impact on color recognition. Don't be fooled; depth perception (choice B) takes place in the parietal lobe.

ENDOCRINE SYSTEM

The endocrine system is the system of glands that produce and secrete the chemical messengers called hormones. Each hormone plays a particular role in the body's metabolism.

Key Parts

The part of the brain called the **hypothalamus** regulates endocrine control. When it recognizes an imbalance, it stimulates the production of hormones in the master gland, the **pituitary**.

Table 8.6 gives the names and locations of the major endocrine glands.

Table 8.6 Locations of Endocrine Glands

Gland	Location
adrenals	above the kidneys
hypothalamus	forebrain
ovaries	pelvic cavity (females)
pancreas	behind the stomach
parathyroids	neck
pineal	hindbrain
pituitary	forebrain
testes	in the scrotum outside the pelvic cavity (males)
thymus	upper thorax
thyroid	neck

WHY DO I NEED THIS?

Endocrine disorders are common and can have major effects on health.

Certain glands are further segmented, with different segments producing different hormones. For example, the adrenals are divided into the **adrenal cortex** and the **adrenal medulla**. The pancreas encloses clusters of cells called the **islets of Langerhans**.

Figure 8.7 shows the location of some key glands.

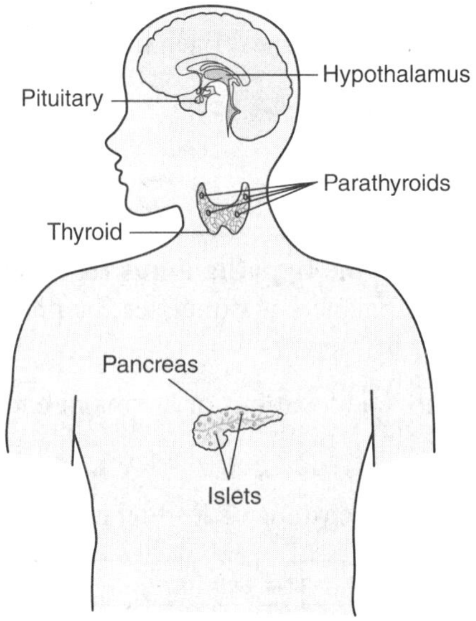

Figure 8.7 Some Endocrine Glands

Key Functions

Hormones may be classified structurally into steroids, fatty acid derivatives, amino acid derivatives, and proteins or peptides. They travel through the bloodstream after being released by the gland that produced them. Steroid hormones enter a target cell; nonsteroid hormones bind to receptors on the membrane of the target cell. Each hormone has a specific function in the body.

Table 8.7 delineates some major hormones, their sources, and their importance to body metabolism.

Table 8.7 Hormones and Their Functions

Gland	Hormone(s)	Function
adrenals	adrenalin	stimulates fight-or-flight reactions
	noradrenalin	stimulates stress response
	corticosteroids	stimulate metabolism of carbohydrates, fats, and proteins; regulate salt and water balance
hypothalamus	releasing/inhibiting hormones	stimulates the pituitary
ovaries	estrogen	stimulates female sexual development and egg production
	progesterone	stimulates growth and function of sex organs
pancreas	glucagon	increases glucose quantities in the blood
	insulin	regulates glucose amounts and conversion to glycogen and fatty acids
parathyroids	parathormone	regulates the distribution of calcium and phosphate
pineal	melatonin	synchronizes the body's day/night rhythms
pituitary	adrenocorticotrophic hormone (ACTH)	stimulates the adrenals to produce corticosteroids
	antidiuretic hormone (ADH)	stimulates reabsorption of water by the kidneys
	follicle-stimulating hormone (FSH)	stimulates the development of ovarian follicles or sperm cells in the testes
	gonadotrophins	stimulate secondary sex characteristics
	human growth hormone (HGH)	stimulates growth
	intermedin	stimulates melanocyte production
	interstitial cell-stimulating hormone (ICSH)	stimulates estrogen or testosterone production
	luteinizing hormone (LH)	stimulates ovulation
	melanocyte-stimulating hormone (MSH)	stimulates melanocytes to produce melanin
	oxytocin	stimulates uterine contraction and milk release
	prolactin (PRL)	stimulates milk production
	thyroid-stimulating hormone (TSH)	stimulates the thyroid to release thyroxin

Table 8.7 Hormones and Their Functions (*Continued*)

Gland	Hormone(s)	Function
testes	testosterone	stimulates male sexual development
thymus	thymosin	activates T cells in the immune system
thyroid	calcitonin	regulates levels of calcium and phosphate
	thyroxin	regulates the body's basal metabolic rate

Finally, here are some ways in which the endocrine system works with some other systems of the body.

The Endocrine System Works with the . . .

integumentary system	by stimulating the production of melanin
skeletal system	by stimulating skeletal growth and strength
muscular system	by influencing the development of muscle mass
nervous system	by reacting to information regarding homeostasis in the body
respiratory system	by stimulating increased respiratory activity in times of stress
digestive system	by producing and disseminating digestive enzymes and controlling the rate of digestion
urinary system	by monitoring levels of fluids to control urine production
reproductive system	by controlling sex drive and the production of gametes

Test Yourself

1. The ___________ glands release hormones in reaction to stress.

2. The hormone ___________ stimulates uterine contraction in childbirth.

3. The pineal gland produces ___________.

4. The pancreas is located behind the ___________.

5. The ____________ and ____________ are located in the forebrain.

6. The ovaries produce ____________ and ____________.

7. Insulin regulates ____________ amounts in the body.

8. Where is the gland located that stimulates the production of T cells?
   A. Above the kidneys
   B. In the thorax
   C. In the brain
   D. In the neck

9. To determine the cause of infertility, a patient might be tested for levels of which hormones?
   A. ADH and HGH
   B. MSH and TSH
   C. FSH and LH
   D. PRL and gonadotrophins

10. Overexertion and excess sweating might stimulate the release of which hormone?
   A. ADH
   B. TSH
   C. HGH
   D. PRL

Answers

1. adrenal. These glands produce adrenalin and noradrenalin.
2. oxytocin. This is one of many hormones produced by the pituitary gland.
3. melatonin. This hormone regulates sleep.
4. stomach. Review the diagram to confirm.
5. pituitary, hypothalamus. Review the diagram to confirm.
6. estrogen, progesterone. Both sex hormones are involved in the female reproductive system.
7. glucose. This hormone is created in the pancreas and regulates the use and storage of glucose.
8. B. The thymus is located in the upper thorax.
9. C. Follicle-stimulating hormone and luteinizing hormone are both involved in reproduction.
10. A. ADH prevents dehydration by helping the kidneys retain water.

CIRCULATORY SYSTEM

The organs and vessels of the circulatory system move gases, nutrients, and hormones to and from the cells in the body. The system uses the fluid blood as a tool for transport.

Key Parts

The circulatory system is made up of the heart and a vast network of blood vessels, which include veins, arteries, and capillaries. The cells in blood are created in the bone marrow and mature into red blood cells, white blood cells, or platelets. They float in a fluid called **plasma**, which contains water, proteins, sugars, and fat. (See Figure 8.8.)

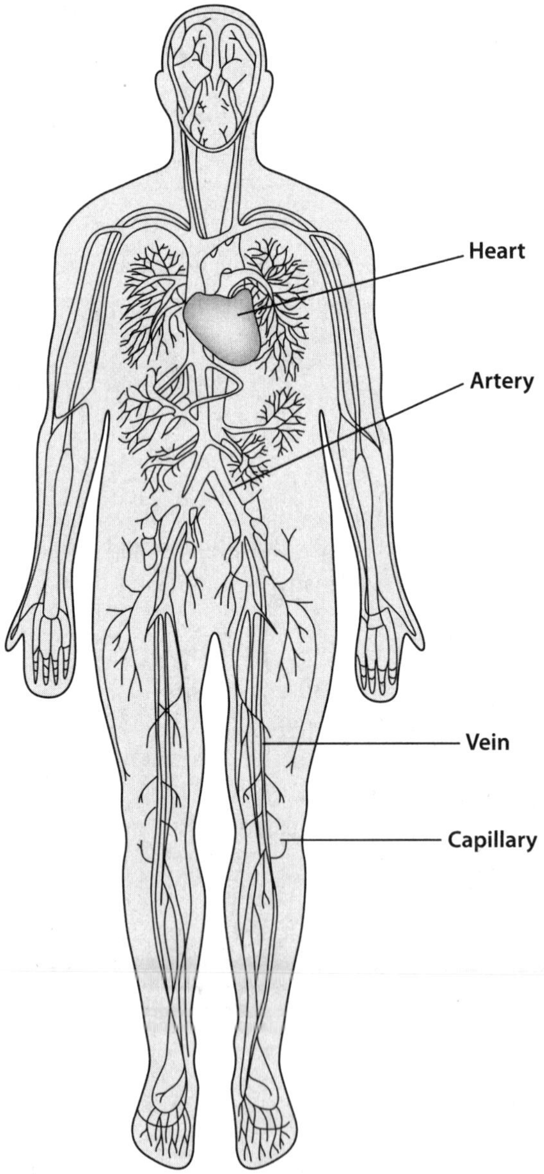

Figure 8.8 The Circulatory System

The heart controls the movement of fluids through the vessels. It contains four chambers: the **left atrium, right atrium, left ventricle**, and **right ventricle**. (See Figure 8.9.)

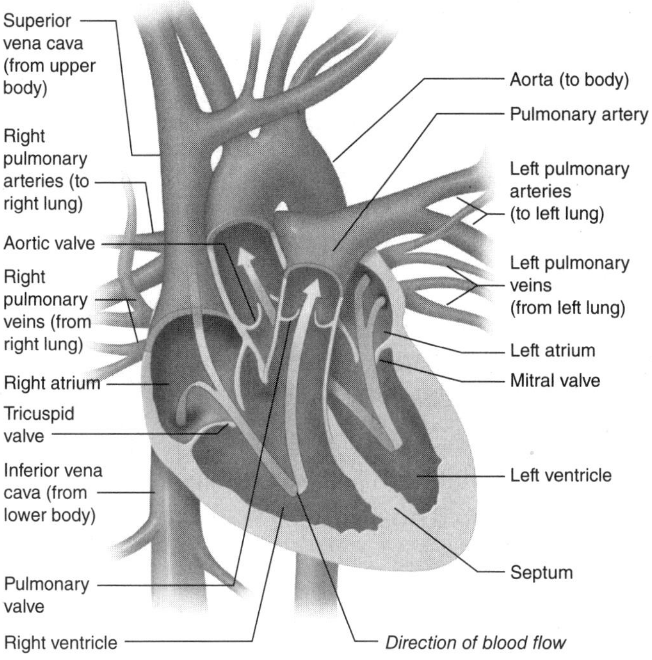

Figure 8.9 The Heart

After the body's cells have used oxygen from the blood, the inferior and superior **vena cavae** carry the oxygen-poor blood back to the heart, into the right atrium and then to the right ventricle. From there, it is pumped to the lungs via the **pulmonary artery**.

After picking up oxygen in the lungs and releasing carbon dioxide, the blood travels back to the heart, passing through the **pulmonary veins** into the left atrium and then into the left ventricle. From there, the heart moves oxygen-rich blood through the heart muscle via the **coronary arteries** and to the rest of the body through the **aorta**.

Valves open and shut to move the blood along and prevent backflow. Figure 8.10 shows how blood passes through the heart.

Atrial contraction

Right side: vena cavae → right atrium → tricuspid valve → right ventricle

Left side: pulmonary vein → left atrium → mitral valve → left ventricle

Ventricular contraction

Right side: right ventricle → pulmonic valve → pulmonary artery → lungs

Left side: left ventricle → aortic valve → aorta → body

Figure 8.10 Movement of Blood in the Heart

Key Functions

As blood circulates through the body, nutrients and oxygen are transported to cells, and carbon dioxide and other waste products are removed. **Hemoglobin** is the protein in red blood cells that performs gas exchange, carrying oxygen to the body and moving carbon dioxide to the lungs to be exhaled. Each molecule of hemoglobin contains four globin proteins and connected iron atoms. Each can carry four molecules of oxygen.

Among the many materials transported in blood are the lipoproteins that carry cholesterol. A high level of low-density lipoproteins can lead to a buildup of cholesterol in the arteries and coronary heart disease. A level of 200 mg/dL (milligram to deciliter) or lower is considered optimal in adults.

White blood cells play a role in the body's immune response. When they receive a signal (for example, from a sudden influx of interleukin 1 or histamine), they move through their blood vessel wall and migrate to the source of that signal to stimulate healing.

Platelets assist in blood clotting. They repair damaged vessels, circulating for a time until they are removed from circulation by the spleen and replaced by new cells from the bone marrow.

This chart shows ways in which the circulatory system works with some other systems of the body.

The Circulatory System Works with the . . .

skeletal system	by using cells developed in the bone marrow
muscular system	by pumping blood using cardiac muscle
nervous system	by reacting to information telling how hard the heart should beat
endocrine system	by moving hormones where they are needed in the body
lymphatic system	by working in tandem to eliminate waste products
respiratory system	by enabling gas exchange to take place in the lungs
digestive system	by moving nutrients, minerals, and vitamins to the cells that need them

Test Yourself

1. Blood moves from the left atrium to the left ventricle through the ____________.

2. A reduction in platelets might mean a reduction in the ability of blood to ____________.

3. ___________ is the protein in blood that performs gas exchange.

4. What separates the left and right chambers of the heart?

A. Ventricle
B. Septum
C. Atrium
D. Vena cavae

5. What is the function of the coronary artery?

A. It carries oxygenated blood to the left atrium.
B. It carries deoxygenated blood to the lungs.
C. It distributes white blood cells to the body.
D. It moves oxygenated blood to the heart muscle.

Answers

1. mitral valve. This movement is part of the atrial contraction.
2. clot. Spontaneous bleeding can happen if the platelet count dips too low.
3. Hemoglobin. This iron-rich protein makes up a good percentage of red blood cells. The Greek word *haima* means "blood."
4. B. The nasal septum is a cartilaginous structure that divides two chambers. The cardiac septum is a muscular structure with the same purpose.
5. D. Choice A describes the pulmonary vein, and choice B describes the pulmonary artery.

LYMPHATIC SYSTEM

Circulating near the vessels of the circulatory system but not pumped by the heart is the body's lymph. Lymph is a clear fluid filled with the white blood cells the body needs to fight off infection.

Key Parts

Graduated sizes of lymphatic vessels connect to **lymph nodes** throughout the body. Major nodes are located in front of and behind the ears, along the jaw, under the arms, and in the pelvic cavity. Other, deep-tissue nodes appear in much of the chest and abdomen.

Other important parts of the lymphatic system are the tonsils, the thymus, and the spleen. The tonsils are at the rear of the throat, the thymus is in the chest, and the spleen lies near the stomach on the left side of the abdomen.

Key Functions

The major functions of the lymphatic system are draining fluid from the tissues, transporting the lymph to nodes that filter out pathogens and other harmful substances, and then carrying filtered lymph to the superior vena cava. Once there, the lymph reenters the circulatory system.

The tonsils trap pathogens that the body inhales. Immune cells in the tonsils produce **antibodies**, blood proteins that combine chemically with and counteract invading pathogens and other substances.

The thymus is an endocrine gland that stores and develops T cells, which hunt down and destroy cells that are infected or cancerous.

The spleen filters the blood, and it stores and activates two kinds of **lymphocytes**, the white blood cells that fight infection. B cells produce antibodies that attack pathogens and toxins. T cells eliminate infected or cancerous cells.

Antibodies come in five **immunoglobulin** classes in the human body. IgA is commonly found in secretions (tears, mucous, saliva). IgD assists with B cell development. IgE helps to bind to and repel allergens. IgG is the most common antibody in the blood and protects against a variety of pathogens. IgM appears at the onset of an infection.

This chart shows ways in which the lymphatic system works with some other systems of the body.

The Lymphatic System Works with the . . .

skeletal system	by transporting white blood cells developed in the bone marrow
nervous system	by reacting to information about potential invaders
endocrine system	by transporting T cells stored in the thymus
circulatory system	by working in tandem to eliminate waste products
respiratory system	by filtering or attacking infectious agents that are inhaled
digestive system	by absorbing and transporting fatty acids and fats

Test Yourself

1. The ____________ gland is considered part of the lymphatic system.

2. ____________ are lymphocytes that attack infected cells, and ____________ are lymphocytes that attack invading pathogens.

3. The tonsils trap ____________ and produce ____________.

4. Which class of antibody is the first line of defense in an infection?

   A. IgA
   B. IgB
   C. IgG
   D. IgM

5. How does the lymphatic system differ from the circulatory system?

   A. It does not transport blood cells.
   B. It does not transport nutrients or waste.
   C. It does not feature a pump to move fluid along.
   D. It does not feature a network of large and small vessels.

Answers

1. thymus. The thymus's function as a storage unit for T cells makes it a critical part of the lymphatic/immune system.
2. T cells, B cells. Both kinds of lymphocytes are important to the body's immune system.
3. pathogens, antibodies. The tonsils are soft tissue masses that trap viruses and bacteria. They contain immune cells that produce antibodies.
4. D. IgM is usually the first antibody produced in an infection.
5. C. The heart pumps the blood, but lymph moves via contractions of the muscles and vessels that surround it.

RESPIRATORY SYSTEM

The respiratory system takes in the oxygen the cells need to survive. It expels carbon dioxide, a waste product of the cells. The upper respiratory tract is in the head and neck. The lower respiratory tract continues down into the **thorax**, or chest.

Key Parts

As air is inhaled, it follows the path shown in Figure 8.11.

Mouth or nostrils: takes in air
↓
Nasal cavity: warms and humidifies the air
↓
Pharynx: diverts air to the larynx
↓
Larynx (voice box): vibrates with passing air
↓
Trachea (windpipe): filters the air and moves mucus and dust out
↓
Primary and secondary bronchi: regulate air flow and direct air to lungs
↓
Lungs: fill with air as they relax
↓
Tertiary bronchi: direct air to bronchioles
↓
Bronchioles: dilate and contract to carry air to alveoli
↓
Alveoli: exchange gases via diffusion from the capillaries

Figure 8.11 Pathway of Air in the Body

Figure 8.12 shows the location of some of these features.

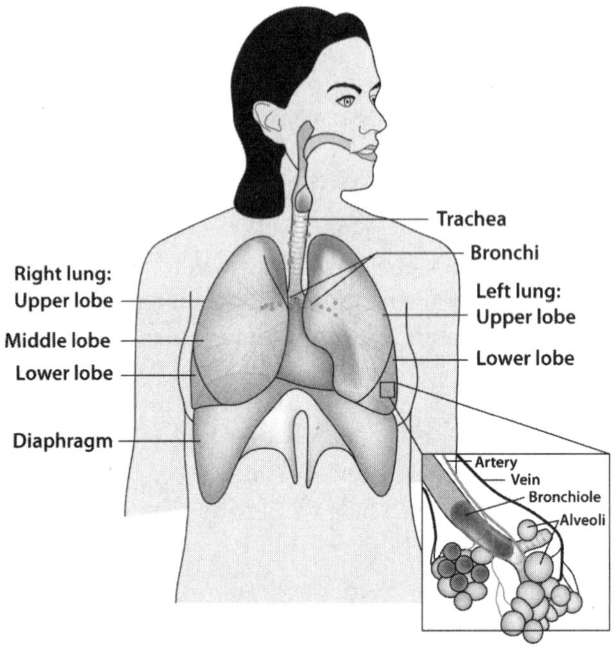

Figure 8.12 The Respiratory System

The thorax is surrounded by ribs, with a muscular partition called the **diaphragm** that separates it from the abdomen. Between each pair of ribs are **intercostal muscles**, which contract with the diaphragm to change the size of the thorax, forcing air into and out of the lungs.

Key Functions

The respiratory system works to move gases into and out of the circulatory system. The alveoli are designed to offer maximum surface area for gas exchange. With each inhale, oxygen diffuses from the alveoli into the capillaries, where the hemoglobin in red blood cells captures it and transports it to the cells of the body. Carbon dioxide moves in the opposite direction as air is exhaled.

WHY DO I NEED THIS?

Measuring respiration rates is a fundamental part of nursing care.

This chart shows ways in which the respiratory system works with some other systems of the body.

The Respiratory System Works with the . . .

integumentary system	by relying on nasal hairs to filter particles from air
skeletal system	by relying on cartilage to maintain air pathways
muscular system	by reacting to contraction and expansion of the diaphragm and intercostals
nervous system	by activating expulsion responses such as coughing or sneezing
endocrine system	by reacting to adrenaline by speeding up breathing
circulatory system	by transporting oxygen to red blood cells and capturing carbon dioxide to be exhaled
urinary system	by reacting to messages from the kidneys regarding blood oxygen levels

Test Yourself

1. Another word for the windpipe is the ____________.

2. Oxygen from the air enters the bloodstream through the ____________ in the respiratory system.

3. Inhaled air is humidified in the ____________.

4. Which system works with the respiratory system to move O_2 and CO_2?

   A. Nervous system
   B. Skeletal system
   C. Endocrine system
   D. Circulatory system

5. Which of the following describes a partial pathway of inhaled air?

   A. Larynx, pharynx, trachea, bronchiole, bronchi
   B. Pharynx, larynx, trachea, bronchi, bronchiole
   C. Trachea, larynx, pharynx, bronchi, bronchiole
   D. Pharynx, trachea, larynx, bronchiole, bronchi

Answers

1. trachea. This hollow tube begins under the larynx and runs to the sternum, where it divides into bronchi.
2. alveoli. Diffusion moves gases from alveoli to and from capillaries.
3. nasal cavity. Cold air is warmed in the nasal passages, and moisture is added to protect the lungs.

4. D. Oxygen is inhaled via the respiratory system and transported from the lungs to the rest of the body via the circulatory system. The same process happens in reverse with carbon dioxide.
5. B. Check the diagram in Figure 8.11 to review the pathway.

DIGESTIVE SYSTEM

The digestive system takes in food and converts it into energy and nutrients for the cells of the body. It consists of a series of hollow organs that extend from the head to the anus.

Key Parts

As food moves through the body, it follows the path shown in Figure 8.13.

Mouth: teeth chew; saliva digests starch

↓

Pharynx: epiglottis flap diverts food to esophagus

↓

Esophagus: swallows food and routes it to the stomach

↓

Stomach: uses stomach acid to digest protein; sends chyme to intestines

↓

Small intestine: made up of **duodenum, jejunum**, and **ileum**; peristalsis moves food along; uses digestive fluids from **pancreas** and **liver** to break down food and absorb nutrients, with some excess fluid stored in the **gallbladder**

↓

Large intestine: made up of **cecum, colon**, and **rectum**; moves undigested food, absorbs excess water, and stores stool

Figure 8.13 Pathway of Food in the Body

Figure 8.14 shows the location of some of these features.

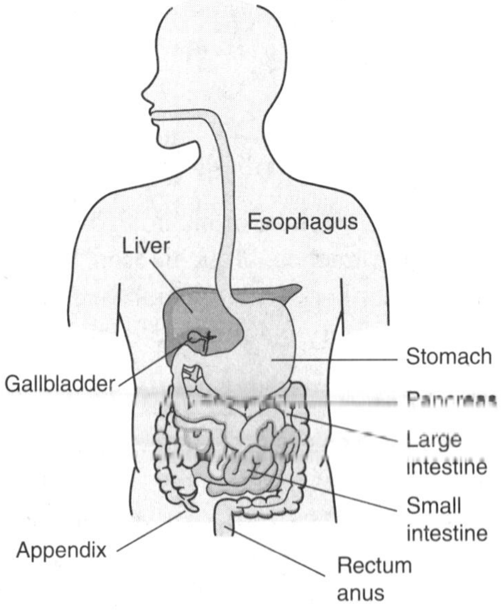

Figure 8.14 The Digestive System

Key Functions

The processes that take place along the long corridor of the digestive system include ingestion of food, secretion of enzymes, mechanical digestion, chemical digestion, absorption of molecules, and excretion of waste.

Mechanical digestion starts with chewing and continues with the churning and grinding that take place in the stomach and intestines. Chemical digestion takes place in the mouth, stomach, and small intestine using digestive juices and enzymes produced in the salivary glands, stomach, pancreas, liver, and small intestine. (See Table 8.8.)

Table 8.8 Some Major Digestive Juices and Enzymes

Produced In	Juice or Enzyme	Digests	Forms
mouth	amylase	starch	maltose
stomach	hydrochloric acid	—	activates pepsinogen into pepsin
	pepsin	protein	peptides, amino acids
pancreas	amylase	starch	maltose
	lipase	fat	fatty acids, glycerol
	protease	protein	peptides, amino acids
liver	bile	fat	fat droplets
small intestine	lactase	lactose	glucose, galactose
	maltase	maltose	glucose
	peptidase	peptides	amino acids
	sucrase	sucrase	glucose, fructose

The digestive system takes in the vitamins and nutrients that allow the body to function well. Vitamin deficiencies can cause disease and other problems. (See Table 8.9.)

Table 8.9 Some Examples of Vitamin Deficiencies

Deficiency	Result	Symptoms
vitamin A		night blindness
vitamin B1 (thiamine)	beriberi	weight loss, weakness, edema, cardiac failure
vitamin B3 (niacin)	pellagra	sun sensitivity, hair loss, rash, dementia
vitamin C	scurvy	lethargy, bone pain, skin changes, jaundice
vitamin D	rickets	bone pain, muscle weakness, skeletal deformity

This chart shows ways in which the digestive system works with some other systems of the body.

The Digestive System Works with the . . .

integumentary system	by assimilating and distributing digestive fats and oils that protect the skin and hair
skeletal system	by using the teeth to start the breakdown of food
muscular system	by relying on muscles to chew, swallow, and move the products of digestion
endocrine system	by receiving digestive enzymes from the pancreas
circulatory system	by delivering digested nutrients to be transported in the bloodstream
lymphatic system	by releasing chylomicrons of fat and fatty acids to be absorbed and transported
urinary system	by releasing excess water and undigested compounds into the urine

Test Yourself

1. The ___________ stores excess bile produced by the liver.

2. The three parts of the small intestine are the duodenum, jejunum, and ___________.

3. The enzyme that helps to break down starch is known as ___________.

4. Which of the following is *not* a site of mechanical digestion?

A. Liver
B. Mouth
C. Stomach
D. Small intestine

5. Because it is largely starch, a piece of toast starts being digested in the mouth. Where does the butter on the toast get digested?

A. Stomach
B. Esophagus
C. Small intestine
D. Large intestine

Answers

1. gallbladder. This small organ above the stomach is primarily a storage unit.
2. ileum. The ileum links the small intestine to the large intestine at the ileocecal sphincter.
3. amylase. Amylase is produced by the salivary glands and the pancreas.

4. A. The liver produces bile, which aids with chemical digestion, but food is not broken up physically in the liver.
5. C. The small intestine uses bile salts from the liver to break down the fat in butter into small globules through emulsification.

URINARY SYSTEM

The urinary system filters out fluid and waste from the bloodstream, releasing it in the form of urine. Along with other body systems, it regulates the balance of body chemicals and water.

Key Parts

Two **kidneys**, located below the ribs in the back, perform the main chores of the urinary system. Kidneys are made up of microscopic units called **nephrons**, which are each in turn composed of a **renal corpuscle** and a **renal tubule**. (*Renal* is from the Latin word for "kidney.") Within each corpuscle is a **glomerulus**, a tiny ball of capillaries. The glomerulus in the nephron is where the process of filtering takes place. Once the glomerulus filters out waste, substances pass through the renal tubules.

From the kidneys, tubes called **ureters** carry urine to the **bladder**. This elastic organ expands and contracts to store urine or release it through the **urethra**. **Sphincter muscles** contract to hold urine in or relax to release it from the bladder.

Figure 8.15 shows the parts of the urinary system in males and females plus the construction of a kidney and nephron.

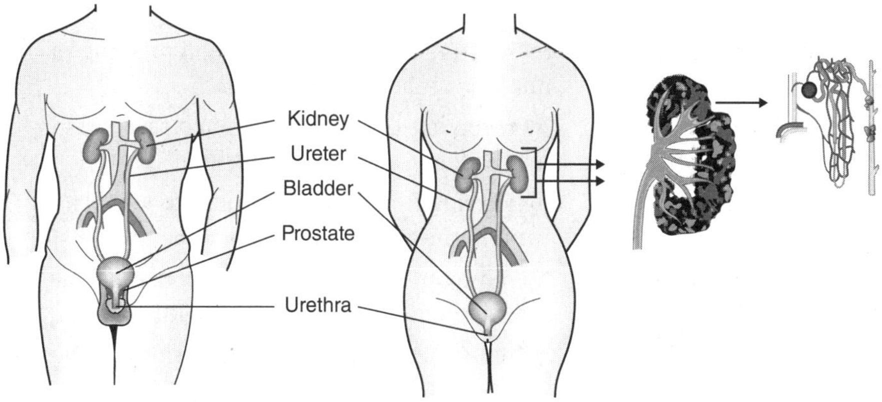

Figure 8.15 The Urinary System

Key Functions

Once the digestive system extracts nutrients from food, waste products remain in the blood and the bowel. A liquid byproduct of protein breakdown called **urea** moves from the bloodstream into the kidneys. Along with water and other waste products, urea passes from the body in the urine through the process of **micturition**, or urination. With normal fluid intake, an adult passes from 800 to 2,000 milliliters of urine daily.

The glomerulus screens out blood cells, proteins, and other needed materials, returning them to the bloodstream. Chemical regulation takes place in the renal tubules. If the body needs more sodium, potassium, or other minerals, the tubules pass these chemicals back into the bloodstream. If the body does not need such substances—if it is chemically balanced—the tubules move the excess minerals to the ureters to be expelled.

The kidneys perform a useful function in regulating blood pressure as well. When the nephrons sense that sodium has decreased and blood pressure has dropped, they release an enzyme called **renin**. Renin breaks down a peptide from the liver, which then is further converted in the lungs into a vasoconstrictor. As the heart works against this new resistance, blood pressure rises.

WHY DO I NEED THIS?

Changes in urinary outflow or content can be indicators of underlying disease.

This chart shows some ways in which the urinary system works with some other body systems.

The Urinary System Works with the . . .

integumentary system	by reacting to water loss through sweat by reducing urine flow
muscular system	by reacting to the tightening and relaxing of muscles in the bladder
nervous system	by receiving signals from stretch receptors in the bladder to initiate micturition
endocrine system	by altering function in response to signals from hormones about chemical balance
circulatory system	by removing waste from the bloodstream and assisting with blood pressure regulation
digestive system	by removing excess byproducts from the body

Test Yourself

1. What happens when the bladder relaxes? ____________

2. When would a kidney release renin? ____________

3. Another word for urination is ____________.

4. Which structure connects the kidney to the bladder?
   A. Ureter
   B. Renal tubule
   C. Urethra
   D. Sphincter
5. Damage to the glomeruli would most likely lead to which of the following symptoms?
   A. Leakage of urine
   B. Sodium imbalance
   C. Low blood pressure
   D. Excess protein in the urine

Answers

1. It releases urine. The bladder expands to store urine and relaxes to release it.
2. When blood pressure drops. Renin works with peptides to constrict blood vessels, causing the heart to work harder and raising blood pressure.
3. micturition. Other synonyms include *uresis* and *voiding*.
4. A. The ureters are tubes that move urine from each kidney to the bladder.
5. D. If the glomeruli cannot perform their screening of blood cells and protein, either may find their way into the urine.

REPRODUCTIVE SYSTEM

Whereas most body systems ensure the survival of the organism, the reproductive system ensures the survival of the species. All of the organs in this system play a part in procreation.

Key Parts

The organs of the reproductive system are often referred to in terms of their location. (See Tables 8.10 and 8.11.)

Table 8.10 External Genital Organs

Male	Female
penis: cylindrical organ attached at the root to the wall of the abdomen	**mons pubis:** fatty tissue that covers the pubic bone
scrotum: sac of skin that contains the testicles	**labia majora:** folds of tissue that enclose the external genitals
testicles: oval organs containing seminiferous tubules	**labia minora:** smaller folds that surround the openings to the urethra and vagina
	Bartholin glands: small glands next to the vaginal opening
	clitoris: sensitive projection at the upper end of the labia minora

Table 8.11 Internal Genital Organs

Male	Female
epididymis: coiled tube in the back of each testicle	**vagina:** tube connecting external genitals to the uterus
vas deferens: long tube extending from epididymis into pelvic cavity	**cervix:** lower part of the uterus extending into the vagina
seminal vesicles: sacs that attach to the vas deferens	**uterus:** muscular organ between the bladder and rectum
ejaculatory ducts: ducts created by the merger of the seminal vesicle with the vas deferens	**fallopian tubes:** two narrow tubes that extend from the upper uterus
urethra: tube that carries urine or semen from inside to outside the body	**ovaries:** oblong organs containing follicles that hold eggs (oocytes)
prostate gland: gland below the bladder	
Cowper's glands: small glands below the prostate	

Figure 8.16 shows the key parts of the reproductive system in males and females.

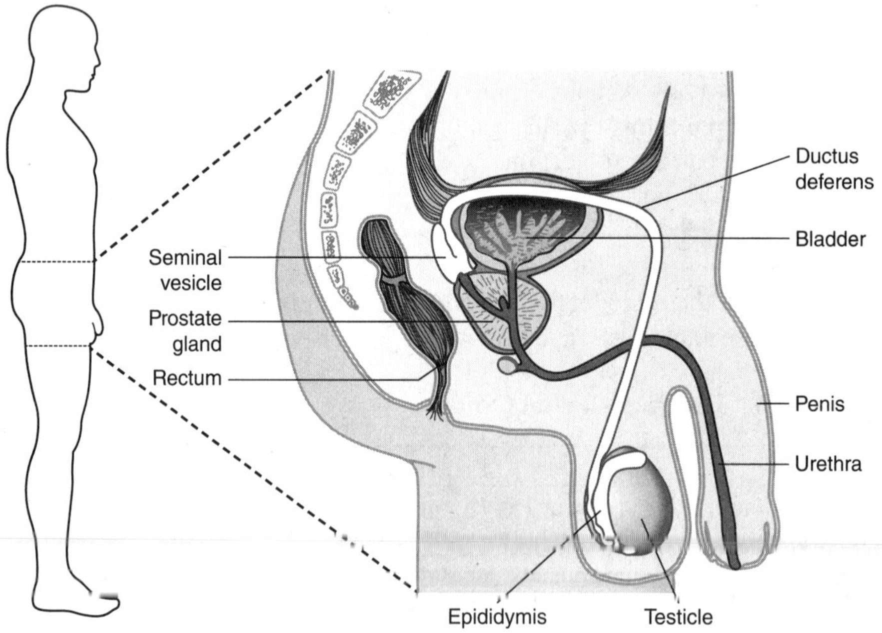

Figure 8.16*a* The Reproductive System—Male

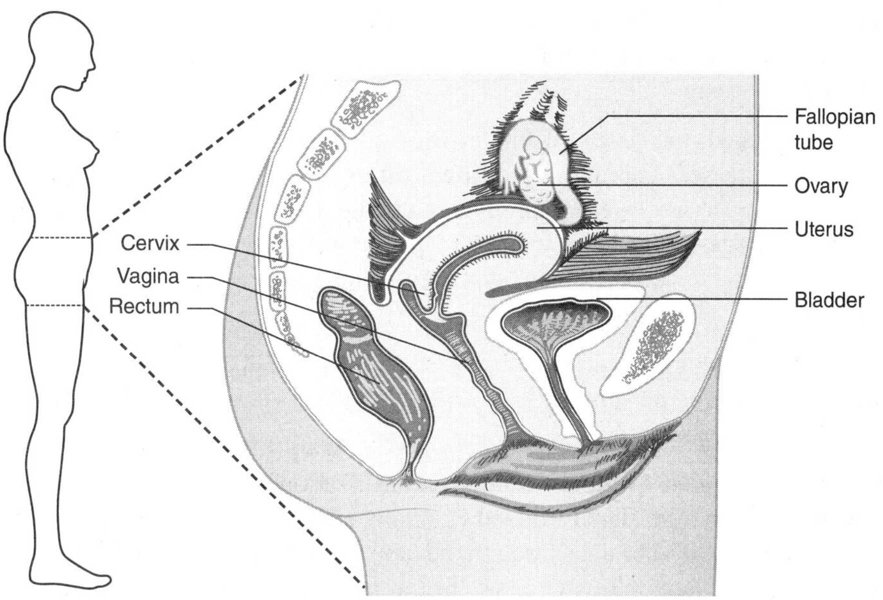

Figure 8.16*b* The Reproductive System—Female

Key Functions

Hormones regulate the reproductive system, with different hormones producing different results. The main function of the male reproductive system is to manufacture, store, and expel sperm, the male gamete. To that end, **follicle-stimulating hormone** stimulates sperm production, aided by **luteinizing hormone**, which helps with the production of testosterone.

Production of testosterone and sperm takes place in the testes (testicles), with sperm produced in the seminiferous tubules. The scrotum keeps the testes at a temperature ideal for sperm production and development.

Sperm from the testes move to the epididymis to mature. They remain there until the male is sexually aroused, at which point contractions move the mature sperm into the vas deferens to be transported to the urethra for ejaculation. Fructose from the seminal vesicles and additional fluid from the prostate provide the sperm with energy and make up most of the semen that is ejaculated. The Cowper's glands (or bulbourethral glands) produce another fluid that lubricates the urethra, making passage by the sperm easier.

In the female, luteinizing hormone (LH) and follicle-stimulating hormone (FSH) have different results. They stimulate the ovaries to produce estrogen, progesterone, and androgens.

Menstruation, the shedding of the **endometrium**, or inner lining of the uterus, is regulated by these luteinizing hormones and follicle-stimulating hormones when fertilization does not take place. Day 1 of the menstrual cycle is the start of the **follicular phase**. Hormone levels are low, the endometrium breaks down, and menstrual bleeding takes place. As menstruation continues, the follicle-stimulating hormone level begins to increase, stimulating follicles in the ovaries. Only one follicle will produce estrogen and develop an egg.

An increase in luteinizing and follicle-stimulating hormones spurs the **ovulatory phase**. Luteinizing hormone causes ovulation, rupturing the follicle and releasing one egg.

Having peaked, the levels of luteinizing and follicle-stimulating hormones quickly decrease, resulting in the **luteal phase**. The ruptured follicle closes up and forms a progesterone-producing **corpus luteum**. If the egg is fertilized, this progesterone helps to prepare the uterus for an embryo. If the egg is not fertilized, the corpus luteum stops producing progesterone, and the cycle begins again.

By the time a woman reaches puberty, she has about 300,000 eggs left in her body. Perhaps 0.1 percent of those will be released via ovulation during her reproductive years.

When a sperm fuses with an egg during fertilization, that action takes place in the fallopian tube. The fertilized egg, now a **zygote**, begins to divide and moves over a period of days through the tube to the uterus, where it implants. (If the egg implants elsewhere, say in the fallopian tube, this is termed an **ectopic pregnancy** and requires medical intervention.) The uterine lining thickens, and a plug of mucus seals the cervix to protect the growing embryo and its surrounding placenta. The placenta starts to produce the hormone hCG, which may be detected in a pregnancy test. As the embryo grows to become a fetus, at about nine weeks post-conception, the uterus expands to hold it. The cervix and vagina increase both in blood supply and in elastic tissue.

As the fetus reaches full term, usually between weeks 37 and 40, the mucus plug at the cervix dissolves, and the cervix begins to dilate. During labor, strong muscle contractions in the uterus move the baby through the cervix, down into the vagina, and through the vaginal opening to be born.

This chart shows some ways in which the reproductive system works with some other body systems.

The Reproductive System Works with the . . .

skeletal system	by producing hormones that aid with maturation of the body and maintaining healthy bone mass
muscular system	by producing testosterone, which builds muscles
nervous system	by receiving signals from the brain that contribute to sexual response
endocrine system	by producing and releasing gametes and developing secondary sex characteristics based on signals from hormones
circulatory system	by receiving nutrition for the growing fetus through the maternal bloodstream

Test Yourself

1. In what part of the body does fertilization take place? ___________

2. In what part of the body are sperm produced? ___________

3. An ectopic pregnancy may occur if the fertilized egg ___________.

4. Which system works with the reproductive system to produce secondary sex characteristics?

A. Skeletal system
B. Nervous system
C. Endocrine system
D. Circulatory system

5. In humans, when does the zygote implant in the uterus?

A. Immediately upon conception
B. Several days after fertilization
C. Toward the end of the first trimester
D. After the cervix is sealed

Answers

1. fallopian tubes. The egg spends about a day hovering at the edge of a fallopian tube, where it may be fertilized if sperm reach it.
2. seminiferous tubules. These tubes in the testicles are the site of sperm production.
3. implants outside the uterus. The typical ectopic pregnancy, which is always a medical emergency, takes place in the fallopian tubes.
4. C. Hormones produced by the endocrine glands stimulate the production of secondary sex characteristics.
5. B. The movement of the zygote can take between one and two weeks between initial fertilization and implantation in the uterus.

CHAPTER 9

Physics

CONTENTS

Only a few programs will require you to include the Physics module in your A2 test. The following pages give you a brief overview of some of the major topics that may appear in that module.

SPEED, VELOCITY, ACCELERATION AND FRICTION

The position of objects in space and the distances those objects move inform the science of velocity and acceleration.

Speed

Speed is a **scalar** quantity, meaning that it has magnitude but not direction. Speed measures the rate of change in position—the rate of motion. Average speed, or rate, is typically reported in terms of distance and time:

$s = d/t$ or $r = d/t$

For example, the average speed of a vehicle might be 35 mi/h, or 35 mph.

Velocity

Velocity is a **vector** quantity, meaning that it has both magnitude and direction. Like speed, velocity measures the rate of motion, but specific to a particular direction. In other words, it measures the rate of **displacement** over time:

$$v = d/t$$

For example, the average velocity of a vehicle might be 35 mph south.

Acceleration

Acceleration is a vector quantity that measures the rate of change of velocity. Acceleration requires the application of a force.

When you measure acceleration, you divide velocity by time. Suppose you start with an object traveling north at a velocity of 10 m/s. Five seconds later, the object is traveling north at a velocity of 20 m/s. Think: Acceleration equals the change in velocity divided by the change in time.

$$a = \frac{\Delta v}{\Delta t}$$

The change in velocity is 20 m/s – 10 m/s, or 10 m/s. The change in time is 5 seconds. If you plug your numbers into the equation, you get

$$a = \frac{10 \text{ m/s}}{5 \text{ s}}$$

So the answer is given in the format distance/time^2. For this problem, it would be

$$a = 2 \text{ m/s}^2$$

Friction

Friction is a force that opposes motion between two surfaces that are in contact with each other. It arises due to the microscopic irregularities present on the surface of objects. When two surfaces are in contact and one of them is in motion, these irregularities interlock with each other, causing resistance to the motion. This resistance force is known as frictional force.

The frictional force depends on the nature of the surfaces in contact, the force pressing them together, and the relative speed between them. Friction can be useful, such as in providing traction between car tires and the road or allowing us to grip objects. However, it can also be a hindrance, such as in causing wear and tear in machinery or slowing down the motion of objects.

Test Yourself

For items 1–3, circle the correct answers in parentheses.

1. (Velocity/Speed) is a vector quantity that includes distance.

2. The measurement 25 ft/s could measure (speed/acceleration).

3. In the equation $v = d/t$, d stands for (distance/displacement).

4. You drive 45 miles west in an hour and then another 15 miles west in half an hour. What is your average speed for the trip? ____________

5. A race car accelerates uniformly from 20.5 m/s to 38.5 m/s in 3 seconds. What is its acceleration?

   A. 6 m/s^2
   B. 9 m/s^2
   C. 18 m/s^2
   D. 19.6 m/s^2

Answers

1. Velocity. Speed is a scalar quantity.
2. speed. Acceleration would involve seconds squared.
3. displacement. Velocity includes direction, so the *d* stands for displacement, not simply direction.
4. 40 m/h. Add the distances and divide by 1.5 hours.
5. A. Subtract the initial velocity from the final velocity and divide by 3 seconds.

MOMENTUM

Objects have mass. When objects with mass move, we say that they have momentum, which essentially means "mass in motion."

Linear momentum, or momentum in one direction, is referred to as p in this equation:

$$p = mv$$

In other words, momentum is the product of the mass of an object in motion and that object's vector velocity. Because linear momentum is a vector quantity, it is measured in mass-distance per time. Usually this is calculated in kilogram-meters per second (kg·m/s).

Since both mass and velocity figure into momentum, changing one variable changes the product. If a large object and a small object are traveling at the same speed, the one with the greater mass will have the greater momentum.

Similarly, if two objects with the same exact mass are traveling, and the first has a velocity twice that of the other, the momentum of the first object will be twice that of the other.

Test Yourself

For items 1–3, circle the correct answers in parentheses.

1. If a rolling cart's mass is doubled by adding a load, but its velocity remains steady, its momentum will be (halved/doubled).

2. In the quantity 36 kg·m/s, "m/s" represents (vector velocity/momentum).

3. Momentum is (directly/indirectly) proportional to an object's velocity.

4. Which has the greater momentum, a train traveling at 90 km/h or a pickup truck traveling at 90 km/h? ___________

5. What is the momentum of a 12-kg ball rolling eastward at 4 m/s?

   A. 3 kg/m
   B. 3 kg·m/s
   C. 48 m/s
   D. 48 kg·m/s

Answers

1. doubled. Try substituting numbers to check: If the mass is 2 kg, and the velocity is 3 m/s, doubling the mass to 4 will double the velocity from 6 to 12 kg·m/s.
2. vector velocity. The unit m/s equals distance per time.
3. directly. Momentum is also directly proportional to the object's mass.
4. train. The train has greater mass, so it has greater momentum at the same velocity.
5. D. Momentum is the product of mass and velocity, measured in mass-distance per time.

NEWTON'S LAWS

After developing his theories of gravitation, Sir Isaac Newton turned his attention to the physics of motion. His three laws of motion are still important to our understanding of force, direction, speed, acceleration, and momentum.

- **First Law of Motion (the law of inertia):** An object at rest will remain at rest unless acted upon by an unbalanced force. An object in motion will remain in motion in a straight line and a steady velocity unless acted upon by an unbalanced force.

- **Second Law of Motion:** Acceleration is the product of a force on a mass. The greater the mass, the greater the force. The greater the force, the greater the acceleration. For any object with constant mass m, the force F is the product of mass times acceleration:

  $F = ma$

  Replacing the variables with metric units, you find

  $1 \text{ N (Newton)} = 1 \text{ kg}\cdot\text{m/s}^2$

- **Third Law of Motion:** For every action (or force), there is an equal and opposite reaction.

Test Yourself

1. A branch falls from a tree and hits the ground. This is an example of Newton's ___________ Law of Motion.

2. When a balloon pops, air rushes out and the balloon streaks away. This is an example of Newton's ___________ Law of Motion.

3. The unit that measures force is the ___________.

4. Given force and acceleration, how do you determine mass?

   A. Multiply force by acceleration.
   B. Divide force by acceleration.
   C. Multiply mass by acceleration.
   D. Divide acceleration by force.

5. A force of 24 N is pushing an object with a mass of 4 kg. What is the acceleration of the object?

   A. 6 m/s^2
   B. 12 m/s^2
   C. 16 m/s^2
   D. 96 m/s^2

Answers

1. First. The branch is the object in motion; it remains in motion until it strikes another object, the ground.
2. Third. The air moving one way will push the balloon the opposite way.
3. Newton. One Newton equals 1 kilogram-meter per second squared. It is the force required to move an object with mass 1 kg 1 meter per second per second.
4. B. The formula for force is $F = ma$, so the formula for mass is $m = F/a$.
5. A. Divide force by mass to get acceleration.

LINEAR AND ROTATIONAL MOTION

The motion we have described thus far in the chapter is motion in one direction. There are other types of motion that are important in physics.

Linear Motion

Linear motion, as you have seen, is defined as a "change in position." It is described using measures of distance (how far the object, point, or particle travels) and displacement (the overall change in position of the object, point, or particle).

When no acceleration takes place, and an object has constant velocity in a straight line, position changes linearly over time:

$$d = vt$$

In the case of a falling object, however, acceleration is caused by gravity, which pulls objects toward the Earth's surface with an acceleration of 9.8 m/s^2. (If friction in the form of air resistance exists, it may slow the acceleration of large, light objects.)

Imagine that you are repairing a roof. If you climb to the roof of a 9-meter house and drop a roofing nail, the nail will accelerate in free fall at 9.8 m/s^2. If you accidentally kick your hammer off the roof, though, the problem changes and becomes a question of **projectile motion**, because the hammer moves horizontally as well as vertically, in a **parabolic** shape.

These "Big Four" equations (also known as "kinematic formulas") are used by physicists to determine information about motion when acceleration is constant. (See Table 9.1.)

Table 9.1 Big Four Equations

Equation	Use when . . .
$v_t = v_i + at$	you do not need to know displacement
$d = \left(\frac{vt + vi}{2}\right)t$	you do not need to know acceleration
$d = v_i t + \frac{1}{2} at^2$	you do not need to know initial velocity
$v_t^2 = v_i^2 + 2ad$	you do not need to know time

KEY: d = displacement
t = time
a = constant acceleration
v_i = initial velocity
v_t = terminal velocity

Think about the roofing nail you dropped from the 9-m rooftop. How fast was it going after 0.7 second?

Because the object was dropped, it has no initial velocity. You know that $v_i = 0$. You know that gravity gave the nail a constant acceleration of 9.8 m/s^2. You know the time: 0.7 second. You do not need to know displacement, so you can choose the first equation.

$$v_t = 0 + (9.8)(0.7) = 6.86 \text{ m/s}$$

So the nail accelerated from a velocity of 0 m/s to 6.86 m/s in 0.7 second.

How fast was the nail going when it hit the ground? Here you do not need to know time. You know initial velocity, acceleration, and displacement (9 m). You can choose the fourth equation.

$$v_t^2 = 2(9.8 \times 9) = \sqrt{176.4} \text{ m/s} \approx 13.28 \text{ m/s}$$

If you picture the nail picking up speed as it falls, the variation between its speed at the beginning (0 m/s), after 0.7 second (6.86 m/s), and at the end (13.28 m/s) makes sense.

Rotation

Rotational motion, rather than dealing with change in position, deals with change in angle, which is represented symbolically using the Greek letter theta (θ).

Objects in rotation spin around an **axis of rotation**. You may use an angle to measure how far the object has traveled. In physics problems, the angle is usually measured in **radians** rather than in degrees, with 360° equal to 2π rad, 180° equal to π rad, 90° equal to $\pi/2$ rad, and 0° equal to 0 rad.

As objects move through a circle, the speed of that movement—how quickly the angle changes—is represented as **angular velocity**, symbolized by the Greek letter omega (ω). It is usually calculated in radians per second. The rate of change of ω is the object's **angular acceleration**, symbolized by the Greek letter alpha (α). It is calculated in radians per second squared.

Figure 9.1 shows how the measurements work together.

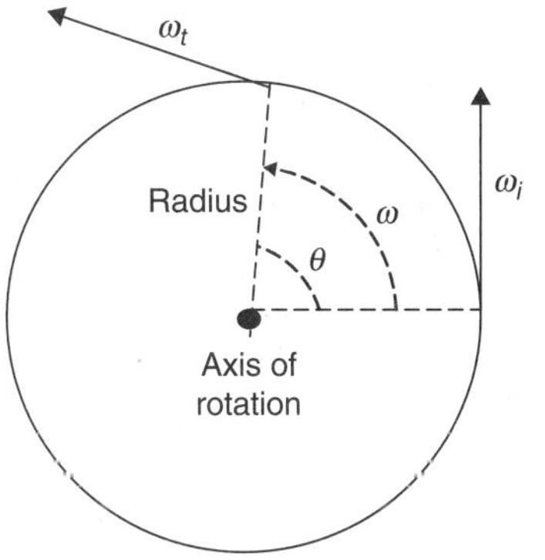

Figure 9.1 Measuring Rotational Motion

Here the object is rotating counterclockwise around an axis of rotation, beginning at initial velocity and ending at terminal velocity. The change in angle is theta, and the angular velocity is omega.

It is important to recognize that any object moving in a circle is accelerating, even if it is at a constant speed, in what is called **uniform circular motion**. Although the object's velocity does not change, its direction constantly changes as it rotates around an axis.

The force that causes an object to rotate is referred to as **torque**. Torque is measured in Newton-meters (N·m). It may be represented by the Greek letter tau (τ). The force that holds the object in a circular path, pulling toward the center of the circle and preventing the object from flying away, is **centripetal force**. It is expressed mathematically this way:

$$F_c = mv^2/r$$

In other words, centripetal force equals mass times velocity squared divided by the radius of the path of motion.

In the case of two identical go-karts on a track, one in the outside lane, and one in the inside lane, with both at the same velocity, the go-kart on the inside lane has a greater **centripetal acceleration** because it has a shorter radius. In the case of a rotating disc such as a CD, velocity increases the farther a point on the disc is from the axis.

Centripetal acceleration may be calculated using this formula:

$$a_c = v^2/r \qquad \text{or} \qquad a_c = \omega^2 r$$

Unlike angular acceleration, centripetal acceleration uses distance units of measure, not radians.

The equations used to calculate rotation are analogous to those used to calculate linear movement, from velocity = distance/time to the equations in Table 9.2.

Table 9.2 Rotational Equations

Equation	Use when . . .
$\omega_t = \omega_i + \alpha t$	you do not need to know displacement
$\theta = \left(\frac{\omega t + \omega i}{2}\right)t$	you do not need to know acceleration
$\theta_t = \theta_i + \omega_i t + ½\, \alpha t^2$	you do not need to know initial velocity
$\omega_t^2 = \omega_i^2 + 2\alpha\theta$	you do not need to know time

KEY: θ = displacement

t = time

α = constant acceleration

ω_i = initial velocity

ω_t = terminal velocity

Test Yourself

For items 1–3, circle the correct answers in parentheses.

1. A car rounds a curve too quickly and skids. This is an illustration of (angular acceleration/centripetal force).

2. A baseball leaves a pitching machine and arcs before it hits the ground. This is an example of (projectile motion/angular velocity).

3. The change in angle as an object rotates is indicated with the letter (θ/ω).

4. A ball bearing is dropped into a long, vertical vacuum tube. What is its velocity after 2 seconds?

   A. 4.9 m/s
   B. 9.8 m/s
   C. 19.6 m/s
   D. 96.04 m/s

5. A race car travels around a track in 60 seconds. What is its angular velocity?

   A. $\pi/30$ rad/s
   B. $\pi/60$ rad/s
   C. π rad/s
   D. 360 m/s

Answers

1. centripetal force. Centripetal force is proportional to the square of velocity, so if you double your driving speed, you need four times the force to keep your car on the road. Excess velocity requires stronger centripetal force.
2. projectile motion. The movement is both horizontal and vertical, forming a parabola.
3. θ. Omega represents angular velocity.
4. C. You don't need to know displacement here, so use $v_t = v_i + at$. Acceleration in a vacuum tube is simply the pull of gravity, or 9.8 m/s^2.
   $v_t = 0 + (9.8 \times 2)$, so $v_t = 19.6$ m/s
5. A. The car travels 2π radians (a complete circle of 360°) in 60 seconds. Its angular velocity is equal to distance (position angle) divided by time: $2\pi/60$, or $\pi/30$ radians per second.

KINETIC AND POTENTIAL ENERGY

Energy is a physical property of objects. It may be defined as the ability of an object to cause change. It is measured in **Joules** (J):

$$1 \text{ Joule} = 1 \text{ kg} \cdot \text{m}^2/\text{s}^2$$

Kinetic Energy

Kinetic energy is the energy of an object in motion. It is affected by the mass and the velocity of the object.

$$K.E. = \tfrac{1}{2}mv^2$$

So a 500-g block moving at 4 m/s would have kinetic energy as follows:

$$K.E. = \tfrac{1}{2}(0.5)(4)^2 = \tfrac{1}{2}(8) = 4 \text{ Joules}$$

A 2,000-kg car moving at 25 m/s would have kinetic energy as follows:

$$K.E. = \tfrac{1}{2}(2{,}000)(25)^2 = \tfrac{1}{2}(1{,}250{,}000) = 625{,}000 \text{ Joules}$$

Kinetic energy may be transferred, as when a rolling bowling ball hits a stationary pin.

Potential Energy

Potential energy is the energy an object has due to its position or state, including its inner tension or electrical charge. Potential energy may be thought of as "stored energy." Examples include the energy in a sled perched at the top of a hill or the energy in a drawn string on a bow before it is released. Batteries and explosives hold potential chemical energy, and certain objects may also contain potential radiant, thermal, magnetic, or sound energy.

Potential energy increases as an object moves farther away from the object pulling on it. An object high above the Earth has more potential energy than the same object close to the ground, because gravity is pulling it downward. So if you drop a ball from a ladder, its potential energy decreases as its kinetic energy increases. Part of its potential energy is converted to kinetic energy. If you toss a ball in the air, the opposite happens. Its potential energy increases as its kinetic energy decreases.

On the other hand, two like objects at the same distance from the ground have similar potential energy. If one object has greater mass than the other, it also has greater potential energy.

For gravitational force, the formula for potential energy is as follows:

$$P.E. = mgh$$

In this formula, m is mass (in kg), g is acceleration due to gravity (9.8 m/s^2), and h is the height of the object in meters.

Work is typically measured as the product of force and distance, or displacement:

$$W = Fd$$

However, not all objects displace energy in one specific direction. Springs are an example of objects that have a complicated motion and a lot of elastic potential energy. We assign a constant, *k*, in units of Newtons per meter, to springs to define how rigid they are. The force required to stretch the spring is directly proportional to the amount of stretch, *x*:

$$F = kx$$

So if a force equal to 12 kilograms stretches a spring 3 centimeters, the constant is 12/3, or 4. You can then apply that constant to determine how far the spring will stretch given a force of 30 kilograms: 30/4, or 7.5 centimeters.

Test Yourself

For items 1–3, circle the correct answers in parentheses.

1. A pendulum has the most potential energy at the (top/bottom) of its swing.

2. Object A may have greater potential energy than object B if object A has (greater/less) mass.

3. As an acorn falls from a tree, its (kinetic/potential) energy increases as its (kinetic/potential) energy decreases.

4. Which has the greatest potential energy?

A. A glider on top of a cliff
B. A kite in a child's hand
C. A ball in a catcher's glove
D. A rubber band

5. Which has the greatest kinetic energy?

A. A 200-kg block moving at 5 m/s
B. A 600-kg block moving at 2 m/s
C. A 25-kg block moving at 40 m/s
D. A 15-kg block moving at 60 m/s

Answers

1. top. It has the most kinetic energy at the very bottom of the arc.
2. greater. Both mass and height add to potential energy.
3. kinetic, potential. Potential energy grows with distance from the ground, and kinetic energy grows with velocity.
4. A. All four have potential energy, but the glider, with more mass and greater height, has the most.
5. D. This is simple math: $K.E. = \frac{1}{2}mv^2$. Because the formula uses the square of velocity, a change in velocity affects the result more than a change in mass does. Choice A has kinetic energy of 2,500 Joules. Choice B has kinetic energy of 1,200 Joules. Choice C has kinetic energy of 20,000 Joules. Choice D has kinetic energy of 27,000 Joules.

FORCE OF ATTRACTION

The force that draws objects together is called "force of attraction." It is measured in Newtons, as other forces are. Forces of attraction include gravitational force, magnetic force, electrostatic force, and electric force.

The formula for gravitational attraction is as follows:

$$F_g = Gm_1m_2/d^2$$

G is the gravitational constant: 6.67×10^{-11} Nm^2/kg^2. The masses of the objects being attracted are represented by m_1 and m_2, and d is the distance between them.

The force between magnets is more complicated to calculate and depends on the magnet. All magnets are dipole, with force of attraction greatest at the poles. The north pole of a magnet is attracted to Earth's North Pole, and the south pole of a magnet is attracted to Earth's South Pole. As two magnetic objects approach each other, a force of attraction pulls the opposite poles together.

French physicist Charles-Augustin de Coulomb studied various forms of attraction in the eighteenth century. He determined that the force of attraction between two magnetic poles is directly proportional to the product of the strength of the magnets and inversely proportional to the square of the distance between them.

Coulomb's important law regarding electrostatic attraction is discussed later in this chapter.

Test Yourself

1. To the nearest hundredth, the gravitational constant is ___________ × 10^{-11} Nm^2/kg^2.

2. In any bar magnet, the strongest force is at the ___________.

3. In the formula for gravitational attraction, *d* represents the ___________ between ___________.

4. The force of attraction between two objects is affected by ___________.

   A. mass and direction
   B. distance and mass
   C. displacement
   D. electrostatic force

5. Two magnets of equal strength lie 2 meters apart. If you reduce that distance by half, what happens to the force of attraction?

   A. It is halved.
   B. It is doubled.
   C. It increases by half.
   D. It is quadrupled.

Answers

1. 6.67. This constant not only figures into Newton's law of universal gravitation, but it is also key to Einstein's theory of relativity.
2. ends or poles. Any kind of magnet has its strongest magnetic force at the poles and its weakest toward the middle.
3. distance, two objects. The mass of the objects is represented by m_1 and m_2.
4. B. The formula contains measures of mass and distance along with the gravitational constant.
5. D. The relationship between force and distance is an inverse square relationship. As distance doubles, force reduces by a factor of four. As distance is halved, force increases by a factor of four.

DENSITY AND BUOYANCY

The density of a substance is the relationship between its mass and its volume.

$$d = m/v$$

Density is usually measured in grams per cubic centimeter, with the density of water equal to 1 g/cm^3. The ratio of the density of a liquid to the density of water at a certain temperature is called that liquid's **specific gravity**.

An object's buoyancy is its ability to float. If the object floats in a fluid (liquid or gas), it is positively buoyant. If it sinks, it is negatively buoyant. Buoyancy depends directly on the density of the material.

If an object has density less than 1 g/cm^3, it will float in water. The greater its density, the more of it will sink below the surface of the water. Gravitational force is pulling downward while **buoyancy force** is holding the object up.

Picture a cylindrical glass of water. The **pressure** at the bottom of the glass is greater than the pressure at the top. Pressure equals force divided by area.

$$P = F/A$$

Now picture a cube submerged but floating in the glass of water. The pressure exerted upward is greater than the pressure exerted downward on the cube. The buoyant force remains the same as the cube gets waterlogged and sinks farther in the glass, because pressure at the top and bottom increase by the same amount.

Archimedes discovered that it is possible to measure volume (and therefore, density) by measuring displaced fluid. This **displacement method** involved putting an object into water and recording the rise of the water level. The object displaces a volume of water equal to its own volume. Another way of looking at **Archimedes' Principle** is that the buoyant force acting on an object in any fluid equals the weight of the volume of fluid displaced by the object.

Temperature has an effect on density. Increasing the temperature of a substance increases its volume while decreasing its density. Such changes are far more evident in gases than in liquids or solids.

Test Yourself

For questions 1–3, circle the correct answer in parentheses.

1. A stick with a mass of 32 grams and a volume of 48 cm^3 will (float/sink) in a lake.

2. If force is applied equally to two objects, the pressure exerted will be (greater/less) on the object with the greater area.

3. Archimedes found that the buoyant force on a submerged object equals the (weight of the displaced fluid/density of the object).

4. When would water have the greatest density?

A. At boiling temperature
B. At simmering temperature
C. At lukewarm temperature
D. At just above freezing

5. In order for a balloon to rise in the air, what must be true?

   A. The balloon must be filled with something lighter than air.
   B. The balloon must have a surface area greater than its volume.
   C. The balloon must be as close as possible to a spherical shape.
   D. The balloon must be launched with a burst of air pressure.

Answers

1. **float.** The density is mass divided by volume—32/48 g/cm^3 (or 2/3 g/cm^3)—making it less dense than water.
2. **less.** Plug examples into the equation $P = F/A$ to check.
3. **weight of the displaced fluid.** The weight of the fluid displaced by the object equals the upward buoyant force on that object.
4. **D.** Density decreases with a rise in temperature. Water is most dense at about 4°C.
5. **A.** The balloon itself is heavier than air, as you can tell before it is inflated. In order to float, it must be filled with a large volume of something very light. This could be helium, a gas with minimal density, or it could be heated air.

WAVE CLASSIFICATION AND THEORY

A wave may be thought of as an organized, regular disturbance of a state of equilibrium or rest. Examples range from ripples from a rock dropped into a pond to visible light when a switch is thrown.

Measurement of Waves

Simple waves are waves that are constant—their motion can be described by a single sine or cosine function. Key measurements involve the **wavelength** (λ), which is the distance from the crest of one wave to the crest of another, and the **amplitude**, which is the height in meters from the rest position to the crest or trough (or half the wave height). (See Figure 9.2.)

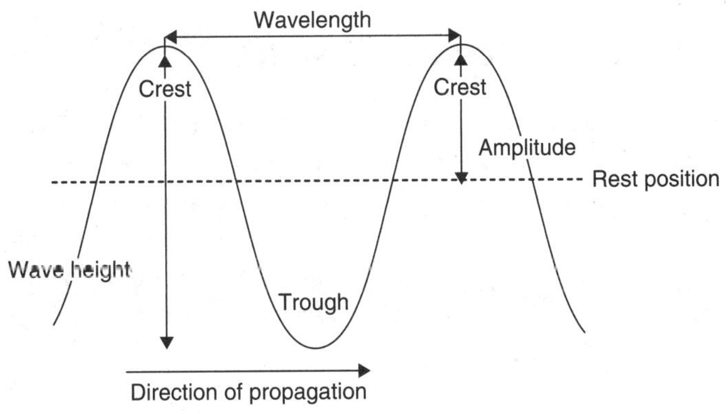

Figure 9.2 Simple Waves

The time in seconds that elapses between one crest and the next is the **period** (T) of a wave. Its reciprocal is the **frequency** (f) of the wave, the rate at which the wave repeats itself, usually given in Hertz (Hz). And the **velocity** (v) or speed of the wave is the rate at which the crest travels in meters per second.

Period = 1/frequency, or $T = 1/f$

Frequency = 1/period, or $f = 1/T$

Velocity = frequency × wavelength, or $v = f\lambda$

If you know that the period of a pendulum is 3.2 seconds, you can determine its frequency.

$f = 1/3.2 = 0.3125$ Hz

If you know that the frequency of a wave is 40 Hz, and its wavelength is 50 centimeters, you can determine its velocity.

$v = 40(0.5) = 20$ m/s (Remember to convert centimeters to meters!)

Wave Classification

Waves may be classified by their energy transfer or by their direction. Here are four types of waves.

- **Mechanical waves** move through a medium, which might be water, air, or earth. Examples include tsunamis, sound waves, and seismic waves (earthquakes).
- **Electromagnetic waves** do not require a medium in order to travel. Examples include UV light, x-rays, and radio waves.
- **Transverse waves** are waves in which the direction of the wave is at right angles to the direction of energy transfer. For example, if the wave moves from left to right, its **oscillations** move up and down. Examples include a plucked guitar string, a ripple on a pond, and an S seismic wave.
- **Longitudinal waves** are waves in which the direction of the wave is parallel to the direction of energy transfer. Examples include sound waves, waves in a stretched spring, and a P seismic wave.

Sound and Light Waves

Sound travels via mechanical, longitudinal waves, also known as **compressional waves**. As a compressional wave passes through the air, it moves air particles together and apart. The number of such compressions per second is the frequency of a sound wave. The faster the vibration, the higher the frequency of the wave. The higher the frequency of a sound wave, the higher the pitch of the sound. The greater the amplitude of a sound wave, the louder the sound.

> **WHY DO I NEED THIS?**
> *Ultrasound uses high frequency sound waves to create images of soft tissues.*

Light waves are a form of electromagnetic wave. On the electromagnetic spectrum, visible light has a wavelength and frequency greater than that of infrared and less than that of ultraviolet light. (See Figure 9.3.)

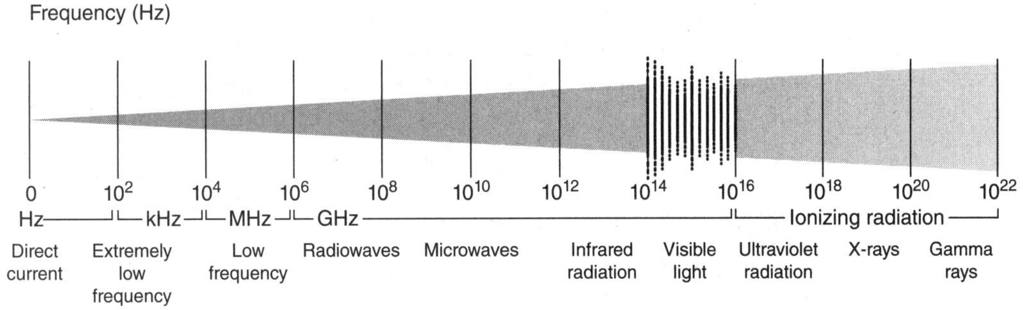

Figure 9.3 Electromagnetic Spectrum

Test Yourself

For questions 1–3, circle the correct answer in parentheses.

1. The (period/frequency) of a wave is the time it takes to complete one cycle.

2. The frequency of (x-rays/microwaves) is lower than that of visible light.

3. When you shake out a rug, the waves that are formed are (parallel/perpendicular) to the direction of energy transfer.

4. In 42 seconds, a pendulum swings back and forth 10 times. What is the period of the pendulum?

   A. 42 s
   B. 4.2 s
   C. 2.1 s
   D. The problem cannot be solved with the information given.

5. Surf along the north shore of Hawaii on one particular day is estimated to contain waves about 7.62 meters (25 feet) long, moving at a speed of around 5.5 m/s. What is the frequency of the waves?

   A. 72 Hz
   B. 1.1 Hz
   C. 0.72 Hz
   D. 0.275 Hz

Answers

1. period. The period is described as the time in seconds that elapses between one crest and the next.
2. microwaves. The frequency of microwaves is lower than that of visible light, which in turn is lower than that of x-rays.
3. perpendicular. Shaking out a rug produces transverse waves that move up and down as the energy moves across the rug.
4. B. The time between one "crest" and the next is 1/10 of 42, or 4.2 seconds.
5. C. Using the equation $v = f\lambda$, divide the velocity by the wavelength to get the frequency in Hertz:

   $$5.5 \text{ m/s} \div 7.62 \text{ m} = 0.72 \text{ Hz}$$

OPTICS

Light passes easily through some matter. It is absorbed by other matter. Some matter bounces or bends light.

Reflection

Light-colored or shiny surfaces reflect light. The path of light as it moves toward an object is called an **incident ray**. The path of light after it is reflected by the object is called a **reflected ray**. At the intersection of these rays is a **point of incidence**, through which you could draw a line perpendicular to the reflecting surface. The **angle of incidence** is equal to the **angle of reflection**.

Picture a flat mirror hanging on a wall. The **virtual image** formed by an object in a flat mirror appears to be as far behind the surface of the mirror as the object is in front of the mirror.

We call the **object distance** d_o and the **image distance** d_i. For a flat, or plane mirror, $d_o = d_i$. The distance from the object to the mirror seems equal to the distance of the image to the mirror.

Convex and Concave Mirrors

The illusion of equal distance between object and mirror and mirror and image changes when the mirror is curved. A **convex** mirror reflects light and spreads it out. The image seen in such a mirror looks smaller than the original object. A **concave** mirror has the opposite effect. The image looks larger in the mirror than it actually is in real life.

For concave or convex mirrors, you may be given the **focal length** of the mirror. The focal length is the distance between the center of the curved mirror or lens and its focus—a measure of how strongly the mirror or lens bends rays of light. A deeply curved mirror bends rays more than a nearly flat mirror does. For such mirrors, given the focal length *f* and one distance, you can figure out the other distance, using the mirror equation:

$$1/f = 1/d_o + 1/d_i$$

So if a vase is placed 30 centimeters from a concave mirror with a focal length of 10 centimeters, you can find the image distance by plugging the numbers into the equation:

$$1/10 = 1/30 + 1/d_i$$

$$3/30 = 1/30 + 2/30$$

$$1/d_i = 2/30 = 1/15$$

$$d_i = 15 \text{ cm}$$

Refraction

The sort of bending of light that takes place with a concave or convex lens or mirror is refraction. We often think of the speed of light as constant, but that is not accurate. As light passes between one substance and another, it changes direction at the point of intersection, and it changes speed as well. If the speed of light in a vacuum is 1, the speed of that light when it enters tepid water is 1.33 times slower. The degree to which a substance causes light to slow is its **refractive index**.

Test Yourself

1. Suppose that light strikes a shiny flat surface at an angle of incidence of 45 degrees. It then forms an angle of reflection equal to ____________.

2. Actors use a mirror that is ____________ as a makeup mirror that magnifies their faces.

3. For a flat mirror, the image distance is ____________ the object distance.

4. An object in a mirror with focal length 4 cm forms an image distance of 20 cm. How far is the object from the mirror?

   A. 3 cm
   B. 5 cm
   C. 12 cm
   D. 40 cm

5. A box 6 cm high forms a 3-cm-high image in a mirror. What is the focal length of the mirror?

   A. 28 cm
   B. 12 cm
   C. 4 cm
   D. 2 cm

Answers

1. 45 degrees. For a flat surface, the angle of incidence is equal to the angle of reflection.
2. concave. The image in a concave mirror looks larger than the original image.
3. equal to. For a flat, plane mirror, the distances are equal.
4. B. Plug the numbers into the mirror formula, $1/f = 1/d_o + 1/d_i$:

   $1/4 = 1/d_o + 1/20$
   $5/20 = 4/20 + 1/20$
   $1/4 = 1/5 + 1/20$
   $d_o = 5$ cm

5. D. Plug the numbers into the mirror formula, $1/f = 1/d_o + 1/d_i$:
   $1/f = 1/6 + 1/3$
   $1/f = 1/6 + 2/6$
   $1/f = 1/2$
   $f = 2$ cm

STATIC ELECTRICITY

All matter is made up of particles with electric charges. Static electricity is an imbalance between the negative and positive charges in objects. The imbalance may be the result of friction between two objects, contact between differently charged objects, or bringing an uncharged object near a charged object (**induction**).

WHY DO I NEED THIS?

The dangers of static electricity in ORs has led to changes in medical clothing and equipment.

Electric Force

Excess electrons give an object a negative charge. Lack of electrons gives an object a positive charge. Like charges—two positives or two negatives—repel each other. Unlike charges—a positive and a negative or a negative and a positive—attract each other. The electric force that occurs when charged objects repel or attract each other is represented as F_{elect}.

Some objects are less likely than others to allow electrons to flow between them. Such objects are called **insulators**. Other objects make the movement of electrons especially easy. Such objects are called **conductors**.

Coulomb's Law

Imagine rubbing a balloon against your clothing. The balloon takes some electrons from the clothing and leaves the clothing positively charged, becoming negatively charged itself. The negatively charged balloon is then attracted to the positively charged clothing and sticks to it temporarily.

French physicist Charles-Augustin de Coulomb applied Newtonian principles to this sort of occurrence. He determined that electric force has both magnitude and direction (in other words, it is a vector force), and that the force between two charged objects is both directly proportional to the product of the magnitude of charge on the objects and inversely proportional to the square of the distance between the objects.

Coulomb's law is expressed this way:

$$F_{\text{elect}} = \frac{k \times Q_1 \times Q_2}{d^2}$$

Q_1 is the charge on the first object in coulombs (C). Q_2 is the charge on the second object. The distance in meters between the objects is d, and k is a constant equal to:

$$\frac{9.0 \times 10^9 \,\text{N} \cdot \text{m}^2}{\text{C}^2}$$

Generally, the charges represented by Q_1 and Q_2 are small. They might be measured in microcoulombs. One microcoulomb (1 μC) equals 10^{-6} coulombs.

Imagine two objects, each with a charge of 2 microcoulombs, placed 1 meter apart. You can find the magnitude of the electric force between them by using this formula:

$$F_{\text{elect}} = \frac{k \times (2 \times 10^{-6}\,\text{C}) \times (2 \times 10^{-6}\,\text{C})}{(1\,\text{m})^2}$$

$$F_{\text{elect}} = \frac{\dfrac{9.0 \times 10^{9}\,\text{N} \cdot \text{m}^2}{\text{C}^2} \times (2 \times 10^{-6}\,\text{C}) \times (2 \times 10^{-6}\,\text{C})}{(1\,\text{m})^2}$$

Cancel out the like variables to express the answer in Newtons (N):

$$F_{\text{elect}} = \frac{\dfrac{9.0 \times 10^{9}\,\text{N} \cdot \cancel{\text{m}^2}}{\cancel{\text{C}^2}} \times (2 \times 10^{-6}\,\cancel{\text{C}}) \times (2 \times 10^{-6}\,\cancel{\text{C}})}{\cancel{(1\,\text{m})^2}}$$

$$F_{\text{elect}} = (9.0 \times 10^{9}\,\text{N}) \times (4 \times 10^{-12})$$

$$F_{\text{elect}} = (36 \times 10^{-3}\,\text{N})$$

$$F_{\text{elect}} = 0.036\,\text{N}$$

Test Yourself

1. 1 coulomb = ___________ microcoulombs

2. Materials that resist the flow of electrons make good ___________.

3. Coulomb determined that electric force has both magnitude and ___________.

4. The force between two charged objects is ___________.

A. directly proportional to the distance between them
B. directly proportional to the magnitude of the charge
C. directly proportional to the product of the magnitude of the charge
D. directly proportional to the square of the magnitude of the charge

5. A balloon with a charge of 4 μC is placed 10 centimeters from another balloon with a charge of 3 μC. What is the magnitude of the resulting repulsive force?

A. 0.108 N
B. 1.08 N
C. 1.8 N
D. 10.8 N

Answers

1. 10^6. A microcoulomb equals 10^{-6} coulombs.
2. insulators. Conductors allow flow of electrons; insulators resist flow of electrons.
3. direction. Electric force is a vector force.
4. C. Multiply the magnitude of the charge on one object (Q_1) by the magnitude of the charge on the other object (Q_2).
5. B. Convert 10 centimeters to 0.1 meter for the denominator of the formula.

$$F_{elect} = \frac{(9.0 \times 10^9 \text{ N}) \times (12 \times 10^{-12})}{0.1}$$

$$F_{elect} = \frac{(108 \times 10^{-3} \text{ N})}{0.1}$$

$$F_{elect} = 1.08 \text{ N}$$

ELECTRIC FIELDS AND CHARGES

Objects do not need to connect directly to attract or repel each other. Electric force reaches across the space between them. Such a force is called a **field force**. Gravity is another example of a field force.

Each charged object creates its own electric field in the space that surrounds it. The electric field from a positive charge points away from the charged object. The electric field from a negative charge points toward the charged object. Electric charge, represented as Q or q, may be positive, negative, or zero. It is measured in coulombs.

When charged objects are near each other, their electric fields are affected. Their fields change shape, which changes the potential energy of the objects.

A **test charge** is a charge of negligible size, one that does not have a noticeable effect on a given electric field. Physicists use the concept of test charges to determine the electric force exerted by a field. If a positive test charge moves in the direction of an electric field, it moves without work by an external force and results in the loss of potential energy. If a positive test charge moves in the opposite direction of an electric field, it requires work by an external force and results in an increase in potential energy.

Given E as the electric field, Q as the charge of a test particle, and F as the force that the field exerts on the charge,

$$F_{elect} = QE$$

Test Yourself

For questions 1–3, circle the correct answer in parentheses.

1. As a positive test charge moves away from the positive charge in an electric field, its potential energy (increase/decreases).

2. The electric field from a (positive/negative) charge points toward the charged object.

3. When charged objects are near each other, their fields change (size/shape).

4. What unit is used to measure electric charge?

   A. Volt
   B. Watt
   C. Joule
   D. Coulomb

5. Given a test charge of Q_t, which equation represents the electric field in which the test charge is found?

   A. $E = F_{elect}/Q_t$
   B. $E = F_{elect} \times Q_t$
   C. $E = Q_t/F_{elect}$
   D. $E = k \times Q_t$

Answers

1. decreases. The movement away does not require work and decreases potential energy.
2. negative. Electric field lines move away from positive charges and toward negative charges.
3. shape. As charged objects near each other, their fields interact and change shape.
4. D. Volts measure potential difference. Watts measure power. Joules measure work. Coulombs measure charge.
5. A. Since $F_{elect} = QE$, electric field is force divided by charge.

CURRENTS, VOLTAGE, AND RESISTANCE

Electric charges move when energy is supplied to them. Machines of all sorts function by using the movements of electrons to do work.

Electric Circuit

Energy to move electrons may come from a **dry cell**, or a series of cells in a **battery**. An electric circuit is the path of electrons from a source in a loop to the original position. The electrons move through a pathway of conductors from the negative pole to the positive pole. A switch may be added to a circuit to allow the circuit to be opened and closed.

Current

The rate at which a given charge flows is called the current. In **direct current**, the electrons move in one direction, from negative to positive. In **alternating current**, electrons move back and forth in a repeating cycle. The rate of flow is measured in **amperes** (I).

Voltage

The difference in charge between two points on a circuit is called voltage. It is a measure of potential energy between the two points. If the current in a circuit equals one ampere, and the power equals one **watt**, or one Joule per second, the potential difference equals one **volt** (V). Power (in watts) equals voltage times current:

$$P = V \times I$$

Resistance

It is possible to limit the number of electrons that pass through a circuit by providing resistance. The greater the resistance, the more difficult it is for a charge to pass through the conductor. As the charge is resisted, its energy dissipates. This resistance (R) is measured in **ohms**.

Ohm's Law

George Ohm developed a formula to correlate voltage, current, and resistance. In his formula, V equals voltage in volts, I equals current in amps, and R equals resistance in ohms.

$$V = I \times R$$

So imagine that you have a 5-ohm resistor wired into a 100-volt power supply. What current flows through this circuit?

$$I = V/R$$

$$I = 100/5$$

$$I = 20 \text{ amps}$$

Test Yourself

1. ____________ is the measure of the degree to which movement of a current is restricted.

2. The rate of flow of electrons in a circuit is measured in ____________.

3. In Ohm's formula, I equals ____________.

4. How many volts would produce a current of 12 amps through a 6-ohm resistor?
   A. 2 volts
   B. 6 volts
   C. 36 volts
   D. 72 volts

5. A 110-volt appliance draws 2 amperes. How many watts of power does it require?
   A. 55 watts
   B. 108 watts
   C. 150 watts
   D. 220 watts

Answers

1. Resistance. This is a definition of *resistance.*
2. amperes or amps. The rate of flow is the current, which is measured in amps.
3. current in amps. V equals voltage, and R equals resistance.
4. D. If $I = V/R$, then voltage equals resistance times current.
5. D. Power equals voltage times current.

EVOLVE REACH (HESI) A2 PRACTICE TEST

READING

50 items
Suggested time: 55 minutes

Biosimilars

Generic drugs are usually identical to the original pharmaceutical on which they are based. Biosimilars, on the other hand, are not required to be exactly the same as the reference product. However, they must provide the same therapeutic benefit to patients that the reference product does.

The FDA will not approve a biosimilar unless it has the same dosage form, strength, and mechanism of action as the reference product it imitates. It must be proved to have the same safety and effectiveness as the original, with no additional risks or downsides. The FDA must also approve the factories and laboratories in which the biosimilars are manufactured.

Whereas generic drugs are made through chemical synthesis, biosimilars are produced from living cells. Because of the high costs of testing and manufacturing biosimilars, they will rarely be as inexpensive as generic drugs. However, as the patents on reference products run out, pharmaceutical companies will rush to fill that gap with biosimilars, and the cost will come down as competition grows. Analysts expect biosimilars, despite their complexity compared to generic drugs, to occupy a significant segment of the pharmaceutical market in the years to come.

1. What is the main idea of the passage?

A. A new type of drug, manufactured from living cells and similar in most ways to brand name drugs, will soon develop a significant market share.
B. Generic drugs remain the cheapest and easiest drugs for patients to use and doctors to prescribe.
C. Biosimilars, which are made by the same companies that manufacture generic drugs, have yet to find a market in the United States.
D. In order for biosimilars to take over the market, they will need to come down in price and prove their worth to the FDA.

GO ON TO THE NEXT PAGE

2. Which of the following is *not* listed as a detail in the passage?

A. Biosimilars cost a good deal to manufacture.
B. Generic drugs are not made the same way that biosimilars are.
C. The FDA must approve any factory that makes biosimilars.
D. Current biosimilars are primarily cancer-fighting drugs.

3. What is the author's primary purpose in writing this essay?

A. To persuade
B. To inform
C. To entertain
D. To analyze

4. Which statement would *not* be inferred by the reader?

A. Biosimilars are new.
B. Biosimilars are expensive.
C. Biosimilars are foreign.
D. Biosimilars are effective.

Treatments for Hypertension

Hypertension, or high blood pressure, rarely manifests symptoms. Nevertheless, it puts patients at risk for stroke, heart failure, vascular disease, coronary artery disease, and even blindness.

Although hypertension is frequently an inherited condition, lifestyle can contribute to patient risk. For that reason, patients with high blood pressure are often counseled to quit smoking or drinking and to lose weight and avoid salt. Stress reduction is also often beneficial to patients with hypertension.

The drug therapies for hypertension range in type and mechanism. For example, ACE inhibitors dilate the blood vessels, which increases blood flow and lowers pressure. Calcium channel blockers slow the movement of calcium into the cells that line the heart and blood vessels, easing the heart's pumping and widening the blood vessels. Diuretics release excess water and salt through urine, making it easier for the heart to pump. Beta-blockers block the effects of epinephrine on the heart, causing it to beat more slowly. Vasodilators relax the walls of the arteries, allowing blood to move more smoothly through them. Aldosterone receptor antagonists work by stimulating receptors in the brain to open peripheral arteries.

The choice of drug depends on a variety of factors, from the patient's age and other diseases to the immediate cause of the hypertension. Patients are often taught to monitor their own blood pressure at regular intervals. All patients at risk should receive regular screenings for damage to the heart, arteries, and eyes that may be related to hypertension.

GO ON TO THE NEXT PAGE

5. As used in the third paragraph, what does the term *dilate* mean?

A. Elucidate
B. Widen
C. Elaborate
D. Bloat

6. What is the main idea of the passage?

A. Patients with vascular disease or heart failure often started off with a mild case of hypertension.
B. It is clear that personal lifestyle and choices may be contributing factors in hypertension.
C. Doctors may prescribe from a variety of drugs and therapies to treat hypertension.
D. Treatments for hypertension work by opening the blood vessels and easing pressure on the heart.

7. Which of the following statements is an opinion?

A. Although hypertension is frequently an inherited condition, lifestyle can contribute to patient risk.
B. The drug therapies for hypertension range in type and mechanism.
C. Aldosterone receptor antagonists work by stimulating receptors in the brain to open peripheral arteries.
D. All patients at risk should receive regular screenings for damage to the heart, arteries, and eyes that may be related to hypertension.

8. Identify the overall tone of the passage.

A. Objective
B. Casual
C. Impassioned
D. Personal

9. Choose the best summary of the passage.

A. Hypertension has serious repercussions, but there are a number of different methods of treatment that work in different ways. The correct therapy depends on the situation and the patient.
B. Hypertension is largely left untreated due to its lack of symptoms, but the results can be deadly. Doctors often prescribe a change in diet or some form of medicine.
C. Heart patients can benefit from a variety of drugs that bring blood pressure down and protect the vessels and heart. The most frequently prescribed drugs attack plaque in the arteries.
D. ACE inhibitors and vasodilators act in similar ways to lower blood pressure, but they may not be used by all patients. Luckily, diuretics and beta-blockers often work on patients for whom the other drugs are too potent.

GO ON TO THE NEXT PAGE

The Short but Powerful History of Zika

The Zika virus is not new; it was first isolated in 1947 in Uganda, by scientists studying yellow fever. The first human cases were seen in Africa in 1952, and in 1964, a scientist who fell ill with Zika recorded his symptoms, which included a mild fever and a generalized rash. Limited outbreaks occurred in Asia and Africa over the next few decades. Only in 2013 did scientists start to link the virus to more serious effects in patients in the Pacific Islands. They recorded effects from paralysis to autoimmune problems to microcephaly in children born to patients with Zika infections.

Still, Zika infection was rare enough that doctors in Brazil did not suspect that particular virus when patients started presenting with neurological disorders after having flu-like symptoms. By 2015, the cases in South America were confirmed as Zika, and the World Health Organization posted an alert.

It was the sudden, shocking upsurge in babies born with underdeveloped brains and small heads that led to Zika's notoriety. By the end of 2015, Brazil reported nearly 3,000 such cases, proving that Zika was not only unexpectedly widespread but also extremely dangerous. The growth of Zika infection from a handful of cases in Africa and Asia to tens of thousands of cases in South America and the Caribbean indicated to scientists that Zika had mutated, improving its ability not only to travel but also to infect.

The disease continues to be transmitted mainly through the bites of two types of mosquitoes, and most people still have mild symptoms that vanish within a week. However, it seems clear that pregnant women can transmit Zika to a fetus during pregnancy or birth, and there is also recent proof that Zika may be passed on sexually. Although only a few people end up with neurological symptoms, the dangers to fetuses are grave enough to call for vigilance and protection in all areas where Zika is known to be present.

10. What is the meaning of the word *isolated* as used in the first paragraph?

A. Inaccessible to all
B. Exceptional and rare
C. Separated in pure form
D. Quarantined for health reasons

GO ON TO THE NEXT PAGE

11. Choose the best summary of the passage.

A. As with most of the most contagious virus infections, Zika arose in Africa and traveled around the globe. Soon we can expect cases of Zika to show up in North America.
B. Doctors have long had trouble differentiating Zika from other viruses. Today they are able to recognize it by its effects, including microcephaly in newborns.
C. The Zika virus started off slowly as a minor infectious agent in Africa and then in Asia. Recently it has changed both its range and its potency to become a real danger to the newborn children of infected mothers.
D. The Zika virus was discovered by accident and then forgotten for decades. Suddenly it is in the news again as multiple cases in Brazil indicate that it is transmitted sexually as well as by mosquitoes.

12. What is the author's primary purpose in writing this essay?

A. To entertain
B. To analyze
C. To inform
D. To persuade

13. What is a conclusion that a reader could draw from this passage?

A. The World Health Organization should have posted an alert years earlier.
B. Although it started in Africa, Zika is now found on six of seven continents.
C. Zika is only dangerous to humans if it is transmitted to infants.
D. The Zika of today differs from the Zika discovered in Uganda.

14. Which of the following is *not* listed as a detail in the passage?

A. The date of Zika's discovery
B. The typical symptoms of Zika
C. The average age of Zika patients
D. The methods of Zika transmission

GO ON TO THE NEXT PAGE

Getting the Most Nutrition from Vegetables

It might seem logical to think that eating vegetables raw maximizes their nutritional value, and that the more you cook vegetables, the less nutritious they are. The facts are not quite that simple.

A 2009 study used a variety of cooking methods on a variety of vegetables and measured the antioxidants that remained. Artichokes retained antioxidants through all cooking methods, and green beans and garlic did fairly well whether they were fried, boiled, baked, or microwaved. Celery and peppers lost hydroxyl radicals when cooked. Carrots actually increased antioxidant values during all cooking methods. In general, pressure-cooking and boiling led to the greatest losses of antioxidants.

Eating raw tomatoes is great, but eating them with a little oil is even better, because the oil helps you to digest the nutrients in tomatoes. Cooking actually increases the antioxidant content of tomatoes.

Chopping and cooking vegetables releases nutrients in the cell walls of those vegetables. It also increases the body's ability to absorb the vegetables' calcium, iron, and magnesium.

The rule seems to be that cooking at low temperatures for short times with the least liquid possible preserves the most nutrients while making vegetables easy to consume. Contrary to popular belief, microwaving is a good way to maintain nutrients in vegetables—it allows for a very brief cooking time with little water. Spinach, for example, loses most of its B vitamins when boiled, but it retains nutrients when microwaved.

Finally, the faster vegetables get from farm to table, the more nutrients they preserve. If they are picked unripe and allowed to ripen on a store shelf, they will not be as nutritious as vegetables picked ripe and sold that day at a farmers' market. They will not even be as nutritious as frozen vegetables, which are picked at the peak of ripeness and flash-frozen. You are better off eating frozen vegetables in winter than eating fresh ones flown in from South America.

15. What is the main idea of the passage?

A. Cooking and eating vegetables correctly can enhance their nutritional value.
B. Raw vegetables are best, but quick-cooked vegetables are also nutritious.
C. Vegetables are easiest to eat when cooked in a little water with a bit of oil.
D. The less you cook vegetables, the more nutrition you will retain

GO ON TO THE NEXT PAGE

16. What is the meaning of the word *retained* as used in the second paragraph?

A. Recollected
B. Preserved
C. Engaged
D. Protected

17. Identify the overall tone of the essay.

A. Idealistic
B. Dramatic
C. Indifferent
D. Matter-of-fact

18. Which of the following is *not* mentioned as a benefit of chopping vegetables?

A. Better absorption of magnesium
B. Better absorption of potassium
C. Better absorption of calcium
D. Better absorption of iron

19. Which of the following statements is an opinion?

A. In general, pressure-cooking and boiling led to the greatest losses of antioxidants.
B. Spinach, for example, loses most of its B vitamins when boiled, but it retains nutrients when microwaved.
C. Finally, the faster vegetables get from farm to table, the more nutrients they preserve.
D. You are better off eating frozen vegetables in winter than eating fresh ones flown in from South America.

20. Which is *not* a conclusion a reader might draw from the essay?

A. Microwaving vegetables may be better than boiling them.
B. Frozen vegetables can be surprisingly nutritious.
C. Cooked tomatoes have more antioxidants than raw ones.
D. Peppers retain their nutrients when cooked.

GO ON TO THE NEXT PAGE

Mitochondrial Intervention

You know of mitochondria as the "powerhouses of the cell," the tiny organelles that create the majority of all cellular energy. Mitochondrial diseases are genetic disorders that occur when the mitochondria cannot produce enough energy for cells to function correctly.

Symptoms of mitochondrial disease range from lack of growth and developmental delays to loss of muscle coordination and seizures. Typically, the disease is progressive and incurable.

In 2016, a mother who carried the disease gave birth to a healthy infant via a process called mitochondrial intervention. Previously, the same woman had given birth to two children who died from mitochondrial disease in early childhood. According to a report in *Medscape*, the children had the mutation in more than 95 percent of their mitochondria, compared to their mother's 24.5 percent.

In the intervention, which faces ethical challenges and remains controversial, the nucleus from the mother's oocyte was transferred to a donor oocyte before being fertilized. The resulting egg has most of its DNA from the mother, mitochondrial DNA from a healthy donor, and DNA from the father, in what some people have called a "three-parent" intervention. The resulting newborn has the mutation in fewer than 2 percent of his mitochondria and is expected to survive disease-free.

Proponents of the technique suggest that it will render mitochondrial disease extinct, which is unlikely. It does open up possibilities for parent carriers, but the technique comes with no guarantees at present. It remains to be seen whether mitochondrial intervention is a fad or a fix.

21. What conclusion can a reader draw about the experimental process described in this passage?

A. It works best if the mitochondrial DNA comes from a maternal relative.
B. It succeeds only when mutation percentages are under 30 percent.
C. It is a simple solution for parents who carry the disease.
D. It is controversial and has unpredictable results.

22. Which of the following statements is an opinion?

A. Mitochondrial diseases are genetic disorders that occur when the mitochondria cannot produce enough energy for cells to function correctly.
B. Symptoms of mitochondrial disease range from lack of growth and developmental delays to loss of muscle coordination and seizures.
C. Previously, the same woman had given birth to two children who died from mitochondrial disease in early childhood.
D. Proponents of the technique suggest that it will render mitochondrial disease extinct, which is unlikely.

23. What is the meaning of the word *progressive* as used in the second paragraph?

A. Advanced
B. Radical
C. Ongoing
D. Piecemeal

24. What is the author's attitude toward the use of mitochondrial intervention?

A. Reassuring
B. Scornful
C. Accepting
D. Unconvinced

25. What is the author's primary purpose in writing this essay?

A. To inform readers of a new methodology
B. To persuade readers to reject this new science
C. To entertain readers with a true medical mystery
D. To reflect upon medical discoveries and their effects

GO ON TO THE NEXT PAGE

Compassionate Care: Cicely Saunders and Hospice

Cicely Saunders trained as a nurse during World War II at St. Thomas's Hospital Nightingale School of Nursing in London. Her relationship with a patient who was dying of cancer helped to interest her in end-of-life issues. She began working in a home for the dying poor and after obtaining a degree in social work decided to pursue a career as a doctor. She researched pain control and developed a philosophy of "total pain," which involved not only the physical, but also the emotional and spiritual pain patients may endure when they are seriously ill.

After qualifying as a doctor, Cicely wrote an article calling for a holistic approach to the end of life, one in which health care professionals worked as a team to "relieve where they cannot heal." She advocated using pain medicine to reduce anxiety as well as physical pain.

After many years of planning, Cicely opened a hospice based on her principles of holistic care and pain relief. Her hospice, St. Christopher's, is considered the first of the modern hospices. It featured a teaching component and opportunities for research as well as patient care. It offered home care, which was then a radical change in care for the dying.

Researchers at St. Christopher's studied morphine and other approaches to pain control. Cicely's training in social work contributed to the hospice's development of bereavement services for families and loved ones.

By the end of her life, this one-time wartime nurse had received the title Dame Commander of the Order of the British Empire along with the world's greatest humanitarian award, the Conrad N. Hilton Humanitarian Prize. To this day, hospices around the world rely on the philosophy she developed.

26. What is the author's attitude toward the subject of this essay?

A. Critical
B. Mocking
C. Awestruck
D. Appreciative

27. What is the meaning of the word *relieve* as used in the second paragraph?

A. Ease
B. Release
C. Replace
D. Dispel

GO ON TO THE NEXT PAGE

28. The author describes each of these aspects of St. Christopher's *except* ____________.

A. research opportunities
B. training in social work
C. available home care
D. bereavement services

29. What is the author's primary purpose in writing this essay?

A. To persuade readers to support the efforts of hospice
B. To analyze the effects of hospice on patient care
C. To inform readers of the early development of hospice
D. To reflect on the good that hospice has done over time

30. Which statement could *not* be inferred by the reader?

A. Without Saunders's intervention, end-of-life care would still inevitably take place in hospitals.
B. In Saunders's time, morphine was a known and regularly used drug for pain control.
C. St. Christopher's was the first establishment of its kind in the city of London.
D. Saunders's work as a nurse, social worker, and doctor all contributed to her ideas about end-of-life care.

Pinkeye

Its real name is conjunctivitis, but parents and children know it as pinkeye. When it is caused by bacteria or viruses, this common inflammation of the eye's mucous membranes is powerfully contagious and can spread through a family in a matter of hours.

Although bacteria cause some cases of pinkeye, most conjunctivitis is caused by adenoviruses, so pinkeye often follows a cold. Symptoms include redness and swelling in and around the eye; thick, sometimes sticky drainage; and a burning or itching in the eyelids. Often victims of pinkeye do not know they have it until they wake up with eyes gummed shut.

Bacterial conjunctivitis may disappear quickly with the use of medicated eye drops or creams. Viral conjunctivitis is harder to get rid of, but warm or cool compresses may ease the itching and soreness.

The most notable feature of conjunctivitis is how easy it is to spread. Any contact with drainage from the eye can spread the infection. Moving a compress from one eye to the other can spread the infection. Sharing a pillow can spread the infection. Shaking hands can spread the infection.

It is critical to wash hands frequently when a case of conjunctivitis is in the household. Do not share eye drops, and don't wear contact lenses. Discard tissues immediately after using them. A modicum of care can prevent the infection from spreading throughout the family and beyond.

31. Which of the following is *not* listed as a detail in the passage?

A. Conjunctivitis is most common in school-age children.
B. Washing hands can help stop the spread of pinkeye.
C. The symptoms of pinkeye may include itchy eyes.
D. Conjunctivitis is spread via the drainage from the eye.

32. The word *modicum* as used in the last paragraph of the passage can best be defined as ____________.

A. a progression
B. a small measure
C. a restraint
D. a balance

GO ON TO THE NEXT PAGE

33. Which statement could be inferred by the reader from the last paragraph of the passage?

A. Conjunctivitis does not need to spread throughout a household.
B. People who wear contact lenses are in danger of conjunctivitis.
C. Certain eye drops can make a case of conjunctivitis worse.
D. Conjunctivitis may accompany a runny or stuffed-up nose.

34. Which statement about pinkeye is a fact?

A. Pinkeye is an annoying condition.
B. Pinkeye is spread through human contact.
C. Pinkeye is a good description of the disease.
D. Pinkeye should be referred to as conjunctivitis.

35. What is the main idea of the passage?

A. Conjunctivitis is referred to as pinkeye because of its symptoms.
B. People with conjunctivitis should be careful not to spread it around.
C. Conjunctivitis is an eye condition that is common and easily spread.
D. Although conjunctivitis looks nasty, it is not particularly dangerous.

GO ON TO THE NEXT PAGE

New Casts from 3-D Printing

In the old days, which were not so long ago, a broken leg might be sealed inside a plaster cast for weeks. Today, it is not uncommon to put a broken leg in a waterproof, fiberglass cast that resembles a ski boot. But the cast of the future looks like a lace bootie, and it has a number of benefits for the patient.

The new cast uses amazing 3-D printing technology to scan the patient's broken limb and build a cast from the bottom up that is specifically personalized to the patient's needs. The final cast is made of plastic, is even lighter than a fiberglass cast, and has round openings that permit easy viewing of the broken limb. Doctors can check skin color and health, and physical therapists can use ultrasound or other treatments to stimulate the limb. Most important for the patient, the cast openings allow the skin to breathe, so the uncomfortable, itchy moistness of skin in plaster or fiberglass casts will be a thing of the past.

Right now, prototypes exist mainly for arm casts. The finished product is sturdy and comfortable. Designers believe that the customized 3-D casts may cut rehabilitation time in half, both because the cast is specific to the patient and because the openings in the cast may help to prevent the limb from atrophying.

As 3-D printing technology becomes more commonly used to design prosthetics, medical models, synthetic skin, and even heart valves, we can expect simple casts for broken bones to join the ranks of advancements in medicine through 3-D printing.

36. What conclusion is suggested by this essay?

A. Three-D printed casts will soon be used for everyone from infants to the elderly.
B. Three-D printing is being applied to many areas of medicine.
C. Three-D printed casts are replacing fiberglass casts in the United States.
D. Three-D printing is especially useful for building prosthetics.

37. What is the meaning of the word *atrophying* as used in the third paragraph?

A. Wasting away
B. Shattering
C. Shielding
D. Turning around

GO ON TO THE NEXT PAGE

38. Identify the overall tone of the essay.

A. Cautionary
B. Unconvinced
C. Enthusiastic
D. Unmoved

39. Which detail is *not* given as a benefit of the new casts?

A. Lightness
B. Low cost
C. Open weave
D. Comfort

GO ON TO THE NEXT PAGE

Superfood or Super Marketing Ploy?

Are certain nutritionally dense foods truly "superfoods"? Should we be basing our diet on these magical berries, juices, and grains?

There is no doubt that certain foods are better for you than others. However, although foods such as blueberries have high concentrations of anthocyanins and other antioxidants, no studies have proved that blueberries are any healthier overall than, say, cranberries.

It is the lack of scientific backing that leads many nutritionists to suggest that the lens of "superfood" is not a helpful way to look at overall diet. Yes, we should probably eat foods high in vitamin C and rich in antioxidants, but it is not clear why kiwis are labeled superfoods and other citrus fruits are not. Kale is called a superfood, but most dark vegetables—spinach, collards, broccoli—offer similar levels of vitamins A, C, and K, along with minerals and fiber.

Often, superfoods seem more faddish than healthful. For example, it is not obvious that black soybeans are better than ordinary soybeans or that chia seeds are better than flax seeds—and raisins definitely have more nutrients than dried cranberries do.

So how do you get to be a superfood? Mostly, it seems, you need a good public relations agent. The European Union will no longer let a food be labeled that way unless the claim is supported scientifically. That is not to say that acai berries and pomegranates are not wonderfully nutritious. It is merely to suggest that you can probably find equal nutrition in cheaper, less trendy products.

40. What is the main idea of the passage?

A. The term "superfood" applies to foods of all types that offer loads of vitamins, minerals, and antioxidants.
B. People tend to choose foods that they have seen promoted rather than looking for genuine healthful qualities.
C. Although certain foods labeled "superfood" have high nutritional value, they are not necessarily better than other nutritional foods.
D. It makes little sense to label kale differently than you would any other dark green, leafy vegetable in terms of nutritional benefit.

41. What is the meaning of the word *concentrations* in the second paragraph of the passage?

A. Collections of living things
B. The actions of focusing effort
C. Strength gathered by removing water
D. The amounts of substances per volume

42. Based on this passage, what can the reader infer about dried cranberries?

A. They have high concentrations of anthocyanins and other antioxidants.
B. They may be called "superfoods," but they have fewer nutritional benefits than raisins do.
C. They are neither as popular nor as nutritionally beneficial as blueberries are.
D. They lack the public relations panache of fruits such as pomegranates.

43. Which is *not* listed as an example of a superfood?

A. Pomegranates
B. Collard greens
C. Blueberries
D. Chia seeds

44. What is the overall tone of the essay?

A. Dubious
B. Puzzled
C. Infuriated
D. Optimistic

45. What is the author's primary purpose in writing this essay?

A. To persuade readers to look beyond superfoods for nutrition
B. To entertain readers with amusing anecdotes about superfoods
C. To inform readers of the potential dangers of superfoods
D. To analyze the effect on consumers of labeling superfoods

GO ON TO THE NEXT PAGE

Neonatal Jaundice

A baby is born with ten fingers, ten toes, and a healthy cry, but in a day or two, he develops a yellow tinge to the eyeball and face. What is going on?

The physical examination nearly every newborn receives will provide the answer. The health care worker checks for cataracts, heart murmurs, and hip dysplasia, but she will also look for signs of jaundice, the cause of such yellowing in the skin and sclera. Jaundice is very common. The March of Dimes estimates that 60 percent of newborns have the condition. It is caused by an accumulation of bilirubin, a yellow substance that is produced as red blood cells break down. All babies have a high level of red blood cells, which rapidly break down and are replaced. Normally, the liver takes care of removing bilirubin. However, in newborns, the liver is immature and not fully functioning.

Parents really ought not to panic if they see a bit of yellow in their baby's eyes or skin. Usually, jaundice is mild and disappears in a matter of days or weeks. Nevertheless, any jaundice should probably be checked out by a doctor, especially in cases where the soles of the feet turn yellow, an indication of high levels of bilirubin. If left untreated, high levels of bilirubin may cause complications from deafness to brain damage. Such complications are quite rare, though.

If bilirubin levels do not decrease on their own, the jaundiced baby is whisked away and placed under fluorescent light in a process called phototherapy. As the light excites the bilirubin molecules, they react with oxygen, and the byproduct is rapidly excreted in urine.

46. Which of the following is *not* listed as a detail in the passage?

A. Bilirubin is a byproduct of red blood cell breakdown.
B. Jaundice may result from an infection or deficiency.
C. Yellow feet indicate high levels of bilirubin.
D. Phototherapy may cure jaundice in newborns.

47. What is the meaning of the word *accumulation* as used in the second paragraph of the passage?

A. Buildup
B. Hoard
C. Addition
D. Swelling

48. Which of the following statements is an opinion?

A. The March of Dimes estimates that 60 percent of newborns have the condition.
B. Parents really ought not to panic if they see a bit of yellow in their baby's eyes or skin.
C. All babies have a high level of red blood cells, which rapidly break down and are replaced.
D. As the light excites the bilirubin molecules, they react with oxygen, and the byproduct is rapidly excreted in urine.

49. Identify the overall tone of the essay.

A. Disheartened
B. Exasperated
C. Agitated
D. Soothing

50. Choose the best summary of the passage.

A. Because the liver does not function fully in a newborn, bilirubin accrues, which may lead to brain damage. Phototherapy is one good way to address this problem.
B. Jaundice causes yellowing of the skin and sclera. If it causes the soles of the feet to turn yellow, parents should rush their babies to the doctor for phototherapy.
C. Within days of birth, babies may develop jaundice due to excess bilirubin. It is usually harmless and clears up quickly, but at times it requires intervention.
D. The yellow skin of jaundiced babies may be frightening for parents, but health care professionals know that it is nothing to worry about and will go away in time.

STOP. IF YOU HAVE TIME LEFT OVER, CHECK YOUR WORK ON THIS SECTION ONLY.

VOCABULARY AND GENERAL KNOWLEDGE

50 items
Suggested time: 45 minutes

1. Select the meaning of the underlined word in the sentence.

She had an <u>adverse</u> reaction to the new medication.

A. Harmful
B. Opposed
C. Hostile
D. Unforeseen

2. What is another word for *resilient*?

A. Ludicrous
B. Hardy
C. Capable
D. Evocative

3. What is the meaning of *penumbra*?

A. Enclosure
B. Discipline
C. Finality
D. Shadow

4. Select the meaning of the underlined word in the question.

When will the tracheal cartilage begin to <u>ossify</u>?

A. Distend
B. Harden
C. Straighten
D. Recede

5. Which word meaning "remedy" best fits in the sentence?

Exercise is not always a ____________ for stiffness in the limbs.

A. retrogress
B. proviso
C. panacea
D. badinage

6. *Succinct* is best defined as being ____________.

A. exact
B. brief
C. accurate
D. contradictory

7. Select the meaning of the underlined word in the sentence.

The doctors recorded measurements of the <u>anomalous</u> lump.

A. Atypical
B. Outsized
C. Noteworthy
D. Surgically removed

8. A medical report that is prolix is ____________.

A. expertly done
B. rambling or wordy
C. widely publicized
D. negative or pessimistic

9. Which word meaning “decay” best fits in the sentence?

If the medical waste were not removed hourly, it might start to ____________.

A. pulverize
B. percolate
C. putrefy
D. proscribe

10. If a disease is rampant, it is ____________.

A. fatal
B. hidden
C. widespread
D. controlled

11. What is another word for *quaff*?

A. Hack
B. Imbue
C. Probe
D. Drink

12. Select the meaning of the underlined word in the sentence.

His doctor is sanguine about the chances for recovery.

A. Silent
B. Optimistic
C. Vague
D. Apprehensive

13. Select the meaning of the underlined word in the sentence.

Her symptoms may be due to senescence rather than to disease.

A. Advanced age
B. Emotional response
C. Nonconforming lifestyle
D. Basic human nature

14. Which word names a small injury resulting in discoloration?

A. Contusion
B. Rash
C. Hive
D. Boil

15. What would you always expect to see in a suppurating wound?

A. Stitches
B. Scabs
C. Pus
D. Gangrene

16. What is the meaning of *prognosis*?

A. Actuality
B. Prediction
C. Malfunction
D. Identification

17. Select the meaning of the underlined word in the question.

How does the efficacy of herbal remedies compare to that of pharmaceuticals?

A. Ability to produce a desired result
B. Quality of moving with great speed
C. Amount of money spent on a purchase
D. Quality of being worthy of attention

GO ON TO THE NEXT PAGE

18. If a blow to the head stupefies the recipient, what does it do?

A. Stuns him
B. Kills him
C. Infuriates him
D. Punctures him

19. If bones are carpal, they are found in the ___________.

A. hand
B. wrist
C. foot
D. jaw

20. Select the meaning of the underlined word in the sentence.

The tablets evanesce when dropped in a glass of water.

A. Lose potency
B. Melt away
C. Float
D. Fizz

21. What is the best definition of the word *extricate*?

A. To disentangle
B. To isolate
C. To scrutinize
D. To clarify

22. Select the meaning of the underlined word in the sentence.

The chemical has a particular acrid odor.

A. Floral
B. Citrusy
C. Woody
D. Bitter

23. What is the meaning of *aberration*?

A. Objection
B. Elimination
C. Irregularity
D. Repugnance

GO ON TO THE NEXT PAGE

24. Select the meaning of the underlined word in the sentence.

The exercise regimen seemed to enervate the surgical patient.

A. Enliven
B. Weaken
C. Frighten
D. Relax

25. Which word meaning "toward the front" best fits in the sentence?

That ____________ vessel feeds into a series of capillaries above the abdomen.

A. dilatory
B. caudal
C. ventral
D. proximal

26. If cough medicine is palatable, it ____________.

A. is blended
B. tastes fine
C. looks tainted
D. seems essential

27. Where might a papule develop on the body?

A. Blood vessel
B. Stomach
C. Brain
D. Skin

28. Someone with cyanosis might appear ____________.

A. infected
B. confused
C. bloody
D. blue

29. Select the meaning of the underlined word in the question.

Germs may enter through a fissure in the skin.

A. Inoculation
B. Protrusion
C. Crack
D. Pore

GO ON TO THE NEXT PAGE

30. What is the meaning of the word *gratuitous*?

A. Appreciative
B. Unwarranted
C. Energizing
D. Unobtrusive

31. Another word for *pregnant* might be ___________.

A. limpid
B. gelid
C. languid
D. gravid

32. What is another word for *gullible*?

A. Impaired
B. Sensitive
C. Trusting
D. Superficial

33. Select the meaning of the underlined word in the sentence.

The patient was <u>obdurate</u> when it came time for physical therapy.

A. Stubborn
B. Reliable
C. Industrious
D. Preoccupied

34. If you are asked to modulate your voice, you should ___________.

A. speak up
B. use good diction
C. remain silent
D. change your tone

35. Select the meaning of the underlined phrase in the sentence.

Some of the patients seem <u>impervious to</u> the change in temperature.

A. Susceptible to
B. Bothered by
C. Unaffected by
D. Attentive to

36. A homemade tonic that is innocuous is ____________.

A. harmless
B. untested
C. mediocre
D. effective

37. If a patient appears lethargic, she may seem ____________.

A. hungry
B. exhausted
C. distracted
D. agitated

38. What is the best definition of the word *distention*?

A. Distribution
B. Complaint
C. Swelling
D. Turmoil

39. Select the meaning of the underlined word in the question.

Who will be attending the <u>postmortem</u> examination?

A. Surgical
B. Graduation
C. End-of-semester
D. After death

40. What word meaning "porous" best fits in the sentence?

The new fiberglass cast has a ____________ membrane underneath.

A. malleable
B. watertight
C. permeable
D. viscous

41. Select the meaning of the underlined word in the sentence.

The nurses worked quickly to <u>stanch</u> the flow of blood.

A. Strengthen
B. Restrict
C. Swab
D. Ease

42. What is the best definition of the word *predilection?*

A. Preference
B. Expression
C. Monitoring
D. Vernacular

43. What word meaning "aid" best fits in the sentence?

Several off-duty EMTs provided ____________ for the victims of the explosion.

A. hegemony
B. patronage
C. counsel
D. succor

44. What is the best definition of *stoic*?

A. Uncomplaining
B. Oppressive
C. Wearisome
D. Lifeless

45. An MI is likely to involve the ____________.

A. eardrum
B. skull
C. kidneys
D. heart

46. Select the meaning of the underlined word in the sentence.

The patient was feeling <u>vertiginous</u> on the ride up in the elevator.

A. Confused
B. Impatient
C. Fatigued
D. Dizzy

47. Which word meaning "dependent" best fits in the sentence?

The speed of her recovery is ____________ on her following the doctor's instructions.

A. precipitant
B. contingent
C. vouchsafed
D. mitigated

GO ON TO THE NEXT PAGE

48. An irascible patient is ____________.

A. grumpy
B. unresponsive
C. suffering
D. disrespectful

49. If a surgeon is meticulous, what must be true?

A. She is alert and observant.
B. She is eccentric and difficult to work with.
C. She is well-trained and professional.
D. She is careful and thorough.

50. Select the meaning of the underlined word in the sentence.

Any coronary <u>occlusion</u> must be dealt with immediately.

A. Incompatibility
B. Dysfunction
C. Blockage
D. Variation

STOP. IF YOU HAVE TIME LEFT OVER, CHECK YOUR WORK ON THIS SECTION ONLY.

GRAMMAR

50 items
Suggested time: 45 minutes

1. Which sentence is written correctly?

   A. Having read the instructions twice Jen felt confident.
   B. Having read the instructions twice Jen, felt confident.
   C. Having read the instructions twice, Jen felt confident.
   D. Having read, the instructions twice, Jen felt confident.

2. Select the phrase that will make this sentence grammatically correct.

   Before we had investigated the menu, Stuart ____________.

   A. is ordering for the whole table
   B. had ordered for the whole table
   C. orders for the whole table
   D. ordering for the whole table

3. What part of speech is the underlined word in the sentence below?

   Isabella's promotion was not <u>unexpected</u>; it was bound to happen sooner or later.

   A. Adjective
   B. Adverb
   C. Noun
   D. Verb

4. Which sentence is grammatically correct?

   A. The restaurant stood on the corner with a blue awning advertising its name.
   B. Advertising its name with a blue awning, the corner held a restaurant.
   C. Advertising its name, the restaurant with a blue awning stood on the corner.
   D. On the corner stood the restaurant, with a blue awning advertising its name.

5. Which word is used incorrectly in the following sentence?

   Countless patients laid on this gurney over the past decade.

   A. patients
   B. laid
   C. gurney
   D. past

GO ON TO THE NEXT PAGE

6. Select the correct word for the blank in the following sentence.

The head nurse and ____________ placed the records in neat stacks.

A. she
B. me
C. him
D. them

7. What word is best to substitute for the underlined words in the following sentence?

Dr. Ricardo asked the patient a question <u>the patient</u> could not answer.

A. her
B. he
C. it
D. they

8. Which word is used incorrectly in the following sentence?

To who should we inquire to learn about options for further study?

A. who
B. inquire
C. options
D. further

9. Which of the following words fits best in the sentence below?

____________ a later inspection, the office will be closed.

A. Amongst
B. Despite
C. Pending
D. While

10. What punctuation is needed in this sentence to make it correct?

The surgeon required certain things in his operating room soft music, slow movement, and an aura of calm.

A. Period
B. Semicolon
C. Comma
D. Colon

11. Which of the following words is spelled correctly?

A. Asthma
B. Azhma
C. Astma
D. Ashtma

GO ON TO THE NEXT PAGE

12. Select the word or phrase that makes this sentence grammatically correct.

To help pay her tuition, Lucy ____________ in a research laboratory.

A. employs
B. employing
C. is employed
D. has employed

13. Select the word in the sentence that is *not* used correctly.

An aural examination before a panel of experts may produce anxiety in the examinee.

A. aural
B. panel
C. anxiety
D. examinee

14. Select the word that makes this sentence grammatically correct.

After having ____________ several bottles of root beer, Chuck felt gassy and uncomfortable.

A. drinking
B. drank
C. drunk
D. drink

15. Which sentence is grammatically correct?

A. Slowing to a crawl, the bus maneuvered through heavy traffic.
B. The bus maneuvered through heavy traffic slowing to a crawl.
C. The bus maneuvered, slowing to a crawl, through heavy traffic.
D. Slowing to a crawl, through heavy traffic the bus was maneuvered.

16. Select the word that makes this sentence grammatically correct.

One out of four students ____________ the meal plan.

A. use
B. uses
C. using
D. are using

17. Which word is best to substitute for the underlined word in the following sentence?

The therapist and I reviewed <u>the therapist's and my</u> responses.

A. his
B. their
C. our
D. mine

GO ON TO THE NEXT PAGE

18. Which word is *not* spelled correctly in the context of the sentence?

The doctors maintain a sweet of offices on the twelfth floor.

A. maintain
B. sweet
C. twelfth
D. floor

19. What punctuation is needed in this sentence to make it correct?

The teaching assistant was not prepared for the question he mumbled an answer and then offered to look it up.

A. Colon
B. Apostrophe
C. Comma
D. Semicolon

20. Which of the following words is spelled correctly?

A. Criticle
B. Critical
C. Criticall
D. Critticle

21. Which sentence is written correctly?

A. Since receiving an A on the prelim, Chung has stopped studying so hard.
B. Since receiving an A on the prelim Chung has stopped studying so hard.
C. Since receiving, an A on the prelim, Chung has stopped studying so hard.
D. Since receiving an A on the prelim; Chung has stopped studying so hard.

22. Select the word or phrase that makes this sentence grammatically correct.

There is a long hallway ____________ the laboratory and the main operating room.

A. among
B. between
C. by way of
D. In conjunction with

23. What part of speech is the underlined word in the sentence below?

Tomatoes have a surprising effect on Kim; she immediately breaks out in a rash.

A. Noun
B. Verb
C. Adjective
D. Adverb

24. Select the word that makes this sentence grammatically correct.

Julianne calls ____________ "the fastest shopper in the West."

A. oneself
B. itself
C. herself
D. themselves

25. Which sentence is the clearest?

A. On the hall table there was a card from Aunt Helen.
B. From Aunt Helen, there was a card on the hall table.
C. There was on the hall table a card from Aunt Helen.
D. On the hall table there was from Aunt Helen a card.

26. Select the word or phrase that is misplaced in the sentence.

From Chicago, the suitcase with the brass buckles and lock belongs to my friends.

A. From Chicago
B. with the brass buckles
C. and lock
D. to my friends

27. Select the word or phrase that makes this sentence grammatically correct.

The doctor's children like ____________ themselves up in her scrubs.

A. dress
B. are dressing
C. to dress
D. to be dressed

GO ON TO THE NEXT PAGE

28. Select the phrase in the sentence that is *not* used correctly.

If someone wants to work in a maternity ward, you must take Human Development 302 or its equivalent.

A. wants to work
B. in a maternity ward
C. you must take
D. or its equivalent

29. Select the word or phrase that makes this sentence grammatically correct.

If Selena takes the course online, she ____________ a good deal of time and money.

A. save
B. saves
C. will save
D. will be saved

30. What punctuation is needed in this sentence to make it correct?

Due to the terrible traffic this morning half of the staff arrived late.

A. Period
B. Comma
C. Exclamation point
D. Semicolon

31. Select the phrase that will make this sentence grammatically correct.

Dr. Kapoor has a twinkle in his eye whenever he ____________.

A. address a small child
B. is addressing a small child
C. will address a small child
D. has addressed a small child

32. Which word is used incorrectly in the following sentence?

Her financial adviser gloomy described the current slump in the market.

A. adviser
B. gloomy
C. current
D. slump

33. Select the sentence that is grammatically correct.

A. Professor Zhang showed she and I the model.
B. Professor Zhang showed me and her the model.
C. Professor Zhang showed her and me the model.
D. Professor Zhang showed her and I the model.

34. What word is best to substitute for the underlined words in the following sentence?

Ms. Renfrew's husband holds <u>Ms. Renfrew's</u> power of attorney.

A. her
B. him
C. hers
D. his

35. Which sentence contains an example of euphemism?

A. Everybody should wear his or her oldest clothing.
B. The situation did not warrant a "whatever" from her.
C. He will be ready in two shakes of a lamb's tail.
D. They had their beloved dog Marnie put to sleep.

36. What punctuation is needed in this sentence to make it correct?

After chairing the offices welcoming committee, she felt connected to each of the new employees.

A. Period
B. Comma
C. Apostrophe
D. Semicolon

37. Which of the following words is spelled correctly?

A. Insicion
B. Insition
C. Incision
D. Incition

38. Which of the following sentences contains a preposition?

A. I met him for the first time yesterday.
B. Can you remember his name?
C. Dr. Liu and he will work together.
D. They will be studying parasitology.

GO ON TO THE NEXT PAGE

39. Which of the following words or phrases fit best in the sentence below?

If Bonita ____________ early, she ____________ the number 2 bus to the mall.

A. finished; will be taking
B. finishes; will take
C. finish; is taking
D. had finished; will have taken

40. Which word is *not* used correctly in the context of the sentence?

Does your enormous grin infer that you relished the celebration?

A. enormous
B. celebration
C. relished
D. infer

41. Which sentence is grammatically correct?

A. I found a book lying on the driveway bound in leather.
B. On the driveway, I found a book lying bound in leather.
C. Lying on the driveway, I found a book bound in leather.
D. I found a book bound in leather lying on the driveway.

42. Select the word that makes this sentence grammatically correct.

Only one of my friends ____________ watched the entire series.

A. have
B. has
C. are
D. is

43. What punctuation is needed in this sentence to make it correct?

You may order the books online or you might find some at the library.

A. Period
B. Apostrophe
C. Colon
D. Comma

44. Which of the following words is spelled correctly?

A. Paralysis
B. Paralisys
C. Paralisis
D. Paralyzis

GO ON TO THE NEXT PAGE

45. Which word is the best substitute for the underlined words in the following sentence?

<u>Our colleagues'</u> reputations in the field are beyond reproach.

A. His
B. Hers
C. These
D. Their

46. Which word in the following sentence is an adverb?

The jolly elf is often used as a symbol of the Christmas holidays.

A. jolly
B. often
C. symbol
D. Christmas

47. Which sentence is the clearest?

A. With their newborn baby, she spotted her neighbors in the park.
B. She spotted in the park her neighbors with their newborn baby.
C. In the park, the neighbors with their newborn baby were spotted by her.
D. In the park, she spotted her neighbors with their newborn baby.

48. Select the phrase or clause that is misplaced in the sentence.

After a brief introduction, the professor turned his seminar over to the visiting from France lecturer.

A. After a brief introduction
B. the professor
C. turned his seminar over
D. from France

49. Which is an example of a run-on sentence?

A. Without receiving any forewarning at all.
B. An interesting but terribly lengthy article.
C. The runner was tired but still on his feet.
D. Del recited the number, I wrote it down.

50. Which sentence is clearest?

A. Scott created a small study in a closet off the hallway.
B. The study created by Scott in a closet off the hallway was small.
C. Scott, in a closet off the hallway, created a study that was small.
D. In a closet, Scott created a small study off the hallway.

STOP. IF YOU HAVE TIME LEFT OVER, CHECK YOUR WORK ON THIS SECTION ONLY.

BASIC MATH SKILLS

50 items
Suggested time: 45 minutes

1. Multiply and simplify: 1/3 × 3 1/9 =

A. 31/27
B. 11/3
C. 1 1/27
D. 26/27

2. Ninety percent of the class passed with a 75 or higher. If that percent equaled 27 students, how many students were in the whole class?

A. 28
B. 30
C. 36
D. 40

3. If a party planner assumes 2 bottles of sparkling water per 5 guests, how many bottles must she purchase for a party of 65?

A. 26
B. 33
C. 49
D. 58

4. Kayla purchased 4 paperbacks and 3 hardcover books at the library sale. The paperbacks were 15 cents apiece, and the hardcovers were 75 cents apiece. If Kayla paid with a $5 bill, how much change was she owed?

A. $2.00
B. $2.15
C. $2.25
D. $3.05

5. Express 5.75 as a fraction in lowest terms.

A. 5 1/25
B. 5 2/5
C. 5 1/2
D. 5 3/4

GO ON TO THE NEXT PAGE

6. How many milliliters are there in 6 liters? (Enter numeric value only.)

____

7. At the Bella Day Spa, a manicure costs $35 and a pedicure costs $49. If on Tuesday, x patrons request manicures, and y patrons request pedicures, what does the spa collect for manicures and pedicures on Tuesday?

A. $\$35x + \$49y$
B. $\$39(x + y)$
C. $\$9(xy)$
D. $(\$35 + x)(\$49 + y)$

8. Approximately how many pounds are there in 12 kilograms?

A. 2.2
B. 5.45
C. 12.0
D. 26.4

9. There are a total of 450 employees at WINK, Inc. The company recently hired 65 new employees and laid off 35 employees. After these changes, the company decided to form teams of 25 employees each for a new project. How many employees will be left without a team assignment?

A. 5
B. 12
C. 19
D. 30

10. At a pet shelter, there are 23 cats and 40 dogs up for adoption. If 5 more cats are brought in, what is the ratio of dogs to cats at the shelter?

A. 40:23
B. 10:7
C. 7:10
D. 23:40

11. If a recipe for custard calls for 200 mL of heavy cream, approximately how many ounces is that?

A. 6.8
B. 12.5
C. 25.0
D. 29.6

GO ON TO THE NEXT PAGE

12. A bakery wants to make some shortbread cookies for a charity event. Each batch of 24 cookies requires 2 cups of flour, 1 cup of powdered sugar, and $\frac{1}{2}$ cup of butter. The bakery has 20 cups of flour, 18 cups of sugar, and 8 cups of butter in stock. How many batches of cookies can the bakery make with the ingredients it has in stock? (Enter numeric value only.) ________________

13. During basic training, cadets eat at 5:30 P.M. What would that be in military time?

A. 530
B. 1230
C. 1730
D. 2330

14. At one summer camp, there is a ratio of 8 campers per counselor. Which of the following is a possible actual number of counselors and campers at the camp?

A. 9:126
B. 12:96
C. 16:208
D. 24:216

15. Divide and simplify: 2 1/2 ÷ 1 7/10 =

A. 11/20
B. 1 1/5
C. 1 8/17
D. 2 2/3

16. Franklin's weekly paycheck is $673.08. Of that, he puts one-third aside for rent and utilities and spends $85 on groceries. What is left from his weekly paycheck?

A. $363.72
B. $309.36
C. $224.36
D. $139.36

17. Nurse Espinal ordered 40 boxes of exam gloves at $9 a box and 2 glove dispensers at $30 apiece. How much did she spend in all? (Enter numeric value only.) ________________

GO ON TO THE NEXT PAGE

18. Of the 975 vehicles sold by Dukakis Auto last year, Samuel sold 117. What percentage of the vehicles did he sell?

A. 12%
B. 14%
C. 18%
D. 22%

19. How many centimeters are there in 1 yard?

A. 30.48 centimeters
B. 60.96 centimeters
C. 91.44 centimeters
D. 120 centimeters

20. In a scale drawing for a shed, 1 inch = 2 feet. If the shed floor is 3 inches by 4 inches on the drawing, what will its area be in reality?

A. 12 square inches
B. 12 square feet
C. 36 square feet
D. 48 square feet

21. Add: 2.35 + 4.38 + 1.44 =

A. 6.73
B. 7.07
C. 8.17
D. 8.37

22. Express 5% as a fraction.

A. $\frac{1}{5}$
B. $\frac{1}{10}$
C. $\frac{1}{15}$
D. $\frac{1}{20}$

23. Add and simplify: 4/15 + 5/6 =

A. 9/15
B. 9/10
C. 1 1/10
D. 1 29/30

24. Which of the following is a solution to the equation $|x-4|=3$?

A. 3
B. 1
C. −1
D. −7

25. Noah weighs 77 kilograms. Approximately how many pounds does he weigh?

A. 170 pounds
B. 177 pounds
C. 189 pounds
D. 193 pounds

26. How many grams are in 25 kilograms?

A. 0.25 gram
B. 2.5 grams
C. 250 grams
D. 2,500 grams

27. What is 40 percent of 95?

A. 24
B. 26
C. 34
D. 38

28. Divide: $612 \div 8 =$

A. 74 r1
B. 76 r4
C. 76 r5
D. 86 r2

29. If Wilbur spends 45 minutes every day practicing the violin, how much time does he spend practicing over a period of two weeks?

A. 5 hours 15 minutes
B. 8 hours 30 minutes
C. 10 hours 30 minutes
D. 10 hours 45 minutes

GO ON TO THE NEXT PAGE

30. What is 65 percent of 80?

A. 50.5
B. 52
C. 50
D. 60.5

31. Express 13/5 as a decimal.

A. 0.026
B. 0.26
C. 2.6
D. 26

32. Laura needs to cover a cut that is 2.4 inches long. The bandages are measured in centimeters. How many centimeters is the cut? Round your answer to the nearest centimeter. (Enter numeric value only.)

____

33. Express the ratio 24:80 as a percentage.

A. 19.5%
B. 22%
C. 25.5%
D. 30%

34. If home blood pressure kits are on sale for $24.99 for 2, how much would it cost to buy 10 home blood pressure kits?

A. $99.96
B. $124.95
C. $125.00
D. $249.90

35. What date in Arabic numerals is Roman numeral MCMIX? (Enter numeric value only.) ____________

36. Caleb is 5 years younger than his brother, who is 9 years older than their 15-year-old cousin. How old is Caleb?

A. 24
B. 21
C. 19
D. 1

37. If Jim's truck needed 7.2 quarts of oil for an oil change, about how many liters is that?

A. 6.14 liters
B. 6.79 liters
C. 7.63 liters
D. 8.26 liters

38. Multiply: $0.7 \times 0.07 =$

A. 0.0049
B. 0.049
C. 0.49
D. 4.9

39. If the outside temperature is currently 15 degrees on the Celsius scale, what is the approximate temperature on the Fahrenheit scale?

A. 44°F
B. 52°F
C. 56.5°F
D. 59°F

40. A hospital blueprint is drawn on a 1:250 scale. If a staff parking lot in the blueprint measures 10 cm by 16 cm, how large is the parking lot in real life?

A. 5 m by 8 m
B. 10 m by 25 m
C. 25 m by 40 m
D. 250 m by 400 m

41. If $2x - 4 = 6y$, what is the value of x when $y = 3$? (Enter numeric value only.) ______________

42. Divide: $7.2 \div 0.9 =$

A. 0.085
B. 0.8
C. 8
D. 80

43. Subtract and simplify: 7/8 – 1/12 =

A. 1/2
B. 7/10
C. 19/24
D. 54/96

44. If a high-speed train averages about 140 mph, how long will it take to travel 455 miles?

A. 3 hours 15 minutes
B. 3 hours 20 minutes
C. 3 hours 30 minutes
D. 3 hours 45 minutes

45. Subtract and simplify: 8 1/4 – 6 5/6 =

A. 2 1/6
B. 1 1/2
C. 1 7/24
D. 1 5/12

46. Express 43.5% as a decimal.

A. 0.435
B. 4.35
C. 43.5
D. 435

47. There are 4,370 people attending a square dance contest in Lakeville. Each dance requires four couples. If the attendees are divided into groups of 8, how many people will be left over? (Enter numeric value only.) ______________

48. Express 0.165 as a percent.

A. 165%
B. 16.5%
C. 1.65%
D. 0.165%

49. The usual ratio of flour to water in bread dough is 5:3. If a recipe calls for 2 1/2 cups of flour, how much water will be required? (Enter numeric value only, and record in decimal form.) _____________

50. Randy is 6 feet 2 inches tall. How many total inches is that? (Enter numeric value only.) _______________

STOP. IF YOU HAVE TIME LEFT OVER, CHECK YOUR WORK ON THIS SECTION ONLY.

BIOLOGY

25 items
Suggested time: 21 minutes

1. Which is *not* a form of passive transport?
   A. Diffusion
   B. Endocytosis
   C. Filtration
   D. Osmosis

2. What is missing from this reaction for photosynthesis?
   carbon dioxide + water → glucose + ___________
   A. carbon
   B. enzymes
   C. oxygen
   D. sucrose

3. Which is an example of parthenogenesis?
   A. Female snakes produce clones of themselves without fertilization using a polar body.
   B. Hydras develop genetically identical polyps that break off to form new organisms.
   C. Bacteria replicate their genetic material and divide into offspring cells.
   D. Strawberries produce tiny plantlets along runners extending from the parent plant.

4. Which base appears in DNA but *not* in RNA?
   A. Guanine
   B. Cytosine
   C. Thymine
   D. Adenine

5. Cystic fibrosis is carried on the recessive allele. In a situation where two heterozygous parents are healthy carriers of the disease, what percentage of their offspring are predicted to be healthy carriers?
   A. 0%
   B. 25%
   C. 50%
   D. 100%

GO ON TO THE NEXT PAGE

6. If you place a red blood cell into a hypotonic solution, what will happen?

A. The cell will shrink.
B. The cell will release chloride.
C. The cell will release saline.
D. The cell will swell.

7. Which animal has an open transport system?

A. Crayfish
B. Trout
C. Earthworm
D. Penguin

8. How are lipids different in structure and function from carbohydrates?

A. They are more diverse chemically, are insoluble in water, and store energy better.
B. They contain no oxygen, have a polar region, and are not sources of energy.
C. They provide fewer calories, are hydrophilic, and are more easily absorbed.
D. They are inorganic, undergo lipogenesis, and contribute to the synthesis of hormones.

9. Which does *not* name a female part of a flowering plant?

A. Style
B. Pistil
C. Stigma
D. Anther

10. After proteins are synthesized by the ribosomes, what often happens?

A. They are recycled via the lysosomes.
B. They move to the Golgi complex for sorting and transport.
C. They deposit mRNA on the surface of the smooth endoplasmic reticulum.
D. They travel through the outer and inner nuclear envelope into the cell nucleus.

11. Which gives the order of four taxonomic categories from least to most specific?

A. Family, phylum, class, order
B. Phylum, class, order, family
C. Order, phylum, class, family
D. Phylum, order, family, class

GO ON TO THE NEXT PAGE

12. What are two components of all amino acids?

A. COOH and NH_2
B. CO_2 and NH
C. Na and OH
D. CH_2 and H_2N

13. Plants use vaculoles to digest unwanted material in the cytoplasm. Which structure works with vacuoles to perform a similar function in animal cells?

A. Lysosome
B. Micronucleus
C. Cytoplasm
D. Cell membrane

14. Which is *not* a key difference between aerobic and anaerobic respiration?

A. Only one produces ATP.
B. The site of the reactions differs.
C. The energy produced differs.
D. Only one involves the Krebs cycle.

15. What is the result of telophase in mitosis?

A. Chromosomes begin to move to opposite ends of the spindle.
B. Nuclear membrane and nucleoli disintegrate.
C. Chromatids line up at the center of the spindle.
D. Nuclear membrane and nucleoli form.

16. Which is *not* a type of genetic mutation?

A. Substitution
B. Deletion
C. Recombination
D. Frameshift

17. Colorblindness is a sex-linked trait carried on the X chromosome. In an example of a male with colorblindness and a female carrier, what ratio of the offspring is predicted neither to carry nor to manifest the disease?

A. 0 female : 1 male
B. 1 female : 1 male
C. 1 female : 0 male
D. 2 female : 1 male

GO ON TO THE NEXT PAGE

18. Which is *not* a product of glycolysis?

A. ATP
B. NADH
C. Pyruvate
D. Oxygen

19. A social scientist developed a testing instrument to determine the correlation between parental home ownership and student success in school. She tested every child in her local school district and found a close correlation. Which does *not* represent one way she might ensure the reliability of her testing instrument and results?

A. Repeat the testing five years later.
B. Repeat the testing in a second district.
C. Ask a second scientist to assess covariation in the study.
D. Ask a second scientist to apply the instrument in a different district.

20. What is the genus of human beings?

A. Chordata
B. Homo
C. Mammalia
D. Primates

21. Students at a vet school are participating in a longitudinal study to determine the effect of the size of a dog on its lifespan. They feed the dogs similar foods, and the dogs receive similar attention and exercise over the course of the experiment. In this experiment, what is the independent variable?

A. The dogs' lifespan
B. The amount of exercise
C. The amount of food
D. The dogs' size

22. Which is an example of deductive reasoning?

A. Ten of the 100 birds we tested have mites; therefore, 10 percent of the population of birds on the island must have mites.
B. Most of the birds we found to have mites were seagulls; therefore, seagulls must be susceptible to mites.
C. Seagulls are susceptible to mites. Specimen A is a seagull. Therefore, specimen A must be susceptible to mites.
D. Specimen A was found on the north shore. Specimen A has mites. Therefore, all birds found on the north shore have mites.

GO ON TO THE NEXT PAGE

23. In a eukaryotic cell, where does the Krebs cycle take place?

A. Lysosome
B. Nucleolus
C. Centriole
D. Mitochondria

24. What is the shape of the bacteria known as *bacilli*?

A. Spherical
B. Rod-shaped
C. Star-shaped
D. Spiral

25. An elk has 68 chromosomes in each parent cell. Following meiosis I, how many chromosomes are in the daughter cells of an elk?

A. 23
B. 34
C. 46
D. 68

STOP. IF YOU HAVE TIME LEFT OVER, CHECK YOUR WORK ON THIS SECTION ONLY.

CHEMISTRY

25 items
Suggested time: 21 minutes

1. In sulfur dioxide, sulfur shares four valence electrons with two oxygen atoms, with each oxygen atom sharing two valence electrons with sulfur. This is called ____________.

A. covalent bonding
B. electronegativity
C. London dispersion force
D. ionization energy

2. On the periodic table, carbon's atomic number is 6, and magnesium's atomic number is 12. Which of the following can you predict from that information?

A. Both carbon and magnesium are nonmetals.
B. Magnesium has fewer neutrons than carbon.
C. Magnesium has a greater atomic mass than carbon.
D. Carbon is a major element, whereas magnesium is a trace element.

3. An amount equaling 28 kilograms of a radioactive substance has a half-life of 10 years. How many years will it take the substance to decay naturally to only 7 kilograms?

A. 15
B. 20
C. 25
D. 30

4. Which compound contains a polar covalent bond?

A. O_2
B. F_2
C. Br_2
D. HCl

5. $A + BC \rightarrow B + AC$ represents what type of chemical reaction?

A. Single replacement
B. Decomposition
C. Synthesis
D. Double replacement

6. Among the following elements, which is a nonmetal?

A. Cobalt
B. Zinc
C. Nitrogen
D. Sodium

7. What is the correct name for $Ca(OH)_2$?

A. Calcium hydroxide
B. Calcium oxide
C. Calcium hydroxate
D. Calcium hydrogen carbonate

8. Which of these elements has no allotropes?

A. Tin
B. Carbon
C. Phosphorus
D. Mercury

9. Why might ginger ale taste flat if the can were taken from a cooler and left on a picnic table in the sun?

A. In the heat, its carbon dioxide would no longer dissolve.
B. The pressure outside the can would be greater than the pressure inside.
C. The carbon dioxide molecules in the liquid would move more slowly in heat.
D. The sugar in the ginger ale would separate from the flavorings under pressure.

10. Which is *not* a primary gas in human blood?

A. Nitrogen
B. Helium
C. Oxygen
D. Carbon dioxide

11. Balance this equation: $Fe + Cl_2 \rightarrow FeCl_3$

A. $2Fe + 3Cl_2 \rightarrow 2FeCl_3$
B. $4Fe + 6Cl_2 \rightarrow 6FeCl_3$
C. $2Fe + 2Cl_2 \rightarrow 2FeCl_3$
D. $4Fe + 3Cl_2 \rightarrow 2FeCl_3$

GO ON TO THE NEXT PAGE

12. Which is *not* a feature of the noble gases?

A. Oxidation number of zero
B. Low boiling point
C. Low reactivity
D. Flammability

13. How many electrons are shared in a double covalent bond?

A. 1
B. 2
C. 4
D. 8

14. How many neutrons are in an atom of carbon-14?

A. 2
B. 6
C. 8
D. 24

15. What is the correct electron configuration for oxygen?

A. $1s^2 2s^2$
B. $1s^2 2s^2 2p^4$
C. $1s^2 2s^2 2p^6 3s^1$
D. $1s^2 2s^2 2p^6 3s^2$

16. Given the number of moles of a solute and the volume of a solution, how do you calculate the molarity?

A. Convert moles to grams and multiply by liters of solution.
B. Divide moles by mass and multiply by liters of solution.
C. Calculate mass of solute and divide by liters of solution.
D. Divide moles of solute by liters of solution.

17. Where would you expect human blood to fall on the pH scale?

A. Between 1 and 3
B. Between 4 and 5
C. Between 7 and 8
D. Between 9 and 10

18. To the nearest whole number, what is the mass of one mole of carbon dioxide?

A. 36 g/mol
B. 44 g/mol
C. 58 g/mol
D. 72 g/mol

19. Which is *not* a form of ionizing radiation?

A. Alpha particles
B. Gamma rays
C. Microwaves
D. X-rays

20. Sodium hypochlorite is the active ingredient in bleach. What is its chemical formula?

A. ONaCl
B. NaOCl
C. ClNaO
D. NaClO

21. What is the oxidation state of each oxygen atom in CO_2?

A. −2
B. −1
C. 0
D. +2

22. Which of these intermolecular forces is weakest?

A. Dipole–dipole interaction
B. London dispersion force
C. Ion–ion interaction
D. Hydrogen bonding

23. Concentrated HCl has a molarity of 12.0. What volume of concentrated HCl should be used to prepare 250 mL of a 6.0 M HCl solution?

A. 41.7 mL
B. 62.5 mL
C. 125 mL
D. 175 mL

GO ON TO THE NEXT PAGE

24. Which of these reactions is an example of combustion?

A. $FeS + HCl \rightarrow FeCl_2 + H_2S$
B. $Na_2CO_3 \rightarrow Na_2O + CO_2$
C. $CaO + CO_2 \rightarrow CaCO_3$
D. $C_6H_{12}O_6 + O_2 \rightarrow CO_2 + H_2O$

25. Which of these metals has the greatest atomic mass?

A. Fe
B. Au
C. Cu
D. Ag

STOP. IF YOU HAVE TIME LEFT OVER, CHECK YOUR WORK ON THIS SECTION ONLY.

ANATOMY AND PHYSIOLOGY

25 items
Suggested time: 21 minutes

1. If a patient has a cut on her forearm, which part of the arm is distal to the cut?

A. The fingers
B. The elbow
C. The bicep
D. The shoulder

2. What is the name of the tissue that lines the chest cavity and covers the lungs?

A. Pleura
B. Trachea
C. Viscera
D. Alveoli

3. Where does diffusion of oxygen and carbon dioxide take place?

A. Along the terminal bronchioles
B. Within the thoracic cavity
C. In the alveolar capillaries
D. Inside the tertiary bronchi

4. Where does the process of peristalsis begin?

A. Mouth
B. Small intestine
C. Stomach
D. Esophagus

5. Where in the body would you be likely to find adipose tissue?

A. Blood vessels
B. Lymph
C. Breast
D. Brain

6. What is the function of the dendrite in the nervous system?

A. It excites or inhibits the neurons.
B. It increases the speed of impulses.
C. It transmits information to neurons.
D. It receives electrical messages.

GO ON TO THE NEXT PAGE

7. How does the integumentary system work with the digestive system?

A. The integumentary system absorbs vitamin D, which the digestive system uses to absorb and use calcium.
B. The digestive system circulates minerals outward to the integumentary system.
C. Touch input via the integumentary system sends messages about caloric needs to the digestive system.
D. Nerves and glands in the integumentary system help to regulate excretory functions in the digestive system.

8. When the tricuspid valve snaps shut, blood cannot flow backward from the ____________ to the ____________.

A. right atrium; right ventricle
B. left ventricle; left atrium
C. right ventricle; right atrium
D. left atrium; left ventricle

9. Patient A is allergic only to ragweed. Patient B is allergic to ragweed and to several other plant pollens. What is definitely true of Patient B compared to Patient A?

A. Patient B has a relatively depressed immune system.
B. Patient B produces more types of IgE antibodies.
C. Patient B is more at risk of anaphylaxis.
D. Patient B is symptomatic at more times of year.

10. The human foot contains about how many bones?

A. About 9
B. About 26
C. About 54
D. About 128

11. The thymus is part of the ____________.

A. nervous system
B. digestive system
C. lymphatic system
D. cardiovascular system

12. Where are phagocytes produced?

A. Blood
B. Bone marrow
C. Lymph nodes
D. Kidneys

13. Which is an example of a sesamoid bone?

A. Patella
B. Skull
C. Vertebra
D. Ulna

14. After entering the heart through the vena cavae, blood flows from the right atrium into the ____________ through the ____________.

A. left atrium; pulmonary valve
B. right ventricle; tricuspid valve
C. left atrium; mitral valve
D. right ventricle; aortic valve

15. Pellagra is a disease caused by lack of ____________.

A. thiamine
B. vitamin C
C. protein
D. niacin

16. How does the endocrine system work with the digestive system?

A. The digestive system produces the building blocks of endocrine hormones.
B. The endocrine system uses digestive products to stimulate growth.
C. The digestive system recycles hormones from the endocrine system.
D. The endocrine system produces chemicals that regulate digestion.

17. A disorder of the pineal gland may have an adverse effect on ____________.

A. sleep
B. growth
C. heart rate
D. bone strength

18. Which part of the skull is most anterior?

A. Occipital bone
B. Temporal bone
C. Parietal bone
D. Nasal bone

GO ON TO THE NEXT PAGE

19. Which of the following is a total cholesterol level that might be considered desirable for an adult?

A. Under 40 mg/dL
B. Under 200 mg/dL
C. 200–239 mg/dL
D. 240–279 mg/dL

20. How does a sagittal section divide the body?

A. Into right and left regions
B. Into upper and lower regions
C. Into front and back regions
D. Between the dorsal and ventral cavities

21. Which enzyme breaks down starch into maltose?

A. Amylase
B. Pepsin
C. Lactase
D. Maltase

22. About how much urine is produced by the adult kidneys daily?

A. 1–2 cups
B. 1–2 pints
C. 1–2 quarts
D. 1/2–1 gallon

23. Which mineral is important for fluid balance in the body?

A. Sulfur
B. Fluoride
C. Copper
D. Potassium

24. The esophagus is ____________ to the trachea.

A. medial
B. ventral
C. posterior
D. anterior

25. Which organ system contains the channels known as Volkmann's canals?

A. The nervous system
B. The skeletal system
C. The digestive system
D. The integumentary system

STOP. IF YOU HAVE TIME LEFT OVER, CHECK YOUR WORK ON THIS SECTION ONLY.

PHYSICS

25 items
Suggested time: 50 minutes

1. Which of these liquids would likely have the least specific gravity?

   A. Alcohol
   B. Sea water
   C. Vinegar
   D. Mercury

2. An airplane travels 200 miles northwest and then, on the return trip, travels 200 miles southeast. Which of the following is true?

   A. The displacement of the plane is 400 miles, and the distance traveled is 0 miles.
   B. The displacement of the plane is 400 miles, and the distance traveled is 400 miles.
   C. The displacement of the plane is 0 miles, and the distance traveled is 0 miles.
   D. The displacement of the plane is 0 miles, and the distance traveled is 400 miles.

3. A little girl is walking her pony around a ring. Both are traveling at a rate of 3 km/h. Which statement is true?

   A. The pony has more kinetic energy than the girl.
   B. The pony has less kinetic energy than the girl.
   C. The walkers have equal amounts of kinetic energy.
   D. Neither of the walkers has kinetic energy.

4. A car's acceleration is 5 m/s^2. How long does it take to change velocity from 10 m/s to 25 m/s?

   A. 2 s
   B. 3 s
   C. 4 s
   D. 5 s

5. A rolling 7.5-kg bowling ball has a momentum of 15 kg·m/s. What velocity must a tennis ball with a mass of 53 grams have to equal the bowling ball's momentum?

   A. 2 m/s
   B 4 m/s
   C. 28 m/s
   D. 283 m/s

GO ON TO THE NEXT PAGE

6. Which substance's volume would be most affected by temperature change?

A. Gasoline
B. Ozone
C. Copper
D. Blood

7. A box is moved by a 12 N force over a distance of 3 meters. What is the amount of work that has been done?

A. 4 J
B. 4 N·m
C. 36 W
D. 36 N·m

8. A 120-volt space heater delivers 1,500 watts of power. How many amperes does it draw?

A. 180,000 amperes
B. 180 amperes
C. 12.5 amperes
D. 8 amperes

9. How do you determine the frequency of a wave?

A. Multiply the speed by the wavelength.
B. Add the speed and the wavelength.
C. Divide the period by 1.
D. Divide the speed by the wavelength.

10. Which is true of kinetic energy but not of potential energy?

A. Height and distance may be determining factors.
B. It can be transferred from one object to another.
C. Mass may be a determining factor.
D. It may be measured in Joules.

11. A Ferris wheel at the county fair has a diameter of 50 meters. If it makes one complete turn at a speed of about 16 km/h, what is the approximate centripetal acceleration of the riders?

A. 10.24 m/s^2
B. 3.15 m/s^2
C. 0.64 m/s^2
D. 0.18 m/s^2

GO ON TO THE NEXT PAGE

12. Which best illustrates a transverse wave?

A. A plucked string on a guitar
B. Surf breaking close to shore
C. A released spring
D. Initial wave in an earthquake

13. Unlike scalar quantities, vectors have ____________.

A. magnitude
B. direction
C. quantity
D. speed

14. Which object will be most buoyant in water with a density of 1 g/cm^3?

A. A block with a mass of 3 g and a volume of 2 cm^3
B. A block with a mass of 4 g and a volume of 2.5 cm^3
C. A block with a mass of 5 g and a volume of 4.5 cm^3
D. A block with a mass of 10 g and a volume of 9.8 cm^3

15. If the mass of each of two objects is doubled, what happens to the gravitational force between them?

A. It is halved.
B. It is doubled.
C. It is quadrupled.
D. It remains constant.

16. Three 1.5V batteries are connected in a series. What is the total voltage of the circuit?

A. 1.5V
B. 3.0V
C. 4.5V
D. 6.0V

17. The relationship between force and reaction force is expressed in ____________.

A. Newton's First Law of Motion
B. Newton's Second Law of Motion
C. Boyle's Law
D. Newton's Third Law of Motion

GO ON TO THE NEXT PAGE

18. A 10-cm candle is placed 20 centimeters away from a mirror with a focal length of 10 centimeters. What is the image distance of the candle?

A. 20 cm
B. 40 cm
C. 60 cm
D. 75 cm

19. A wave in a vibrating wire travels at 15 m/s and has a wavelength of 2.5 meters. What is the frequency?

A. 37.5 Hz
B. 17.5 Hz
C. 6 Hz
D. 2.4 Hz

20. Four children are riding their soapbox cars down an incline. Which car has the greatest momentum?

A. Abner, weighing 75 pounds, is driving a car with a mass of 155 pounds at 15 mph.
B. Bai Minh, weighing 68 pounds, is driving a car with a mass of 172 pounds at 12 mph.
C. Caitlyn, weighing 70 pounds, is driving a car with a mass of 165 pounds at 15 mph.
D. Darrell, weighing 78 pounds, is driving a car with a mass of 162 pounds at 14 mph.

21. A light wave strikes a boundary and is reflected again, with the angle between the incident ray and the reflected ray measuring 80 degrees. What is the angle of reflection?

A. 40 degrees
B. 80 degrees
C. 120 degrees
D. 160 degrees

22. A force of 15 Newtons stretches a spring 3 centimeters. How far will the spring stretch given a force of 22 Newtons?

A. 4.4 cm
B. 5 cm
C. 7 cm
D. 7.2 cm

23. A 1,500-kg car runs around a track at 20 m/s with a centripetal acceleration of 4 m/s^2. What is the radius of the track?

A. 400 m
B. 100 m
C. 75 m
D. 40 m

24. Four 5-ohm resistors are placed in a series and wired into a 100-V power supply. What current flows through this circuit?

A. 2 amp
B. 5 amp
C. 20 amp
D. 50 amp

25. An object with a charge of 3 μC is placed 1 meter from another object with a charge of 1 μC. What is the magnitude of the resulting force between the objects?

A. 0.03 N
B. 0.027 N
C. 270 N
D. 3×10^{-6} N

STOP. IF YOU HAVE TIME LEFT OVER, CHECK YOUR WORK ON THIS SECTION ONLY.

EVOLVE REACH (HESI) A2 PRACTICE TEST ANSWER KEY

Reading

1. A	11. C	21. D	31. A	41. D
2. D	12. C	22. D	32. B	42. B
3. B	13. D	23. C	33. A	43. B
4. C	14. C	24. D	34. B	44. A
5. B	15. A	25. A	35. C	45. A
6. C	16. B	26. D	36. B	46. B
7. D	17. D	27. A	37. A	47. A
8. A	18. B	28. B	38. C	48. B
9. A	19. D	29. C	39. B	49. D
10. C	20. D	30. A	40. C	50. C

Vocabulary and General Knowledge

1. A	11. D	21. A	31. D	41. B
2. B	12. B	22. D	32. C	42. A
3. D	13. A	23. C	33. A	43. D
4. B	14. A	24. B	34. D	44. A
5. C	15. C	25. C	35. C	45. D
6. B	16. B	26. B	36. A	46. D
7. A	17. A	27. D	37. B	47. B
8. B	18. A	28. D	38. C	48. A
9. C	19. B	29. C	39. D	49. D
10. C	20. C	30. B	40. C	50. C

Grammar

1. C	11. A	21. A	31. B	41. D
2. B	12. C	22. B	32. B	42. B
3. A	13. A	23. D	33. C	43. D
4. D	14. C	24. C	34. A	44. A
5. B	15. A	25. A	35. D	45. D
6. A	16. B	26. A	36. C	46. B
7. B	17. C	27. C	37. C	47. D
8. A	18. B	28. C	38. A	48. D
9. C	19. D	29. C	39. B	49. D
10. D	20. B	30. B	40. D	50. A

Basic Math Skills

1. C	11. A	21. C	31. C	41. 11
2. B	12. 10	22. D	32. 6	42. C
3. A	13. C	23. C	33. D	43. C
4. B	14. B	24. B	34. B	44. A
5. D	15. C	25. A	35. 1909	45. D
6. 6,000	16. A	26. D	36. C	46. A
7. A	17. 420	27. D	37. B	47. 2
8. D	18. A	28. B	38. B	48. B
9. A	19. C	29. C	39. D	49. 1.5
10. B	20. D	30. B	40. C	50. 74

Biology

1. B	6. D	11. B	16. C	21. D
2. C	7. A	12. A	17. A	22. C
3. A	8. A	13. A	18. D	23. D
4. C	9. D	14. A	19. C	24. B
5. C	10. B	15. D	20. B	25. B

Chemistry

1. A	6. C	11. A	16. D	21. A
2. C	7. A	12. D	17. C	22. B
3. B	8. D	13. C	18. B	23. C
4. D	9. A	14. C	19. C	24. D
5. A	10. B	15. B	20. D	25. B

Anatomy and Physiology

1. A	6. D	11. C	16. D	21. A
2. A	7. A	12. B	17. A	22. C
3. C	8. C	13. A	18. D	23. D
4. D	9. B	14. C	19. B	24. C
5. C	10. B	15. D	20. A	25. B

Physics

1. A	6. B	11. C	16. C	21. A
2. D	7. D	12. A	17. D	22. A
3. A	8. C	13. B	18. A	23. B
4. B	9. D	14. D	19. C	24. B
5. D	10. B	15. C	20. C	25. B

EVOLVE REACH (HESI) A2 PRACTICE TEST EXPLANATORY ANSWERS

MODULE 1: READING

1. (A) Remember that the main idea is the most important theme, one that carries throughout the passage. If someone asked you what this passage was about, you would be most likely to answer "biosimilars and their future marketing," making A the best answer.

2. (D) Details A and B appear in paragraph 3, and detail C is in the last sentence of paragraph 2. Detail D is never mentioned or implied.

3. (B) The author is not trying to convince you of anything, as a persuasive essay might do (choice A). The basic purpose here is to provide information on a topic.

4. (C) Options A, B, and D all find support somewhere in the passage, but option C has no support at all.

5. (B) Find the word in context: ". . . ACE inhibitors dilate the blood vessels, which increases blood flow and lowers pressure." To release pressure and increase flow, the vessels must be widened, making choice B the correct answer.

6. (C) Choices A, B, and D all have some support in the passage, but they are details rather than the main idea. Choice C covers every aspect of the passage and could apply to any part of it.

7. (D) A statement of fact can be proved or checked. A statement of opinion is what someone thinks or believes. In this case, statements A, B, and C could be proved scientifically, but statement D is simply someone's belief. The word *should* is a clue that this is a judgment rather than a fact.

8. (A) An objective essay is one that sticks to the facts without inserting the author's bias or excessive opinions. That is the best description of this fact-based essay.

9. (A) A summary should select the most critical parts of the essay and put them together to review the main ideas. Choice A does this without being overly specific or injecting information or opinions not included in the essay.

10. (C) In the case of a word that has multiple meanings, you must always look back at the word in context. Here, the author is telling about a virus being isolated, meaning discovered and separated from other viruses or from surrounding living matter—possibly grown in a pure culture.

11. (C) Choice A contains information not implied by the passage. Choice B is on topic but not comprehensive enough for a summary. Choice D is more specific than a summary should be and does not include the important fact that the virus has changed its range and its danger to humans.

12. (C) The author is not trying to convince the reader of anything, as choice D would indicate. The essay primarily transmits facts.

13. (D) It is not clear that having WHO post an alert earlier would have made a difference (choice A). Choice B is not supported by the facts in the essay, and choice C is belied by facts in the essay. The conclusion that is best supported is choice D.

14. (C) Choice A is found in the first paragraph, choice D appears in paragraph 4, and choice B is discussed throughout. The average age of patients is never mentioned.

15. (A) This choice best covers all of the information in the passage without being either too specific or too vague.

16. (B) Find the word in context: "Artichokes retained antioxidants through all cooking methods. . . ." The clearest synonym is choice B: "Artichokes *preserved* antioxidants through all cooking methods."

17. (D) Think about the author's attitude toward the subject matter. The tone is not idealistic (choice A), which would imply a dreamy sort of romanticism. Nor is it dramatic (choice B), which would indicate intensity. Rather than seeming uncaring, or indifferent (choice C), the author seems to be straightforward, or matter-of-fact (choice D).

18. (B) Find the part of the essay that mentions chopping vegetables (paragraph 4) and look for the minerals listed.

19. (D) An opinion cannot be checked or proved. Here, choice D may seem true, but it is impossible to prove because "better off" is such a vague description.

20. (D) Choices A, B, and C have support in the paragraph, but choice D is contradicted in paragraph 2.

21. (D) Choices A, B, and C are unsupported by details in the passage. Choice D is close to being the main idea.

22. (D) Calling the conclusion of proponents "unlikely" is the writer's personal opinion, not a statement of fact.

23. (C) A progressive disease is one that is ongoing and getting worse over time.

24. (D) The writer seems to be interested in the procedure, but the fact that "the technique comes with no guarantees at present" emphasizes that the writer remains unconvinced that it will be a true panacea for parent carriers.

25. (A) The author may not be convinced of the procedure's value, but there is no call upon the reader to reject it (choice B). The story is true, but it is not a mystery (choice C). Primarily, the purpose is informational—to give facts about a new procedure and to allow readers to draw their own conclusions.

26. (D) The author does not use fawning adjectives that would indicate being awestruck (choice C), but the attitude toward Saunders is definitely appreciative (choice D).

27. (A) The word *relieve* has a variety of meanings, but the one that best fits paragraph 2 is *ease* (choice A).

28. (B) In this sort of question, you must look for the one detail that does not appear in the passage. Cicely's training in social work is mentioned, but it is not an aspect of St. Christopher's, making choice B correct.

29. (C) The passage is largely informational and describes how one woman developed the idea of hospice.

30. (A) It is not possible to know whether Saunders's work is wholly responsible for the removal of end-of-life care from hospitals. Someone else might have developed hospice if she had not done so. Choice A goes beyond the specifics of the passage, but choices B, C, and D all have support in the passage.

31. (A) Although choice A may be true, it is not mentioned in the passage. Choice B is mentioned in paragraph 5, choice C in paragraph 2, and choice D in paragraph 4.

32. (B) A modicum of care is a small amount of care.

33. (A) The question refers only to the last paragraph in the passage, which states that "a modicum of care can prevent the infection from spreading throughout the family and beyond." In other words, the disease does not need to spread, if a modicum of care is used.

34. (B) The words *annoying* (choice A), *good* (choice C), and *should* (choice D) are all judgment words that indicate a writer's opinion. Choice B can be proved one way or the other, and thus it is a fact.

35. (C) What is the passage mostly about? It is about a condition that is common and easily spread. Choices A, B, and D are too narrowly focused to be main ideas.

36. (B) A conclusion must be supported by details in the essay. Choice A goes beyond what the writer suggests, as does choice C. Choice D is a judgment the author never makes. Choice B, however, has support in the final paragraph of the essay.

37. (A) If a limb atrophies, it weakens and withers from lack of use.

38. (C) The author uses words such as *amazing, benefits, sturdy, comfortable,* and *advancements* to indicate an attitude of enthusiasm for this new technology.

39. (B) The cast is described as lighter than fiberglass (choice A), with openings that allow the skin to breathe (choice C) and a design that is sturdy and comfortable (choice D). The cost (choice B) is never mentioned.

40. (C) Think about the choice that fits every aspect of the passage. Choice A is not the focus of the passage—it is about superfoods but not about their benefits. Choices B and D are too limited to be the main idea. Choice C is precisely the focus of the passage.

41. (D) This is a specific use of the word *concentrations*—here it is used to describe antioxidants within blueberries.

42. (B) The author compares cranberries to raisins in paragraph 4 while comparing superfoods to ordinary foods. You can conclude that dried cranberries are superfoods, even though raisins have more nutrients.

43. (B) Collards (choice B) are merely listed with "most dark vegetables," contrasted with kale, which is a superfood.

44. (A) The author is not angry about the labeling of foods, as choice C would suggest, but she is doubtful, or dubious, about the value of calling certain foods "superfoods," making choice A the best answer.

45. (A) Although much of the passage is informative, the author is not informing readers of dangers (choice C). The main goal is to show that other foods can offer just as much nutritional value as superfoods, making choice A correct.

46. (B) Although choice B is true, it is never mentioned in the passage.

47. (A) An accumulation of bilirubin is the same as a buildup of bilirubin.

48. (B) An estimate (choice A) is not an opinion. Choices C and D can be tested. The word *ought* (choice B) is a judgment word that signals an opinion.

49. (D) The author's point is that jaundice in babies is not serious and is easily cured. This is a soothing message for parents.

50. (C) Choice A is much more sensational than the essay seems to be. Choice B is quite narrow. Choice D almost covers everything but does not include the fact that sometimes intervention is required. Only choice C is all-inclusive.

MODULE 2: VOCABULARY AND GENERAL KNOWLEDGE

1. (A) If something is adverse, it is working against you.

2. (B) A resilient plant might go without water for days and then perk up when watered. A resilient patient might recover easily after an operation.

3. (D) *Umbra*, as in *umbrella*, means "shadow." On an x-ray, a penumbra may be a blurred region at the edge of an anatomical structure.

4. (B) The root *os* means "bone." To ossify is to harden to be like bone.

5. (C) From the Greek *pan* ("all") and *akos* ("remedy"), a panacea is a cure-all.

6. (B) Other synonyms for *succinct* include *concise* and *pithy.*

7. (A) If something is anomalous, it is uncharacteristic.

8. (B) The *lix* in *prolix* means "flowing"—it is the same root as in *liquor.* If you are prolix, your words just keep flowing.

9. (C) To putrefy is to rot, decompose, or spoil.

10. (C) *Rampant* has more than one meaning, but here it means "unchecked or proliferating."

11. (D) *Quaff* may refer to the action of drinking or the liquid being drunk.

12. (B) The etymology of *sanguine* connects it to *sang*, meaning "blood." At one time it was supposed that people in whom blood was the predominating humor were unusually cheerful and positive.

13. (A) Adolescence is youth; senescence is old age.

14. (A) The discoloration in a bruise is the result of ruptured blood vessels.

15. (C) A suppurating wound is one that is discharging pus.

16. (B) When a team of doctors make a prognosis, they are predicting the course of a disease or injury.

17. (A) *Effectiveness* and *efficacy* stem from the same root; both mean "the power to produce intended results."

18. (A) To be stupefied is to be knocked senseless.

19. (B) *Carpus* is the Latin word for "wrist." The eight small carpal bones connect the hand to the forearm.

20. (C) A soft drink might fizz or effervesce (choice D), but if the tablets evanesce, they fade or melt away.

21. (A) You can extricate yourself from a spiderweb or from a tricky situation. Either way, you are disentangling yourself.

22. (D) An acrid smell might be described as bitterly pungent. Vinegar has an acrid odor. Acrid odors may make your eyes water and sting your nasal passages.

23. (C) Other synonyms for *aberration* include *deviation* and *anomaly*.

24. (B) Because it looks a bit like *energize*, *enervate* may be misused to mean the opposite of its actual meaning. To enervate is to take away strength.

25. (C) The ventral part of the body is that where the belly is located; *venter* means "belly." In humans, that part is in front.

26. (B) Something palatable is pleasing to the palate.

27. (D) A papule is a small, inflamed bump in the skin.

28. (D) *Cyan* means "blue." When human blood lacks oxygen, the result is a bluish tinge to the body.

29. (C) An earthquake may cause a fissure in the Earth. Extreme dehydration may cause a fissure in the skin.

30. (B) Something gratuitous is given or taken without apparent reason.

31. (D) From a Latin root meaning "heavy" or "burdened," this is a technical adjective meaning "pregnant."

32. (C) A person who is gullible is easily fooled.

33. (A) The root *dur* means "hard." Someone who is obdurate is immovable.

34. (D) The word *modulate* is often used to indicate a lowering of the voice, but in fact, it refers to any change in tone or volume.

35. (C) *Impervious* is from the same root as *permeate.* To permeate is to spread through, or to infiltrate. If people are impervious, they let nothing in, or let nothing bother them.

36. (A) An innocuous tonic does no harm.

37. (B) *Lethargic* is from a root meaning "drowsy." A lethargic patient is sleepy and sluggish.

38. (C) The Latin root *tendere* means "to stretch," as in *extend.* A distention is an expansion through stretching.

39. (D) *Post* means "after," and the root *mort* means "death." A postmortem examination is done on a corpse, usually to determine cause of death.

40. (C) *Malleable* means "adaptable" (choice A), *watertight* is the opposite of *porous* (choice B), and *viscous* means "sticky" (choice D). The correct answer is *permeable*, meaning "able to be penetrated" (choice C).

41. (B) To stanch is to stop the flow of a liquid.

42. (A) If you have a predilection for hip-hop music, you think favorably of it compared to other music.

43. (D) To give succor is to give assistance or relief.

44. (A) The Stoic school of philosophy was developed by Zeno, who believed that people should be free from passion and never complain. A stoic patient accepts treatment without complaint.

45. (D) An MI is a myocardial infarction, commonly called a heart attack.

46. (D) *Vertigo*, from the root *vert*, meaning "turn," refers to a kind of spinning dizziness.

47. (B) *Contingent* has more than one meaning, but it is often used to mean "conditional" or "dependent upon something not yet certain."

48. (A) *Irascible* stems from the same root as *ire* and refers to angry irritability.

49. (D) Someone who is meticulous may seem overly fussy about details, but the more positive meaning of the word has to do with precision and care.

50. (C) To occlude is to stop up or close up.

MODULE 3: GRAMMAR

1. (C) A comma must appear between the introductory phrase *Having read the instructions twice* and the independent clause *Jen felt confident.* No other commas are needed.

2. (B) The verbs in the sentence must be parallel. In this case, that means that both must use a form of the helping verb *to have.*

3. (A) *Unexpected* is an adjective that describes her promotion.

4. (D) Reading the choices aloud may help you determine which choice has a logical order of phrases and clauses. The least convoluted sentence is choice D. In choice A, *with a blue awning* seems to modify *corner.*

5. (B) The verb must be a form of *to lie.* In this case, it could be *lay* or *have lain*, but not *laid*, which is the past tense of *lay* and requires an object, as in *He laid the flowers next to the bed.*

6. (A) The correct pronoun must be a subject pronoun. Only choice A is a subject pronoun.

7. (B) The only possible pronoun that completes the sentence is a singular subject pronoun with gender. It could be *she* or *he*. You would never refer to a patient as "it" (choice C).

8. (A) Use the object pronoun *whom* with a preposition such as *to.*

9. (C) Substitute the choices in the blank to find the one that makes sense in context. The sentence as a whole means "While we await a later inspection, the office will be closed."

10. (D) A colon after *room* would introduce the list of things the surgeon required.

11. (A) This is a frequently misspelled word that must simply be memorized.

12. (C) Lucy is not doing the employing, she is being employed.

13. (A) Examinees are more likely to have an oral (out loud) examination than an aural (hearing) one.

14. (C) *Drunk* is the verb form that goes with *having.*

15. (A) The modifying phrase *slowing to a crawl* should be as close as possible to the subject *bus.*

16. (B) The subject of the sentence is *one*, so the verb should be singular.

17. (C) The responses belong to the therapist and me; they belong to us. The correct possessive pronoun is *our.*

18. (B) The correct word is *suite*, meaning "a set of rooms."

19. (D) Placing a semicolon between the two independent clauses (*The teaching assistant was not prepared for the question* and *he mumbled an answer and then offered to look it up*) makes the sentence correct.

20. (B) Knowing when to use the suffix *-le* and when to use *-al* is often just a matter of memorization.

21. (A) Only the introductory phrase requires a comma to separate it from the independent clause it precedes.

22. (B) If something is a connector of two other things, it is between them.

23. (D) *Immediately* is an adverb that modifies the verb; *immediately* describes the speed with which Kim breaks out into a rash.

24. (C) The reflexive pronoun must correspond to the subject, *Julianne*. Only *herself* is appropriate in number and gender.

25. (A) If in doubt, read the sentences aloud and pick the one that is clearest.

26. (A) It is the friends who should be described as being "from Chicago," so that phrase should move to the end of the sentence.

27. (C) Only the infinitive phrase works with the rest of the sentence.

28. (C) Because the sentence begins with *someone*, the pronoun should match that antecedent. The sentence could be altered to read "If someone wants to work in a maternity ward, he or she must take . . ." or "If you want to work in a maternity ward, you must take. . . ."

29. (C) This sentence is an example of "first conditional"—it starts with a possible event in the future (Selena takes the course) and must end with a future tense verb (Selena will save).

30. (B) Placing a comma after *morning* separates the introductory adverbial phrase from the rest of the sentence.

31. (B) In this type of question, you must make sure that the tense of verbs remains consistent. Because *has* is present tense, the correct answer contains another present-tense verb, which could be *addresses* or *is addressing.*

32. (B) The adviser described the slump *gloomily*, an adverb, not *gloomy*, an adjective.

33. (C) Because the pronouns follow the verb and receive the action, they must be object pronouns. That eliminates choices A and D. Grammatically, it is correct to name oneself last, making choice C the best answer.

34. (A) The power of attorney belongs to Ms. Renfrew; it is her power of attorney.

35. (D) Euphemism is the substitution of a mild expression for one that is harsh or offensive. *Put to sleep* is a euphemism for "killed humanely."

36. (C) A comma is used correctly (choice B), and the sentence has an end mark (choice A). It is missing an apostrophe in *office's.*

37. (C) The word is related to *incisive*, which may help you remember its spelling.

38. (A) *For the first time* is a prepositional phrase headed by the preposition *for.*

39. (B) This is another sentence in the first conditional; the verbs should be present and future tense.

40. (D) To infer is to deduce, or conclude. A person's grin cannot do that. A grin may, however, imply or indicate delight or relish.

41. (D) To be clear and correct, the phrase *bound in leather* should lie as close as possible to the word it modifies, *book*, and the phrase *lying on the driveway* should clearly refer to the book bound in leather, not to the speaker.

42. (B) The subject is *one*, which is singular. Therefore, the correct verb must agree with a singular subject. *Is watched* (choice D) is ungrammatical.

43. (D) A comma after *online* would separate the two independent clauses, which are joined by the conjunction *or.*

44. (A) *Lysis* is a common ending for a medical term; examples include *analysis* and *dialysis*.

45. (D) *Colleagues'* is a plural possessive noun that must be replaced by a plural possessive pronoun. The pronoun *our* should not throw you off here.

46. (B) *Jolly* (choice A) and *Christmas* (choice D) are used as adjectives here to modify *elf* and *holidays*. *Symbol* (choice C) is a noun. *Often* (choice B) is an adverb that tells when something happens.

47. (D) Who had the newborn baby? Only choice D places the modifying phrase next to the word it modifies and maintains both the active voice and the meaning of the sentence.

48. (D) Look for the phrase that, if moved around, would improve the sentence. The lecturer may be visiting from France, but a better sentence would be "After a brief introduction, the professor turned his seminar over to the visiting lecturer from France."

49. (D) Choices A and B are sentence fragments. Sentence C is correct. Sentence D connects two independent clauses with a comma but no conjunction, creating a comma splice, which is a form of run-on sentence.

50. (A) Choice A contains all of the information in a logical order.

MODULE 4: BASIC MATH SKILLS

1. (C) Express 3 1/9 as an improper fraction: 28/9. Then multiply numerators and denominators: $1/3 \times 28/9 = 28/27$. Finally, express this as a mixed number in lowest terms: 1 1/27.

2. (B) Express the percent as a decimal: 0.90. Think: $0.90x = 27$. Solve: $x = 27 \div 0.90$. The answer is 30.

3. (A) Set this up as a proportion: $2/5 = x/65$. You may cross-multiply to solve:

$$2 \times 65 = 5x$$

$$130 = 5x$$

$$x = 130/5, \text{ or } 26.$$

4. (B) First, determine how much Kayla spent for the paperbacks: $\$0.15 \times 4 = \$0.60$. Then find out what she spent for the hardcovers: $\$0.75 \times 3 = \$2.25$. Add those sums: $\$0.60 + \$2.25 = \$2.85$. Finally, subtract that total from \$5.00:

$$\$5.00 - \$2.85 = \$2.15$$

5. (D) 5.75 = 5 75/100, or 5 3/4 in lowest terms.

6. (6,000) One liter = 1,000 milliliters, so 6 liters = 6,000 milliliters.

7. (A) $\$35x$ represents the income from manicures, and $\$49y$ represents the income from pedicures. Adding the two gives you the spa's total income from manicures and pedicures on Tuesday.

8. (D) One kilogram is approximately 2.2 pounds. Set up a proportion: $\frac{1\text{ kg}}{2.2\text{ lbs}} = \frac{12\text{ kg}}{x\text{ lbs}}; 2.2 \times 12 = 26.4.$

9. (A) First calculate the new total number of employees after the changes: $450 + 65 - 35 = 480$. To find the number of employees without a team assignment, we need to calculate the remainder after dividing by 25: $480 \div 25 = 19\ R5$, so 5 employees are left without a team assignment.

10. (B) First, find the new number of cats: $23 = 5 = 28$. There are 40 dogs and 28 cats, so the ratio of dogs to cats is 40:28, which can be reduced to 10:7.

11. (A) One ounce is approximately 29.6 milliliters. Set up a proportion: $\frac{1\text{ oz}}{29.6\text{ mL}} = \frac{x\text{ oz}}{200\text{ mL}}; 200 \div 29.6 \approx 6.8$ ounces.

12. (10) We need to find how many batches can be made with each ingredient and then whichever is the lowest number, that is the maximum number of batches the bakery can make. For flour: $20 \div 2 = 10$ batches. For sugar, $18 \div 1 = 18$ batches. For butter: $8 \div \frac{1}{2} = 16$ batches. The limiting ingredient is the flour, so the maximum number of batches that can be made with the available ingredients is 10.

13. (C) Military time starts with hours before noon. After noon, 1:00 P.M. is 1300, 2:00 P.M. is 1400, and so on.

14. (B) You must find the ratio that is equivalent to 1:8. You may think of each ratio as a fraction and find the fraction that is equivalent to 1/8. It should not require much calculation to recognize that 12/96 = 1/8.

15. (C) Begin by expressing the mixed numbers as improper fractions: 2 1/2 = 5/2, and 1 7/10 = 17/10. To divide by a fraction, multiply by its reciprocal. Therefore, 5/2 ÷ 17/10 = 5/2 × 10/17, or 50/34. Now reduce to lowest terms: 50/34 ÷ 2/2 = 25/17. Finally, express 25/17 as a mixed number: 1 8/17.

16. (A) First, find 1/3 of $673.08 by dividing the total by 3—$224.36. Subtract that from $673.08 to find what Franklin has left after paying for rent and utilities: $673.08 – $224.36 = $448.72. Now subtract the amount he spends on groceries: $448.72 – $85 = $363.72.

17. (420) Forty boxes of gloves at $9 each: 40 × $9 = $360, plus two dispensers at $30 each: 2 × $30 = $60. The total is $360 + $60 = $420.

18. (A) Solve by dividing Samuel's cars sold by the total and expressing the resulting decimal as a percent:

$$117 \div 975 = 0.12, \text{ or } 12\%$$

19. (C) Since 1 inch equals 2.54 centimeters, 36 inches (1 yard) equals 2.54 × 36, or 91.44 centimeters.

20. (D) Think in terms of ratios. If 1 inch is equivalent to 2 feet, 3 inches is equivalent to (3 × 2) or 6 feet, and 4 inches is equivalent to (4 × 2) or 8 feet. A shed floor 6 feet by 8 feet has an area of 48 ft^2.

21. (C) You can eliminate choices A and B here just by estimating the answer.

22. (D) Percent means "per 100," so to convert a percent to a fraction, put the percent as the numerator of a fraction and 100 as the denominator and then reduce if needed: $\frac{5}{100} = \frac{1}{20}$.

23. (C) First, find the lowest common denominator:

$4/15 \times 2/2 = 8/30$

$5/6 \times 5/5 = 25/30$

$8/30 + 25/30 = 33/30$, or 1 3/30. In lowest terms, that is 1 1/10.

24. (B) For the absolute value part of the equation to equal 3, either $x - 4 = 3$ or $x - 4 = -3$. For $x - 4 = 3$, add 4 to both sides: $x - 4 + 4 = 3 + 4; x = 7$. That's not an answer choice, so try the other option: $x - 4 = -3; x - 4 + 4 = -3 + 4; x = 1$. That is choice B.

25. (A) One kilogram is approximately 2.2 pounds. Set up a proportion: $\frac{1 \text{ kg}}{2.2 \text{ lbs}} = \frac{77 \text{ kg}}{x \text{ lbs}}; 2.2 \times 77 \approx 170$ lbs.

26. (D) Since 1 kilogram = 1,000 grams, 250 kilograms = 2,500 grams.

27. (D) Multiply 95 by the decimal equivalent of 40%: $0.40 \times 95 = 38$.

28. (B) The calculation would look like this:

```
  76r4
8)612
  56
   52
   48
    4
```

29. (C) You need to multiply 45 minutes by the number of days in two weeks, 14: $45 \times 14 = 630$. 630 minutes is equal to 10 hours 30 minutes.

30. (B) Use the decimal equivalent: $0.65 \times 80 = 52$.

31. (C) Simply divide to find the decimal equivalent: $13 \div 5 = 2.6$. It should be clear from looking at the answer choices that only choice C makes sense.

32. (6) One inch is approximately 2.54 centimeters. Set up a proportion: $\frac{1 \text{ in}}{2.54 \text{ cm}} = \frac{2.4 \text{ in}}{x \text{ cm}}; 2.54 \times 2.4 = 6.096$ centimeters, which rounds to 6 centimeters.

33. (D) Percentages are essentially ratios where the second number is 100. Divide 24 by 80 to find a decimal equivalent: $24 \div 80 = 0.3$, or 30%.

34. (B) If 2 cost $24.99, 4 cost $24.99 × 2, 6 cost $24.99 × 3, and so on to 10, which cost $24.99 × 5. You can probably figure out the answer without doing the computation.

35. (1909) Reading from left to right, M = 1,000, CM = 900, and IX = 9, making the date 1909.

36. (C) You can do this algebraically or in your head. Algebraically, say that Caleb = C, and his brother = B. C = B – 5, and B = 9 + 15, or 24. Since B = 24, C = 19.

37. (B) One liter is approximately 1.06 quarts. Set up a proportion: $\frac{1\text{ L}}{1.06\text{ qt}} = \frac{x\text{ L}}{7.2\text{ qt}}$; $7.2 \div 1.06 = 6.79$ liters.

38. (B) Since you are multiplying a number with two digits after the decimal point by a number with one digit after the decimal point, the answer should have three digits after the decimal point.

39. (D) The formula is C × 9/5 + 32 = F. 15 × 9/5 + 32 = 59.

40. (C) You can find the answer by setting up the easier of the two possible proportions: 1/250 = 10/x, so x = 2,500 cm. Since 2,500 cm = 25 m, you should be able to rule out all of the choices but choice C.

41. (11) Substitute 3 for y: $2x-4=6(3)$; $2x-4=18$. Now solve for x. Add 4 to both sides: $2x-4+4=18+4$; $2x=22$. Now divide both sides by 2: $\frac{2x}{2}=\frac{22}{2}$; $x=11$.

42. (C) The math is basic; the only problem is where to put the decimal point. Common sense should tell you that 7.2 divided by almost-one will be a bit more than 7.2.

43. (C) Find the least common denominator and subtract: 21/24 – 2/24 = 19/24.

44. (A) Think of this as a proportion: 1 hour/140 miles = x hours/455 miles. Cross-multiply to solve: 455 = 140x; x = 455/140, or 3.25 hours, which equals 3 hours 15 minutes.

45. (D) Express each mixed number as an improper fraction: 33/4 – 41/6. Then find the lowest common denominator and restate those fractions: 99/12 – 82/12. Solve, and express as a mixed number in lowest terms: 17/12 = 1 5/12.

46. (A) Percent means "per 100," so to convert a percent to a decimal, put the percent as the numerator of a fraction and 100 as the denominator and then divide: $\frac{43.5}{100} = 0.435$.

47. (2) Divide 4,370 into groups of 8: $4{,}370 \div 8 = 546\ R2$. There will be 546 groups of 8 with two people left over.

48. (B) Percent means "per 100," so to convert a decimal to a percent, multiply the decimal by 100: $0.165 \times 100 = 16.5\%$.

49. (1.5) The ratio is 5 to 3, so w (water) = 3/5 f (flour).

3/5 × 2 1/2 = 3/5 × 5/2 = 15/10

15/10 = 1 5/10, or 1 1/2, or in decimal form, 1.5.

50. (74) There are 12 inches in a foot, so $6\text{ ft} \times 12\frac{\text{in}}{\text{ft}} = 72$ inches. Add the other 2 inches to get 74 total inches.

MODULE 5: BIOLOGY

1. (B) The four forms of passive transport are diffusion, facilitated diffusion, filtration, and osmosis. Endocytosis (choice B) is active transport in which a cell uses energy to form a vacuole and engulf molecules.

2. (C) The reaction for photosynthesis in plants is

$$6CO_2 + 6H_2O \rightarrow C_6H_{12}O_6 + 6O_2.$$

3. (A) All of the answer choices describe types of asexual reproduction, but parthenogenesis is the development of an embryo from an unfertilized egg cell (polar body). It is far more common in plants and invertebrates than it is in reptiles, but it does occasionally happen in some lizards and snakes.

4. (C) In RNA, the four bases are A, G, C, and U (uracil). In DNA, the four bases are A, G, C, and T (thymine).

5. (C) In this case, we are crossing *Aa* with *Aa*. If the disease is carried on the recessive allele, the *aa* combination of recessive genes represents a diseased offspring, but any *Aa* combination would be a healthy carrier. On a Punnett square, that would be two out of four offspring, or 50%.

6. (D) A hypotonic solution has a lower osmotic pressure and a lower concentration of solutes than the cell it surrounds. Osmotic pressure would achieve balance by diffusing water into the cell, swelling it.

7. (A) Unlike vertebrates, crayfish and other crustaceans have a system in which blood circulates through blood vessels that open into spaces in their body cavities.

8. (A) Lipids, or fats, typically have polar and nonpolar regions and a more complex chemical makeup than most carbohydrates. Because of their combination of polar and nonpolar regions (attracting and repelling water), they do not dissolve easily. This helps to make them useful for long-term storage of energy.

9. (D) The anther produces pollen, which contains the male gametes in plant production.

10. (B) The ribosomes synthesize proteins through the process of translation. Then the proteins typically move to the Golgi complex to be stored in vesicles before being released to their final destinations.

11. (B) The taxonomic categories in order from least to most specific are: kingdom, phylum, class, order, family, genus, species.

12. (A) Every amino acid contains a carboxyl (COOH) and an amine (NH_2).

13. (A) Lysosomes are essentially enzymes wrapped in a membrane whose only function is to digest.

14. (A) Both forms of respiration produce ATP, the coenzyme that transports chemical energy. Although both aerobic and anaerobic respiration may take place in the cytoplasm, only aerobic respiration involves the mitochondria, making choice B a key difference. Aerobic respiration produces more energy, making choice C a key difference. Both involve glycolysis, but only aerobic respiration involves the Krebs cycle, making choice D a key difference.

15. (D) Telophase is the final stage of mitosis, in which the two separate nuclei are formed and the division into two separate cells begins.

16. (C) In a substitution (choice A), one base is exchanged for another. In a deletion (choice B), part of the DNA is lost. In a frameshift (choice D), insertions or deletions change the way the codons are read. All three of these mutations involve changes in small segments of the nucleotide sequence and are caused either by errors in DNA replication or by mutagens that change the structure of nucleotides. Unlike mutation, the exchange of genetic material known as recombination (choice C) takes place during cell division and is catalyzed by enzymes.

17. (A) Picture a Punnett square. Reading the chart clockwise from top left, the cross would yield one female carrier, one female with colorblindness, one male with colorblindness, and one normal male who neither carries nor manifests the disease.

18. (D) Glycolysis converts glucose into pyruvate, releasing energy in the form of ATP and NADH. Oxygen is neither used for the reaction nor released as a byproduct.

19. (C) Reliability can be determined by repeating the test, whether over time (choice A) or in different locations (choices B and D).

20. (B) We are genus *Homo*, species *sapiens*. Others in our genus in the past included *Homo erectus*, *Homo neanderthalensis*, and *Homo habilis*.

21. (D) The dogs' size is the variable that may or may not affect the dependent variable, the dogs' lifespan.

22. (C) In deductive reasoning, a hypothesis follows from a set of premises, which may be true, in which case the reasoning is sound, or not true, in which case the reasoning is unsound.

23. (D) Eukaryotic cells include a number of specialized organelles that are not found in prokaryotes. Among them are mitochondria. Mitochondria are the site of the Krebs, or citric acid, cycle, in which carbon dioxide and water are formed from fuel molecules, generating energy in the form of ATP.

24. (B) Most bacteria are spherical (choice A), rod-shaped (choice B), or spiral-shaped (choice D). *Bacilli* are common rod-shaped bacteria.

25. (B) The parent cell is diploid, with two sets of chromosomes for a total of 68. Meoisis results in daughter cells that are haploid, containing half the number of chromosomes of the parent cell.

MODULE 6: CHEMISTRY

1. (A) A covalent bond involves electron pairs being shared between atoms. In sulfur dioxide, sulfur shares four of its valence electrons with two oxygen atoms, two with each. This shared bonding forms a covalent compound.

2. (C) The atomic number of an atom defines its number of protons (and in its uncharged form, its number of electrons). The first periodic tables were arranged in order of atomic mass, and in today's tables, the atomic mass (or relative atomic mass) increases as atomic number increases—with a few exceptions. Magnesium is a metal, making choice A incorrect. Since carbon has fewer protons, it would also be expected to have fewer neutrons (calculate this by subtracting the number of protons from the atomic weight—magnesium has about 12 neutrons to carbon's 6), making choice B incorrect as well. The terms "major element" and "trace element" only have relevance when you are describing elements within a sample, so choice D does not work either.

3. (B) For a substance to decay from 28 kg to 7 kg, it must undergo two half-lives ($28 \rightarrow 14 \rightarrow 7$). If the half-life of the substance is 10 years, then two half-lives would be 20 years.

4. (D) If the elements in a covalent bond have different electronegativity values, the unequal sharing of electrons causes the bond to be polar. HCl is the only choice with a polar covalent bond.

5. (A) In a single-replacement reaction, one element reacts with a compound and replaces another element in that compound. In the case shown, A replaces B in the compound BC, forming AC instead. For example, imagine combining iron with hydrochloric acid. The reaction binds the iron to chlorine, forming iron chloride and hydrogen.

6. (C) Nitrogen is located on the upper right side of the periodic table. Like other nonmetals, it has a low melting and boiling point and does not conduct heat or electricity well.

7. (A) Ca is calcium, and $(OH)_2$ is hydroxide (an anion consisting of hydrogen and oxygen).

8. (D) When an element exists in two or more different physical forms, it is said to have allotropes. There are only a few elements that have this property; among them are tin (choice A), which can exist as gray tin or white tin; carbon (choice B), which has a variety of forms including diamond and graphite; and phosphorus (choice C), which comes in three main forms known by their colors.

9. (A) Substances that are gases at room temperature decrease in solubility as temperature rises. The carbon dioxide that gives ginger ale its fizz leaves the liquid and concentrates as a gas near the top of the can when it gets too warm.

10. (B) A test for blood gases measures oxygen and carbon dioxide (choices C and D), which are the main gases in the blood. A small amount of nitrogen is inhaled with oxygen, and some is dissolved in the blood. Under pressure, as in scuba diving, that dissolved nitrogen can be problematic, because it cannot be released. Divers must ascend very slowly to allow the nitrogen to come out of solution slowly.

11. (A) The single iron (Fe) atom on either side of the original equation seems balanced, but the chlorine (Cl) does not. There are two chlorine atoms on the left, and three on the right. To balance that, you need to add a coefficient of 3 to the left chlorine and a coefficient of 2 to the right iron chloride. Once you do that, you have:

$$Fe + 3Cl_2 \rightarrow 2FeCl_3$$

But the equation is not entirely balanced until you add a coefficient of 2 to the iron on the left:

$$2Fe + 3Cl_2 \rightarrow 2FeCl_3$$

Now your equation shows two iron atoms on either side and six chlorine atoms on either side. The equation is balanced.

12. (D) The noble gases (helium, neon, argon, krypton, xenon, and radon) were once called inert gases because it was thought that they were completely nonreactive, but under certain circumstances, xenon, krypton, and radon have been found to form molecules. Nevertheless, the noble gases are very close to being nonreactive (choice C), since their valence electron shells are full, making them stable and giving them an oxidation number of zero (choice A). All six have low boiling points (choice B), and they are also nonflammable, making choice D correct.

13. (C) In a single bond, one pair of electrons is shared (choice B). In a double bond, two pairs of electrons are shared.

14. (C) Calculate the number of neutrons by subtracting the atomic number from the mass number. The mass number of carbon-14 is 14, and the atomic number for carbon is 6, so $14 - 6 = 8$.

15. (B) The electron distribution of an atom is divided into shells, which in turn contain subshells composed of the orbitals in which the electrons reside. In electron configuration, the symbols 1s, 2s, 2p, and so on, are used to designate subshells, with superscripts indicating the number of electrons in each subshell. There is a maximum number of electrons per subshell. Oxygen has atomic number 8, meaning that it has 8 protons, and in its balanced state, 8 electrons. Looking at the superscripts alone should tell you that only the superscripts in choice B add up to 8.

16. (D) Molarity = moles of solute/liters of solution. If you were given the mass rather than the moles, you would have to perform more calculations, but here you are given moles, making it a simple division problem.

17. (C) Healthy human blood is fairly neutral, falling between 7.35 and 7.45 on the 0–14 pH scale, where acid is lower in value and alkali is higher.

18. (B) A mole of atoms consists of Avogadro's number of atoms and has a mass in grams numerically equal to the atomic weight of the element. So, one mole of carbon dioxide, CO_2, has a mass in grams equal to the atomic weight of one atom of carbon plus two atoms of oxygen—about $12 + 16 + 16$, or 44 g/mol.

19. (C) Rays at the top of the electromagnetic spectrum are ionizing—they are highly energetic and move at high speeds. Gamma rays (choice B) and x-rays (choice D) are two such rays. The products of radioactive decay include neutrons, beta particles, and alpha particles (choice A). Microwaves (choice C) are further down the spectrum and are considered non-ionizing.

20. (D) The naming of chemical compounds is quite formalized. In this case, sodium is named first, and there is no prefix of any kind, so you can assume that in the formula, Na will precede any other element. That eliminates choices A and C. The second part of the name, *hypochlorite*, has both a prefix, *hypo-*, and a suffix, *-ite*. Sodium *chlorate* would be $NaClO_3$; sodium *chlorite* would have one fewer oxygen atom ($NaClO_2$), and sodium *hypochlorite* would have one fewer oxygen atom than that, making it NaClO.

21. (A) With a few rare exceptions, oxygen has an oxidation number of –2 in a compound.

22. (B) Weak intermolecular forces have a low boiling point. Strong intermolecular forces have a high boiling point.

London dispersion < dipole-dipole < H-bonding < ion-ion

London dispersion is the weakest force of those shown.

23. (C) You can use the molarity/dilution equation to solve this.

$$M_1V_1 = M_2V_2$$
$$12\ M \times x = 6\ M \times 250\ \text{mL}$$
$$2x = 250\ \text{mL}$$
$$x = 125\ \text{mL}$$

24. (D) If you recall that any combustion reaction involves O_2, you can see at a glance that the only possible answer is choice D, which represents the combustion of glucose.

25. (B) Although we think of iron (Fe) as being heavy, its mass is less than that of copper (Cu), silver (Ag), and the metal with the greatest atomic mass on this list, gold (Au).

MODULE 7: ANATOMY AND PHYSIOLOGY

1. (A) Something that is distal is away from the center of the body. The fingers would be distal to the forearm.

2. (A) The pleura line the thorax and wrap around the lungs.

3. (C) The tiny air sacs called the alveoli contain capillaries that are the site of gas exchange in the lungs.

4. (D) Peristalsis is the contraction of muscles that moves food through the digestive system. It begins in the esophagus and continues through the intestines.

5. (C) Adipose tissue stores energy as fat. It is mainly found under the skin, protecting major organs, and in the breasts.

6. (D) A dendrite is a short, branched extension of a neuron. Its function is as a receptor—it receives information at the synapses and stores it or transfers it to the soma or axons.

7. (A) The integumentary system includes the skin, hair, nails, and assorted glands. Vitamin D promotes calcium absorption. It is obtained through diet, but it is also synthesized in the skin following exposure to sunlight.

8. (C) The tricuspid valve is also known as the right atrioventricular valve. Once blood flows from the right atrium to the right ventricle, the valve shuts to prevent backflow.

9. (B) Any of the choices may be true, but only choice B is certainly true. For each allergy, the immune system produces antibodies called Immunoglobulin E (IgE). Different allergens stimulate different allergy-specific IgE antibodies.

10. (B) The foot and base of the ankle contain 7 tarsal bones, 5 metatarsal bones, and 14 phalanges.

11. (C) T cells and lymphocytes are products of the thymus, making it part of the lymphatic system.

12. (B) Phagocytes, which include macrophages and neutrophils, protect the body by ingesting foreign particles. They are produced in the bone marrow and released into the bloodstream.

13. (A) A sesamoid bone is one that is embedded within a tendon or muscle. The patella (kneecap) is the largest of the sesamoid bones. Others are found in the hand, foot, wrist, and ear.

14. (C) Oxygenated blood from the lungs enters the left atrium and flows through the mitral valve into the left ventricle.

15. (D) From the Latin root meaning "skin," this disease of the skin, gastro-intestinal tract, and nerves is usually caused by a lack of vitamin B3, niacin, which is also known as nicotinic acid.

16. (D) The pancreas is the part of the endocrine system that works most closely with the digestive system. It produces insulin to regulate the break-down of sugars.

17. (A) The pineal gland produces melatonin, which helps to support the circadian rhythm of the body. Disturbance of this rhythm due to inadequate melatonin may lead to insomnia and other sleep disorders.

18. (D) The bone that is most anterior is closest to the front of the body. Compared to the other skull bones listed, that would be the nasal bone.

19. (B) Total cholesterol includes LDL ("bad" cholesterol), HDL ("good" cholesterol), and triglycerides. In adults, a total 200 mg/dL or lower is considered an acceptable measurement. Under 40 mg/dL (choice A) would be a good measurement of HDL only.

20. (A) A sagittal section divides the body vertically into left and right halves.

21. (A) Amylase is present in saliva, where it begins to break down starch into sugar.

22. (C) A normal range is between 800 and 2,000 mL daily, or up to about 2 quarts.

23. (D) The level of potassium in the body is controlled by the kidneys. Potassium, along with calcium, chlorine, sodium, phosphate, and magnesium, is a common electrolyte, a substance that assists in the movement of fluid between cells.

24. (C) The esophagus runs behind the trachea, making it posterior (or dorsal).

25. (B) The Volkmann's canals are small channels that lie at right angles to the length of the bone and connect vascular systems within the bone.

MODULE 8: PHYSICS

1. (A) Specific gravity of a liquid is the ratio of the density of the liquid to the density of water at a certain temperature. For example, if water at 4°C has a specific gravity of 1.00, sea water (choice B) has specific gravity of around 1.02. If you think about which of the liquids named is least dense, you can probably estimate that the liquid less dense than water is likely to be alcohol. The other three have a specific density greater than 1.00.

2. (D) The plane traveled a total of 400 miles, but because it ended back where it started, the displacement is 0.

3. (A) Kinetic energy is the energy of an object in motion. The greater the mass of that object, the greater its kinetic energy.

4. (B) The car changes velocity by 15 m/s. Acceleration (5 m/s^2) equals change in velocity (15 m/s) divided by change in time. Therefore, time must equal 3 s.

5. (D) Momentum equals mass times velocity. In this problem, the tennis ball has a mass of 53 grams and a momentum of 15 kg·m/s. So,

$$15 = 0.053x$$ (Notice that grams are converted to kilograms.)

$$15/0.053 = x$$

$$283 \approx x$$

6. (B) Increasing the temperature of a substance increases its volume and decreases its density. Such changes are far more evident in gases than in liquids or solids.

7. (D) Work is the force that is applied to an object over a distance: $W = Fd$. The force is 12 N, and the distance is 3 m, giving a total amount of work equal to 36 N·m.

8. (C) Based on the equation $P = IV$, the current is P/V, or power divided by voltage. Dividing 1,500 watts by 120 volts gives you 12.5 amperes.

9. (D) The frequency of a wave is determined by dividing its velocity by its wavelength.

10. (B) Potential energy is defined by an object's position, inner tension, and electrical charge as opposed to its motion, which defines kinetic energy. Height, distance, and mass may be determining factors in potential energy as in kinetic energy (choices A and C), and all energy is measured in joules (choice D). However, only kinetic energy transfers (choice B), as when one object collides with another.

11. (C) Centripetal acceleration equals the velocity squared divided by the radius. Because it is measured in meters per second squared, and because the diameter of the Ferris wheel is given in meters, begin by converting the speed in the problem:

16 km = 16,000 m

1 hr = 3,600 s

= 16,000/3,600 m/s or about 4.4 m/s

So:

$4^2/25 = a_c$ (Notice that the radius equals 1/2 the diameter given.)

$16/25 = a_c$

$0.64 = a_c$

12. (A) The vibrations in transverse waves move at a 90-degree angle to the wave. Choices C and D represent longitudinal waves, and choice B is a surface wave, in which particles move in a circular motion.

13. (B) Vectors have both direction and magnitude. Scalars have only magnitude.

14. (D) Since the density is 1 and the force of gravity is the same on each object, you need only look at the relative densities of the objects listed. Density equals mass divided by volume, so the densities are 1.5 g/cm^3 (choice A), 1.6 g/cm^3 (choice B), 1.11 g/cm^3 (choice C), and 1.02 g/cm^3 (choice D). The object with density closest to that of water will be most buoyant.

15. (C) If the mass of each object is doubled, the force of attraction is quadrupled.

16. (C) Attaching batteries in a series gives you a voltage equivalent to the combined voltage of all the batteries.

17. (D) Newton's Third Law of Motion states that for every action, there is a reaction that is equal in size and opposite in direction.

18. (A) Look at the relationship between the object distance (d_o), the image distance (d_i), and the focal length (f). Use the equation: $1/f = 1/d_o + 1/d_i$ where $f = 10$ cm and $d_o = 20$ cm.

$1/10 = 1/20 + 1/x$

The image distance is 20 centimeters.

19. (C) Speed equals wavelength times frequency ($v = f\lambda$). In this problem, $15 = 2.5\lambda$, so $\lambda = 6$ Hz.

20. (C) Momentum is the product of velocity and mass. It is usually measured in metric units, but don't let that confuse you, and don't forget to add the weight of both child and car to get the total mass. Abner's momentum is

3,450 lb·m/h (choice A). Bai Minh's momentum is 2,880 lb·m/h (choice B). Caitlyn's momentum is 3,525 lb·m/h (choice C). Darrell's momentum is 3,360 lb·m/h (choice D). Caitlyn has the greatest momentum.

21. (A) Imagine a normal line intersecting the boundary at right angles and dividing the 80-degree angle in half. One-half is the angle of incidence, and the other is the angle of reflection. In this case, both measure 40 degrees.

22. (A) Force equals the extension of the spring times a constant ($F = kx$). If a force of 15 Newtons stretches this particular spring 3 centimeters, the constant is 5. Apply that same constant to the increased force: 22 N = $x \times 5$. The distance of the extension must be 22 ÷ 5, or 4.4 centimeters.

23. (B) Acceleration equals the speed squared divided by the radius ($a = v^2/R$). In this case, a = 4 m/s^2, and v = 20 m/s, so the radius must be 400 ÷ 4, or 100 m. The mass of the car is irrelevant to the problem.

24. (B) According to Ohm's Law, current (I) equals voltage (ΔV) divided by resistance (R), or $I = \Delta V/R$. In this case, you know voltage and resistance, so I = 100/20, or 5 amp.

25. (B) Use Coulomb's Law to find the force. The equation to use is this:

$$F_{\text{elect}} = \frac{k \times Q_1 \times Q_2}{d^2}$$

Remember that 1 Coulomb = 10^6 microcoulombs. Q_1 in this case equals 3×10^{-6} C, Q_2 equals 1×10^{-6} C, and d, distance, equals 1 m. Now, you must recall Coulomb's constant, $k = (9.0 \times 10^9 \text{ N.m}^2/\text{C}^2)$. Once more, it's all about computation:

$$\frac{9.0 \times \frac{10^9 \text{N} \cdot \cancel{\text{m}^2}}{\cancel{\text{C}^2}} (3 \times 10^{-6} \cancel{\text{C}})(1 \times 10^{-6} \cancel{\text{C}})}{(1 \cancel{\text{m}})^2} = \frac{27 \times 10^{-3}}{1} = 0027 \text{ N}$$

Credits

Figure 6.3. Classification Levels (Image copyrighted and used with permission by Peter Halasz)

Figure 6.4. Energy Pyramid (Image copyrighted and permitted to use by Danie1996)

Figure 6.5. Animal Cell (Content provided by the National Human Genome Research Institute)

Figure 6.6. Plant Cell (Content provided by Mariana Ruiz, LadyofHats)

Figure 6.8. Cross-Section of a Leaf (Content provided by U.S. Fish & Wildlife Service)

Figure 6.9. Parts of a Flowering Plant (Content provided by Mariana Ruiz, LadyofHats)

Figure 6.10. Phases of Mitosis (Content provided by Mariana Ruiz, LadyofHats)

Figure 6.11. Phases of Meiosis (Content provided by the NCBI of the National Institutes of Health)

Figure 6.12. Punnett Square (Image used with permission by Madprime)

Figure 6.13. DNA Replication (Content provided by U.S. Department of Energy)

Figure 7.1. The Water Cycle (Image copyrighted and used with permission by Wasserkreislauf)

Figure 8.1. Body Planes (Content provided by the U.S. National Library of Medicine)

Figure 8.2. The Skin (Illustration by Don Bliss from the National Cancer Institute)

Figure 8.3. The Skeleton (Content provided by Mariana Ruiz, LadyofHats)

Figure 8.4. The Muscles
(a) Source: Häggström, Mikael (2014). "Medical gallery of Mikael Häggström 2014". WikiJournal of Medicine **1** (2). DOI:10.15347/wjm/2014.008. ISSN2002-4436. Public Domain
(b) Häggström, Mikael (2014). "Medical gallery of Mikael Häggström 2014". WikiJournal of Medicine **1** (2). DOI:10.15347/wjm/2014.008. ISSN2002-4436. Public Domain

Figure 8.5. The Nervous System (Content provided by the National Institute of Diabetes and Digestive and Kidney Diseases, National Institutes of Health)

Figure 8.6. Neurons (Content provided by the NIA of the National Institutes of Health)

Figure 8.7. Some Endocrine Glands (Content provided by the National Institute of Diabetes and Digestive and Kidney Diseases, National Institutes of Health)

Figure 8.8. The Circulatory System (Content provided by the National Institute of Diabetes and Digestive and Kidney Diseases, National Institutes of Health)

Figure 8.9. The Heart (Content provided by the National Heart, Lung, and Blood Institute, National Institutes of Health)

Figure 8.12. The Respiratory System (Content provided by the National Cancer Institute)

Figure 8.14. The Digestive System (Content provided by the National Institute of Diabetes and Digestive and Kidney Diseases, National Institutes of Health)

Figure 8.15. The Urinary System (Content provided by the National Institute of Diabetes and Digestive and Kidney Diseases, National Institutes of Health)

Figure 8.16. The Reproductive System (Content provided by the Department of Health and Human Services, Centers for Disease Control and Prevention)

Figure 9.3. Electromagnetic Spectrum (Content provided by the National Institute of Environmental Health Sciences, National Institutes of Health)

NOTES

NOTES

NOTES

NOTES

NOTES

NOTES

NOTES

NOTES

NOTES

NOTES

NOTES

NOTES

NOTES

NOTES

NOTES

NOTES

NOTES

NOTES